P9-DFY-830

Between Fetters and Freedom

African American Baptists since Emancipation

The James N. Griffith Series in Baptist Studies

This series on Baptist life and thought explores and investigates Baptist history, offers analyses of Baptist theologies, provides studies in hymnody, and examines the role of Baptists in societies and cultures around the world. The series also includes classics of Baptist literature, letters, diaries, and other writings. For a complete list of titles in the series, visit www.mupress.org and visit the series page.

—C. Douglas Weaver, Series Editor

BETWEEN FETTERS AND FREEDOM

African American Baptists since Emancipation

Edited by

Edward R. Crowther and Keith Harper

With an Afterword by

Wayne Flynt

MERCER UNIVERSITY PRESS | *Macon, Georgia*

MUP/ H906

© 2015 by Mercer University Press
Published by Mercer University Press
1501 Mercer University Drive
Macon, Georgia 31207
All rights reserved

9 8 7 6 5 4 3 2 1

Books published by Mercer University Press are printed on acid-free paper
that meets the requirements of the American National Standard for
Information Sciences—Permanence of Paper for Printed Library Materials.

ISBN   978-0-88146-540-2
Cataloging-in-Publication Data is available from the Library of Congress

For

Lori and Johnnie

MERCER
UNIVERSITY PRESS

Endowed by
Tom Watson Brown
and
The Watson-Brown Foundation, Inc.

Contents

Contributors

APRIL C. ARMSTRONG is Special Collections Assistant and Social Media Manager at Seeley G. Mudd Manuscript Library, Princeton University, Princeton, New Jersey.

EDWARD R. CROWTHER is Professor of History at Adams State University, Alamosa, Colorado.

WAYNE FLYNT is Emeritus Distinguished University Professor of History at Auburn University, Auburn Alabama.

KEITH HARPER is Professor of Baptist Studies, Southeastern Baptist Theological Seminary, Wake Forest, North Carolina.

PAUL HARVEY is Professor of History at the University of Colorado at Colorado Springs, Colorado.

CHARLES F. IRONS is Associate Professor of History and Chair of the Department of History and Geography at Elon University, Elon, North Carolina.

COURTNEY PACE LYON is Assistant Professor of Church History, Memphis Theological Seminary, Memphis, Tennessee

ANDREW M. MANIS is Professor of History at Middle Georgia State College, Macon Georgia.

SANDY DWAYNE MARTIN is Professor of Religion in the Department of Religion at the University of Georgia, Athens, Georgia.

ERIC M. WASHINGTON is Assistant Professor of History and the Director of African and African Diaspora Studies at Calvin College in Grand Rapids, Michigan.

ALAN SCOT WILLIS is Professor of History at Northern Michigan University in Marquette, Michigan.

Between Fetters and Freedom

Introduction

Edward R. Crowther and Keith Harper

Historians have focused on African American Christianity, and especially its largest denominational expression, black Baptists, to understand the ebb and flow of the lives of African Americans in the United States. Prior to the Civil War, African Americans blended their myriad religious structures with European Christianity to create a syncretic faith that helped them forge an identity that preserved important African folkways, offer a moral critique to their European "owners," and nurture a sense of their own humanity as God's chosen people who would one day be delivered for the bondage of slavery through the awesome grace of God. In Mechal Sobel's treatment, an African American Baptist identity emerges as early as 1750. Over time, as she shows, a coherent synthesis of African and European religious thought emerged among black Baptists, one that informed their sojourn through a largely physically enslaved existence but that also shaped white worship experience as well, especially through sermon and song cadences.[1]

Scholars have previously made syncretic African American Christianity a centerpiece of the world that the slaves made. In a recent study, Daniel Fountain suggests that the recovery of both the "invisible institution" of syncretic African American Christianity—biracial congregations—and quasi-independent African American evangelical congregations ignores a much larger fact. Most African Americans at emancipation had limited or no exposure to Christianity, with fewer than 40 percent in Fountain's survey, revealing pre-Civil War conversions. Evidence of a strongly persistent folk cosmology as well as the survival of African Islam competed with a slowly leaching Christianity for the attention of most enslaved people. Persistent Africanisms and folk-culture, especially among enslaved populations in rural areas, were more typical of the religious milieu of early African American religion. Although antebellum African American Christianity did inform the lives of many enslaved people, the rise of the institutional church and the

---

[1] Mechal Sobel, *Trablin' On: The Slave Journey to an Afro-Baptist Faith* (Princeton: Princeton University Press, 1988).

Christianization of African American culture is a post-Civil War phenomenon.[2]

At the conclusion of the Civil War, African American Baptists began to form state level conventions, with their nascent leaders engaging in a remarkable effort of denominational growth and cultural empowerment. Ministerial institutes, Sunday Schools, and even cooperative efforts to promote domestic and international missions helped undergird a series of interrelated transformations. First, African Americans asserted control over their congregations and conventions. Second, they engaged in missionary work in both urban and, especially, underserved rural areas. Third, they supported and nurtured the growth of African American institutions, especially colleges and schools. And finally, they formed a national-level convention. Earlier African American Baptist conventions had largely been confined to the northern states, but the Consolidated American Baptist Missionary Convention represented black Baptists from the north and south during its short existence (1867–79). Class, regional, and economic differences grounded this cooperative effort. Three subsidiary bodies filled the void of the failed national body, and in 1895, the National Baptist Convention, USA, formed, under the leadership of its president, Elias Camp Morris. Although plagued from the beginning with schism—in 1897, 1915, and 1961—the National Baptist Convention became by far the largest African American religious denomination in the United States.[3]

Given the significance of religious leadership in the struggles for African American civil rights, notably remembered through the career of Martin Luther King, Jr., and more accurately and fully through the delineation of the myriad roles of the church women who used the networks to organize challenges to white supremacy, African American religious groups occupy a privileged place in a triumphalist narrative of struggle and deliverance against the dark night of slavery and Jim Crow. In this view, from the end of the Civil War to the 1950s, African American churches were community and spiritual centers that the logic of Christian white supremacy

---

[2] Daniel L. Fountain, *Slavery, Civil War, and Salvation: African American Slaves, and Christianity, 1830–1870* (Baton Rouge: Louisiana State University Press, 2010) 3, 16, 28, 72–90, 112, 114.

[3] Carter G. Woodson, *The History of the Negro Church*, 2nd ed. (Washington, DC: Associated Publishers, 1921) 199–205; C. Eric Lincoln, *The Black Church in the African American Experience* (Durham: Duke University Press, 1990) 26–9.

had to tolerate; hence, white churches provided space for worship and "uplift" for the larger African American community. Denominational ties with the American Baptist Convention and, to a lesser degree, the Southern Baptist Convention permitted the augmentation of an African American leadership class represented by Benjamin Mays and Howard Thurman as well as historically black colleges.[4]

This heroic interpretation of the African American church emerged as a reaction to an earlier view espoused by sociologist E. Franklin Frazier, who posited that African American churches had actually habituated African Americans to a servile status rather than challenged the social order. Far from an institutional Moses leading African Americans to moral and material liberation, Frazier contended that "the Negro church and Negro religion have cast a shadow over the entire intellectual life of Negroes and have been responsible for the so-called backwardness of American Negroes." Frazier's preachers often served the interests of "the white community" and subverted the democratic and educational opportunities for African American organizational life. Although most scholars take a less jaundiced view of African American churches and their role in promoting or inhibiting African American attainments after the civil war, one does well to remember that both Martin Luther King, Jr., and Fred Shuttlesworth criticized a Cadillac-driving ministerial leadership who appeared to accommodate rather than confront white power structures that marginalized African Americans.[5]

Gender further complicates the image of African American Baptist life. Although Baptist women sometimes performed public roles in associ-ational and convention meetings, such as leading in prayer, the leadership structure in congregations and the convention was patriarchal. However, the membership was majority female, and attendance at church functions was even more skewed. Like white Baptists, black Baptists generally held a literal, as opposed to a cultural, interpretation of New Testament passages regarding women's roles in ministry, so they reserved ministerial positions,

---

[4] Paul Harvey, *Through the Storm, Through the Night: A History of African American* Christianity (Lanham: Rowman & Littlefield, 2011) 109–10. See generally William E. Montgomery, *Under Their Own Vine and Fig Tree: The African American Church in the South, 1865–1900* (Baton Rouge: Louisiana State University Press, 1993).

[5] E. Franklin Frazier, *The Negro Church in America* (New York: Schocken Books, 1974) 90.

especially titles, for men. But women, it seemed, did everything else. As Evelyn Brooks Higginbotham and Paul Harvey have shown, African American Baptist women and men believed the church provided an appropriate vehicle for racial uplift, served as a locus for negotiating proper gender boundaries, and provided a space for moral nurture of children. Like white Baptist women, African American Baptist females found formal expression of their role in the Women's Convention, an auxiliary to the National Baptist Convention, which is focused on missions. While deferring to male ministerial leadership, the Women's Convention was a voice for equality before God and the sanctity of home and marriage.[6]

Black Baptist History reflects two important and interrelated questions: What does it mean to be Baptists and what does it mean to be African American? The ongoing negotiation between faith and the material circumstances of the world as well as the discourse between race and place in the United States have shaped black Baptists in the years since emancipation, as they search for spiritual fulfillment and an understanding of ultimate things and seek equitable treatment in a society that has systematically sought to deny them the fruits of their labor and equal justice under law. The nine essays that follow provide case struggles in this larger racial and religious struggle.

Professor Sandy Dwayne Martin contrasts the black Baptist vision of religion as liberation versus the white Baptist vision that sanctified antebellum slavery, civil war, and confederate defeat as a noble lost cause. Like whites, Martin's Baptists saw the hand of God active in history, shaping the destiny of nations, but acting particularly to free them from bondage and permit them to fashion new religious institutions and seek religious betterment, along with other benefits stemming from emancipation. For African American Baptists, the God of the Bible was a liberator; as he had led the Israelites out of Egypt, so he now led African Americans in an exodus from bondage toward freedom and a deeper Christian faith. Even the travails of white supremacy served to remind African Americans of their need to live righteous lives and to engage in and support missionary activity, all while

---

[6] Elizabeth Brooks Higginbotham, *Righteous Discontent: The Woman's Movement in the Black Baptist Church, 1880–1920* (Cambridge: Harvard University Press, 1993) 158–9, 185–8; Paul Harvey, *Redeeming the South: Religious Cultures and Racial Identities among Southern Baptists, 1865–1925* (Chapel Hill: University of North Carolina Press, 1997) 238–43.

showing gratitude to God. The God who worked in history and had compelled emancipation would vindicate continued faith in Him by ridding the United States of white supremacy.

While reasserting the significance of African American Baptists fashioning their own congregational and denominational structures, Charles F. Irons complicates the historiography of the African American exodus from white-controlled Baptist congregations after the Civil War. He uncovers examples of African American Baptists who not only persisted in their antebellum ecclesiastical affiliations long after the Civil War but also identifies a few African Americans who actually joined white-controlled congregations after the collapse of the Confederacy. Irons challenges historians to rethink assumptions about whose behavior was supposedly on the right side of history and suggests that African American Baptists faced many contingent circumstances and made their choices of church membership based on their particular circumstances. Irons's view alters the perception of a racially unified exodus moment from biracial fellowships to African American-controlled fellowships, a view consistent with the concept of freed peoples dealing with the unknown and unknowable in the maelstrom of Reconstruction.

Similarly, Eric Michael Washington demonstrates how a long-standing African American tradition of Ethiopianism, an idea that defined a Providential purpose for the horrors of slavery as a divine means for the conversion of Africans, informed the efforts of African American Baptists after the Civil War to unite in efforts for evangelizing the African continent. Having concluded that white missionaries may not have the best of intentions toward Africans and drawing on the cultural memory of Lott Carey, the first African American missionary to Africa, post-Civil War black Baptists looked to Africa as a primary mission field and as a possible locus for emigration from the South. William Colley, a multi-racial Virginian and Southern Baptist Missionary in Africa, worked with black Baptist leaders in the 1870s to encourage their undertaking of African missions, which led to the formation of the Baptist Foreign Missionary Convention in 1880, the forerunner of the National Baptist Convention.

While much of the historiography of Baptists focuses on men, April Armstrong highlights the important relationship between the white founder of the Women's Missionary Union, Annie Armstrong, and her relationship with the African American founder of the Women's Convention in the National Baptist Convention, Nannie Helen Burroughs. Their cooperation came during the nadir of race relations between the Southern Baptist Convention and the National Baptist Convention and shows that a patriarchal focus obscures how women and women's groups negotiated the tortured terrain of gender and race in the early twentieth century. Armstrong's support proved vital to the creation of the Women's Convention, but the relationship between the Women's Convention and the Women's Missionary Union did not survive Armstrong's decision to give up her missionary work in the face of differing opinions regarding the establishment of a missionary training institute for women. The Armstrong-Burrough's friendship demonstrates both the possibilities and limitations of interracial Baptist friendships in an era of white supremacy.

White expectations of African Americans sometimes informed how black Baptists sought to structure their own worship experiences. A quest for "respectability" sometimes compelled denominational leaders to call on African American Baptists to mimic the norms of urban white churches. Paul Harvey shows how the tension between authentic cultural expression and the desire to appease white cultural norms expressed itself in black Baptist religious expression in the first century following emancipation. Although there were many expressions of this tension, Harvey focuses on the debate over hymnody, whether black Baptists should sing the songs of Isaac Watts or African American spirituals, and the distinctive homiletical stylings of black preachers. With the black migration to northern cities, not only did African American gospel music and recorded sermons undergird black entrepreneurialism, the cadences of African American Baptists illustrate a successful reconciliation of authenticity and a quest for respectability, and even the infusion of African American norms into a larger national mainstream.

Alan Scot Willis examines the extraordinary career and vision of Madison Crencha Allen, editor of the *National Baptist Union*, the denominational paper of the National Baptist Convention, USA, in the 1950s. Heralding the Afrocentrists of later decades, Allen suggests that African Americans were in fact morally superior to their white oppressors, a view of racial uplift that made humble blacks the measuring stick for behavior. Much of the earlier movement for racial betterment had urged African Americans to mimic the behavior and mannerisms of white society. In contrast, the remainder of the publication was devoted to racially neutral articles aimed at female and juvenile readers urging modesty and modeling a Christian lifestyle. In this way, Allen's paper provided a complete spectrum of the day-to-day needs for living a full and Christian life, while setting an Afrocentric vision for a post-racial future in the United States.

Next, Courtney Pace Lyons resurrects the career of Prathia Hall, as her career in Albany, Georgia, and surrounding communities in Southwest Georgia was important in its own right. But Lyon's depiction of Hall serves as a vital metaphor informing the robust scholarship of the civil rights movement. Hall is not just a church woman, she works for the Student Nonviolent Coordinating Committee (SNCC). She not only provides ministerial and organizational support, but also is a voting rights organizer. Northern born, she works in the South with locals, and in the wake of the storied Albany Movement of the Southern Christian Leadership Conference, it was Hall and the SNCC who registered voters and pressed for long-term political change, which her moral vision helped to shaped. A female preacher, Hall also experienced the burgeoning sexism within the male leadership of the movement and in the SNCC specifically. Hall's career illustrates the long and ongoing role of the social-gospel in the African American church and how it informed the activism and vision for important strands of the civil rights movement, as well as the centrality of local leadership and local people in effecting religiously informed and long-term social change.

Edward R. Crowther examines the political culture within the National Baptist Convention and the powerful role played by its presidents, who mixed political and ministerial skills in a very public venue. With the National Baptist Convention being the largest African American organization in the United States through most of the twentieth century, it is unsurprising that the presidential office was a desideratum of ambitious men who parleyed their power to exact concessions from the white power structure even as they pursued evangelistic and educational enterprises. The demands for denominational unity rubbed against the personal and political ambitions of aspirants for the presidency, threatening schism, even at the death of a long-serving president of the convention. The presidency of Joseph H. Jackson shows how the internal political culture struggled with both the politics of accommodation and gradualism against the demands of younger preachers for limitations on presidential power and tenure. The internal pressures within the denomination, occurring against the backdrop of the civil rights movement in the 1950s and 1960s, led to denominational rupture and the founding of the Progressive National Baptist Convention.

Finally, Andrew Manis details the career and especially the funeral of Fred Shuttlesworth, whose death marks the passing of the ministerial leadership of the civil rights era and highlights something more fundamental in the black-and-white world of the Baptist denomination. Manis, who is Shuttlesworth's biographer, was also among his eulogists. As a white scholar and a Baptist, Manis, following his long encounter with Shuttlesworth, is a telling commentary on the divisive role of race in the Baptist Fellowship, but it is also a testament to the continuing possibilities of racial brotherhood under the umbrella of a shared Baptist faith.

Dr. King once describe Sunday mornings as the "most segregated in America." However, in 2012, the Southern Baptist Convention elected Louisianan Fred Luter as president, the first African American to hold that office. Whether Luter's election represents a substantial movement toward a full reconciliation among white and black Baptists, carrying forward the 1995 apology by the Southern Baptist Convention for racism and slavery, or whether it is a simple anomaly remains to be seen. At the same time, demographic and economic data suggest a persistent gap between black and white Americans. This ongoing division in American society reflects the challenging role of race and history, which is reflected in the Baptist world since emancipation. The needs of cultural identity—African American self-determination and, sadly, white supremacy—have historically kept black and white Baptists separated, even as a common commitment to evangelistic goals has posited opportunities for cooperation and shared visions. For African American Baptists, the historical record is much clearer. The Baptist faith has provided a source of religious and cultural identity for scores of African Americans. At times, the possibility of brotherhood has seemed to point in the direction of full equality, both civil and ecclesiastical. As they contemplate a world not apportioned according to the color of one's skin, black Baptists often find themselves, more than a century and a half after emancipation, between fetters and freedom.

1

Vindicated Faith, Not a Lost Cause:

African American Baptist Identity and Vision in the Civil War and Postwar Eras, 1850–1900

Sandy Dwayne Martin

For African American Christians in general and black Baptists in particular, the Civil War was not a time of defeat and search for theodicy (an explanation or inquiry on how to reconcile faith in the existence of an omnipotent and loving God with unfortunate or tragic circumstances of life), as was the case for Southern white Christians. Rather, the events of the Civil War signaled victory and an answer to questions of theodicy. For both white and black Christians, including Baptists, the Civil War raised the twin issues of self-identity and vision of purpose. Both the "vindicated faith" of African Americans and "the lost cause" religion of whites were expressions of their respective self-identities and their understanding of the mission that lay before them. This essay examines the responses of African American Baptists to the events of the American Civil War, particularly as those responses differed from the mainstream of Southern white Baptists.

The following pages aim to inform and/or remind readers that, broadly speaking, there were two major types of Southerners, two main types of religion, and two overall responses to the Civil War. In other words, this work seeks to examine the alternative black theological perspective on the meaning of the Civil War. In so doing, first, we recognize the agency of black people instead of regarding them as passive recipients or beneficiaries of the events. Second, this essay emphasizes the uniqueness, creativity, and vibrancy of African American religion, realizing that while it shares events with white Christianity, African American religion at this time is far from a simple imitation of white religiosity.

Historical Context: Theological Meanings of the Civil War

The Civil War represented different things to various Americans.[1] To examine these main themes and approaches to the Civil War, one might place Americans during this era in one of three major classes: Southern whites, Northern whites, and African Americans and antislavery whites. Granted, this division of Americans into three categories is over simplified and does not reflect nuances in all three groups. There were white Northerners who were Southern sympathizers. There were white Southerners who were Unionists and enlisted in the federal armed services. Among African Americans, there was a small group of slaveholders and a very small number who labored in the armed ranks of the Confederacy. Of course there were some antislavery whites who on a personal level despised black people about as much as they abhorred the slavery system. Moreover, other groupings of Americans might include Native Americans who held slaves and other Native Americans who found themselves among the "colored" population of the enslaved; some Irish and non-Irish white Northerners who violently opposed the Northern draft for service in the Union cause, persons who saw their own struggle with poverty and security as more pressing than a battle to free descendants of Africa whom they disliked intensely; and Jews and Catholics on both sides of the North-South and slavery-antislavery divides. Nonetheless, the above three-fold categorizing of Americans, while insufficiently nuanced, points to three major trends or themes associated with the Civil War and therefore serves a useful purpose.

For white Northerners, the Civil War was truly a battle over whether the nation would remain united, a concern that rose above all other issues such as slavery. For white Southerners the war was a struggle for Southern (white) independence and the right to establish their own (white) nation with its own laws and customs. For blacks and antislavery whites the war, as it progressed, became a War of Black Emancipation, the end of chattel slavery, and the opportunity for the undisputed citizenship of African

---

[1] For an examination of the issues relating to slavery, Civil War, and the churches, see John Corrigan and Winthrop S. Hudson, *Religion in America*, 8th ed. (Boston: Prentice-Hall, 2010) 181–212; Edwin S. Gaustad, ed., *A Documentary History of Religion in America: To the Civil War* (Grand Rapids: Eerdmans Publishing Co., 1982) 467–52; Albert J. Raboteau, *Canaan Land: A Religious History of African Americans* (New York City: Oxford University Press, 2001) 61–81.

Americans, at least in constitutional terms. To be sure, slavery was the central and defining issue of the conflict, irrespective of how much many Northern and Southern whites through the decades have tried to obfuscate it as the cause. Everyone who fought to have a separate white nation, keep a united nation, or bring about the liberation of black people did not necessarily favor or oppose slavery or like blacks. Nonetheless, the records of the white Southern secessionists and slaveholders, not to mention the debates and conflicts leading up to the Civil War, reveal that had there been no commitment to maintain slavery there would have been no Civil War in the 1860s.[2]

Not all participants in the conflict placed religion as their central concern, either for themselves or for the cause for which they were struggling. Religion, however, played a key role in buttressing the support and even shaping the normative vision of all three categories: white Northerners, white Southerners, and blacks and antislavery white people. White religious Northerners, including Baptists, believed that the nation had indeed been founded with the approval of God and that the Almighty had ordained a purpose for a united nation. To divide that nation, peacefully or through war, was to work against the plan of God for the destiny of the Lord's chosen people to bring Christianity and democracy to the larger world. White religious Southerners, including Baptists, believed that slavery was consistent with the Bible, Christian tradition, and God's plan for the American people. Indeed, the efforts of antislavery people (even those who were not abolitionists) to condemn servitude was indicative, for white Southerners, of a Northern move away from biblically based, traditional, authentic Christianity. The northern version of religion, which white Southerners believed was an increasingly corrupted form of Christianity, threatened the God-ordained destiny of the nation. African American Christians and their antislavery white allies (at least to the extent of being opposed to slavery)—and the Baptists among them—saw slavery as a blight on the Christian faith and the nation's constitutional principles. While many would not agree with the African American abolitionist David Walker's call in the late 1820s and early 1830s for the enslaved to rise up in armed

---

[2] For more on this topic, see Gary W. Gallagher's two classic studies: *The Union War* (Cambridge: Harvard University Press, 2011); *The Confederate War* (Cambridge: Harvard University Press, 1999).

rebellion against their oppressors,[3] they did agree with Walker that slavery was odious to God and that the nation would face the judgment of the Lord if it did not eliminate the practice. Hence, one may conclusively and confidently affirm that the Civil War was a war about liberation (whether pro-black liberation or con-black liberation) and was, to a great extent, a conflict involving varying religious identities and visions.

Of the three broad categories of Americans in the 1860s—white Northerners, white Southerners, and African Americans and antislavery whites—it was the first group, white Northerners, for whom the Civil War brought a long-lasting and definitive resolution to the concerns they had going into battle. Their goal in the war had been to maintain national unity and, for many, to be free of the threat of enslaved labor to white free workers. Militarily defeated and having lost slaveholder status, white Southerners, including Baptists, had more difficulty with the war's end. They found themselves having to accept a new order while trying to maintain the enduring justice of their cause. In the immediate aftermath of the war, black Americans were the most jubilant, followed closely by the antislavery people. For African Americans and some antislavery whites, the end of slavery was truly momentous, although there remained the on-going struggle of acquiring and securing full, equal citizenship and opportunity for freed slaves and black Americans. White Southerners, in dealing with this new order, began discussing the Lost Cause; contrarily, African American Southerners in jubilation of the new order and arranging their lives for the struggle ahead exhibited vindicated faith.[4]

What then was the (white) Southern Lost Cause? In essence, it revolved around remembering and celebrating the participation of the South in the struggle for Confederate independence.[5] While the white South lost

---

[3] David Walker, *David Walker's Appeal, in Four Articles ...* (Boston: David Walker, 1830), http://docsouth.unc.edu/nc/walker/menu.html (accessed 27 September 2013).

[4] For a good summary of contrary ideas of Providence and the Civil War's outcome, see George C. Rable, *God's Almost Chosen Peoples: A Religious History of the Civil War* (Chapel Hill: University of North Carolina Press, 2010) 389–97.

[5] For information on the Lost Cause Myth and the Religion of the Lost Cause, see Charles Reagan Wilson, *Baptized in the Blood: Religion of the Lost Cause, 1865–1925* (Athens: University of Georgia Press, 2009); Gaines M. Foster, "Lost Cause

on the battlefield, it nevertheless affirmed the justice of its cause, continuing to believe that it had fought for the noblest and truest understanding of the original American republic. These individuals held the profound conviction that the sacrifice of life in the war actually made the struggle all the more just and noble. The white South had lost the war and, in a general sense, accepted the results (especially the elimination of chattel bondage but not racial equality or black citizenship in the full sense of the term). There was no admission that the Confederate cause was anything less than just. Additionally, there was a sense that the white South still had a special mission to perfect the nation and thereby influence the world. In more particular terms, this worldview, shaped a great deal by religious ideals regarding the white Southern way of life, was expressed in religious concepts and practices that Charles Reagan Wilson calls "Southern civil religion" or "Religion of the Lost Cause."[6]

In the South and elsewhere at this time, African American Christians, including Baptists, held a diametrically opposed view regarding slavery and the place of blacks in the future of the nation. African American Christians had always rejected the notion that God favored their enslavement or that they should suffer discrimination and unequal treatment in the body of the church. Clearly, one sees this expressed during the slave era in the founding of independent black denominations, associations, and conventions. The Union Church of Africans, the African Methodist Episcopal Church, and the African Methodist Episcopal Zion Church all explicitly based their separation from the white-controlled parent body Methodist Episcopal Church on the principles of racial justice and the deep abiding conviction that racial injustice is inconsistent with the practice of true Christianity. This separation from white-controlled groups may be classified in two ways: (1) those independent bodies who exercised total freedom to shape their religious organizations as they saw fit and, (2) autonomous bodies who mainly, because of the strictures of the slavery system, did not have full organizational freedom but who, on a day-to-day basis, had the opportunity

---

Myth," in *Encyclopedia of Southern Culture*, ed. Charles Reagan Wilson and William Ferris (Chapel Hill: University of North Carolina Press, 1989) 1134–5.

[6] Wilson, *Baptized in Blood*, 10–13.

to exercise great leeway in the construction and execution of their organizations.[7]

Black Baptists were later than the Methodists in organizing independent and autonomous church organizations beyond the congregational level.[8] However, the associations and conventions formed between 1834 and 1865—including the Wood River Baptist Association and the Providence Baptist Association in the Midwest, the Amherstburg Baptist Association in the northern Midwest and Canada, and the American Baptist Missionary Convention in the northeast—promulgated boldly the same perspective that slavery was an injustice to humanity, an affront to God, and that caste religion had no place in the practice of Christianity. Furthermore, Baptists, although they chronologically followed the Methodists in the establishment of regional and aspirant national organizations, actually pioneered independency and autonomy at the local congregational level. Early black Baptist churches, such as Silver Bluff Baptist Church in South Carolina, First African/First Bryan Baptist Church of Savannah, Georgia, sought the same freedom to operate free of racial restrictions, as would later-organized Methodist congregations and denominations. For African Americans in slave states who were not able to establish separate associations, conventions, and denominations, the "invisible institution" (secret meetings and the religious activities of blacks not observed by whites) was a means to practice the Christian faith according to their convictions. In other words, these independent and autonomous groups departed from white-controlled religious bodies to avoid imitating whites congregations, to be free of racially prescribed constraints, and to practice true Christianity—a religion they perceived as not practiced by white congregations.

This historical survey of independency and autonomy among pre-Civil War African American Christians underscores the point that temporal freedom and equity were always a vital part of their understanding of the Christian faith. This tradition continued through the antebellum and Civil War eras. Out of eyesight and earshot of whites, enslaved African American

---

[7] For the rise of independent or autonomous black Christianity, see Raboteau, *Canaan Land*, 21–39; Gayraud S. Wilmore, *Black Religion and Black Radicalism: An Interpretation of the Religious History of Afro-American People*, 2nd ed. (Maryknoll: Orbis Books, 1983) 74–98.

[8] For black Baptist organizational beginnings, see Leroy Fitts, *A History of Black Baptists* (Nashville: Broadman Press, 1985) 41–106.

Baptists, as well as other black Christians, prayed and longed for physical as well as spiritual freedom. Black Baptist associations in the free states made it an explicit part of their organizational responsibility to fight against slavery and to struggle for evangelizing and educationally enlightening the black race, domestically and sometimes abroad. While African American slaves were not naïve to the limits of white Northern sympathy toward them, even in some cases to outright hostility, they prayed that the Union forces would prevail. In his classic, *Slave Religion,* Albert Raboteau refers to slaves who were urged to pray for the Confederate forces by white slaveholders concerned about the advancing federal military. In one instance, when an enslaved woman remarked that she prayed that God's will would prevail, the slaveholding mistress wisely noted that this was not the desired response to their original request (or command). She insisted that the enslaved woman pray specifically that the Confederate forces would prevail.[9] This incident illustrates at least three historical points: First, white Southerners, including Baptists, often signaled their faith in the efficacy of some black people's prayers and, hence, the authenticity of African American Christianity, however flawed they might have imagined black Christianity to be in comparison with white Christianity. Second, perhaps this event demonstrates that some Southern whites had some serious, if unspoken, doubts regarding the rectitude of the slave system and the Confederate cause. Third, and maybe more pertinent to the main thesis of this essay, this episode boldly illustrates how two sets of people, while confessing belief in the same God, the same Bible, and perhaps shared denominational ties, could nonetheless hold diametrically opposed views about the Confederacy and black freedom.

Faith Awaiting Vindication

Amazingly, the African American faithful still believed that the justice of God meant that they would one day be free despite the reality of chattel slavery. However, the reliability of this faith was not always obvious to other black and white observers. Consider the 1850s, the decade immediately preceding the Civil War. This decade indeed held out little hope for black

---

[9] Albert Raboteau, *Slave Religion: The "Invisible Institution" in the Antebellum South,* Updated ed. (New York City: Oxford University Press, 2004) 308–9.

freedom.[10] A passage of the Fugitive Slave Law in 1850 made it a federal crime to harbor slave refugees or impede their return to their slaveholders, even when those refugees had reached free territory. In some communities, whites and blacks made bold, dangerous, even violent stances that often proved to be successful at thwarting authorities sent to forcibly retrieve refugees. Yet, such pro-refugee support was not always forthcoming. As a matter of fact, some Northern communities legally prohibited free blacks from remaining in their midst. Given such realities, some African American refugees understandably chose to flee all the way to Canada for guaranteed safety. Some of these ex-slaves maintained or adopted the Baptist faith, and some, such as Anthony Binga, Jr., would return to the American South during and after the Civil War to play leadership roles in religious and/or political circles.[11]

It was not simply the Fugitive Slave Law, however, that clouded the vision of black freedom during the 1850s. In 1857, just four years prior to the advent of the sectional conflict, the US Supreme Court under the leadership of Chief Justice Roger Taney handed down the Dred Scott Decision. Essentially, this decision held that blacks escaping to free territory could not sue for their freedom because the citizenship status of all blacks was questionable, and that the Founding Fathers never intended that black people should be a full part of the body politic. Additionally, it was not absolutely certain to everyone that the 1860 election of Abraham Lincoln would bring about the freedom of the enslaved. Lincoln had made it clear that his goal was not to stop the practice of servitude where it already existed

---

[10] For the history of African Americans regarding issues and events during the Antebellum and Civil War years, see John Hope Franklin and Alfred A. Moss, Jr., *From Slavery to Freedom: A History of African Americans*, 8th ed. (Boston: McGraw Hill Higher Education, 2000) 167–244. Regarding black Christians' prayers for and belief that they would eventually be freed from enslavement, see Raboteau, *Slave Religion*, 289–318. For a brief description of missionary efforts at this time, especially the work of Anthony Binga, Jr., see Sandy D. Martin, *Black Baptists and African Missions: The Origins of a Movement, 1880–1915* (Macon, GA: Mercer University Press, 1989) 109–10.

[11] Carter G. Woodson, *The History of the Negro Church*, 2nd ed. (Washington, DC: Associated Publishers, 1921) 171, 240.

but to stem its spread into new areas, making it obvious that the candidate from Illinois was not an advocate of racial equality.[12]

Faith Vindicated

With the advent of the Civil War, many African Americans and antislavery whites dearly hoped, but had no certain basis for believing, that the conflict would result in freedom for the enslaved. As the war progressed (and not to the advantage of the federal forces), it became clear to Union leaders that certain steps amenable to black freedom must be undertaken. First, black soldiers were permitted to participate in the war effort. Many African American Christians, including Baptists, who had fled north from a life of slavery eagerly recruited black soldiers and/or enlisted themselves. Second, the Emancipation Proclamation was announced, becoming effective 1 January 1863. This singular event cemented the conviction that God had acted in history to vindicate divine justice and set the Lord's faithful people free.

Later, in the 1970s, an African American thinker, William R. Jones, took issue with James Cone, J. Deotis Roberts, and other advocates of black theology who were asserting that the Christian gospel is one of liberation for the oppressed.[13] Jones asked a piercing question: What proof is there that God has acted in history to liberate African Americans from oppression? For that matter, could not one just as easily argue that God was on the side of white racists rather than the supporter of the black oppressed given the persistence of racial subjugation? This line of theodicy was proposing that a more rational and realistic theology or philosophy stemmed from a humanistic perspective (which includes the understanding that human beings must solve their own problems) rather than from a theistic worldview (which holds an expectation that a personal, omnipotent, omniscient, and benevolent God rules the universe). Unfortunately, the leading black theologians did not provide an answer to that question of theodicy, except to

---

[12] The literature on Lincoln, race, and slavery is vast, but an authoritative source on this point specifically is James Oakes, *The Radical and the Republican: Frederick Douglass, Abraham Lincoln, and the Triumph of Antislavery Politics* (New York: Norton, 2007) 87–132.

[13] Gayraud S. Wilmore and James H. Cone, eds., *Black Theology: A Documentary History, 1966–1979* (Maryknoll, NY: Orbis Books, 1979) 620–2.

say something to the effect that the nature of faith calls for confidence in the revelation of God's eventual justice.

Nineteenth-century Civil War-era black Christians, including Baptists, would have had a ready reply to such humanistic arguments. Just as God had freed the Hebrews from bondage in Egypt against all humanly understood odds, keeping the promise to Abraham after centuries of servitude, so this same God in the 1860s was acting in history to free Israel once again, this time African Americans who walked in faith. These Christians were not naïve to humanity's mixed and selfish motives, even when acting in the interests of justice and freedom. Rather, these African American faithful firmly believed traditional Christian teachings about divine sovereignty and benevolence: the God of justice and freedom would not forever permit the continuation of brutality and injustice. Only a few years earlier, it seemed that the reign of chattel slavery would continue throughout the land, that prospects for freedom were getting worse not better. However, then came the unlikely freedom of a people who had been enslaved for centuries; it is no wonder that many enslaved people stayed up all night on 31 December 1862 awaiting the dawn of the New Year when they would be legally free. Nor is it surprising that for decades African American churches continued to celebrate what they termed *Jubilee*, a biblical term for a holy day celebrating the Emancipation Proclamation. Even today, many African American churches, including Baptist congregations, continue a tradition of holding worship services lasting from the night of December 31 to the midnight arrival of the New Year. Regrettably, many black Christians, Baptists and otherwise, are unmindful of the historical significance of this practice.

It is not the decades-old theological or philosophical argument of William Jones or the contemporary challenge of Anthony Pinn that questions the conviction of the practical or even theological significance of the Emancipation Proclamation.[14] In academic circles, many have come to the position of downplaying or missing the powerful significance of emancipation for Civil War- and postwar-era blacks. Critics make the following charges: (1) The Proclamation concerned itself less with a humanitarian quest for justice and freedom and more with taking a practical

---

[14] Anthony B. Pinn has written a number of books from a humanistic perspective on African American religion; see, for example, *Why, Lord? Suffering and Evil in Black Theology* (New York City: Continuum, 1995).

war-time measures to rally support in the North and defeat the Confederacy. (2) Some have argued in the past that the Proclamation did not actually free any slaves, since it applied only to states in rebellion where the decree could not be enforced and exempted the enslaved in border states still aligned with the Union. (3) The Proclamation and even the Thirteenth, Fourteenth, and Fifteenth Amendments to the Constitution were of little long-term value until the impact of the twentieth-century civil rights movement because the federal government walked away from Reconstruction and the enforcement of the amendments and other civil rights laws, resulting in a nation that replaced a brief period of black freedom with one of segregation, disfranchisement, economic exploitation, racial lynching and terrorism, and white supremacy. Moreover, many critics contend that especially after Reconstruction ended in approximately 1877, the life of African Americans in the South returned to a type of enslavement as exemplified in the sharecropping system.[15] If assertions from humanist critics are correct, then that would seemingly undercut the thesis of this essay that a major result of the Civil War era was that black Baptists, as other African American Christians, experienced a vindicated faith.

Of course, there is a great deal of truth in the above three contentions. Regardless of how contemporary historians might judge the emancipation moment, the historical events of emancipation and the Civil War for African American Baptists and other Christians at the time and thereafter were some of the most significant events in American history. Furthermore, there are historical, extra-theological responses that belie or severely mitigate these three humanist assertions. First, in reply to the assertion regarding a marshal rather than humanitarian motivation behind the Proclamation, it matters little about the political intentions; what matters is the change that the Proclamation brought about for the lives of those enslaved and for others who opposed slavery. Second, the Proclamation did in fact free enslaved people. Prior to the proclamation, individual Union commanders could (and sometimes did) opt to return refugees to the slaveholder or regard them as "contraband." With President Lincoln's Proclamation, those escaping from

---

[15] The author is not referring to any detailed argument set forth by a particular scholar or group of scholars. The above simply summarizes alternative viewpoints regarding the impact of Emancipation and the Civil War on African American thought.

slavery would, in fact, legally be regarded as refugees, i.e., human beings escaping slavery. Additionally, as the Union forces victoriously advanced over Confederate strongholds, former slaves would gain their freedom. It is true that all branches of the federal government—Legislative, Executive, and Judicial—refused to support the civil rights of African Americans in the decades following the Civil War. Nevertheless, even segregated, second-class citizenship in an environment of white dominance was a far cry from the brutalities of chattel slavery. While the system of sharecropping was economically exploitative and disfranchisement a direct assault on the black people's constitutional rights, it was far more progressive than a system of chattel enslavement wherein one might lose one's children or spouse on the auction block. Yes, African Americans, including Baptists, felt betrayed by the negligence and indifference of the federal government, but, sufficient progress had been made and retained to secure their vindicated faith, which holds that God had acted in history on their behalf and continued to do so.

Despite the harsh experiences they encountered, especially after Reconstruction, African American Baptists, as did other blacks, continued to hold out hope for a better day well into the twentieth century. Some African American Christians, including Baptists, even interpreted the injustice and oppression visited upon them in the late 1800s and early 1900s as an opportunity to reclaim a closer fellowship with Christ and repent from wrongdoing. Those who employed this type of theodicy credited whites, not God, with injustice. They held on to a biblically based conviction that God often uses human sinfulness to advance his divine will. W. Bishop Johnson, pastor of Second Baptist Church in Washington, DC, was one such Baptist. Rev. Johnson had played important leadership roles among Virginia Baptists and in the recently organized National Baptist Convention. In the early 1900s, when white supremacy dominated the South, Johnson published a book of sermons, one of which bore the name of the book title, *The Scourging of a Race*. In this publication, Johnson quite candidly and graphically notes the oppressed state of African Americans.[16]

---

[16] W. Bishop Johnson, *The Scourging of a Race and Other Sermons and Addresses* (Washington, DC: Beresford Printers, 1904), http://archive.org/details/scourging-ofrace00john (accessed 27 September 2013). For a short biography of Johnson, see Edward M. Brawley, introduction to *The Scourging of a Race*, by Johnson, iii–vi.

However, it was the pastor's conviction that God was employing these injustices and sufferings, inflicted by sinful people to "scourge" the race, to teach African Americans to return to the true worship and service of God. In his judgment, African Americans had departed from certain core values and practices and stood guilty of a number of flaws, including ingratitude to the Lord for divine blessings, desertion from the type of manhood that respected and protected African American women, a loss of racial togetherness, disrespect for race leaders, lack of growth in faith, and not giving proper attribution to God for prosperity. Nevertheless, Johnson wrote (and preached) that God wished to correct these defects in the race so that the Lord might use African Americans to make a great contribution to the world: "[God's] wisdom is gradually fitting [African Americans] to play a might part in the world's history." This would entail some sacrifice and suffering, and "there has always been an inseparable connection between sacrifice, service, and suffering ... and God has not called any people to sacrifice, service, and suffering without crowning their lives with rich and abundant reward when they have been faithful."[17]

Johnson held firmly to a vindicated faith. The Baptist pastor believed that the enslaved people of faith had dearly prayed for freedom and that God eventually acted in history in response to their prayers. It was no accident or mere human endeavor that had brought freedom to black people in America. From their perspective, God had moved antislavery spokespersons, white and black, to condemn the practice. After the Civil War, the Lord had raised up friends of the race who established institutions of learning, which an impoverished and formerly enslaved people so desperately needed. The progress of the race is thus seen as having been under the hand of Providence. Johnson believed that African Americans had progressed because of their strong faith in God, a faith that even racially prejudiced people had to recognize in the race. "Providence has led thus far. Let no one think," he intoned, "that we do not figure in the divine economy, or that we are not an element, in the divine scheme for the world's enlightenment and civilization." As scripture says, God chastens or disciplines those for whom the Lord cares. Hence, while Johnson critiqued the African American community for its failures and faults, he held to the steadfast conviction that

---

[17] Johnson, *Scourging of a Race*, 13.

"God is still with us. His sleepless eye is ever upon us. He is still our Sun and Shield. He still gives grace and glory ..."[18]

Building Institutions with Vindicated Faith

African American Christians, including Baptists prior to the Civil War who had awaited the vindication of their faith that God was acting in history on their behalf, saw their faith in this cause vindicated in the outcome of the war. Thus, as the remainder of this essay demonstrates, African American Christians proceeded to build institutions based in large part on that vindicated faith. Emerging from the bonds of slavery (and witnessing their brothers and sister do so), African American Christians, including Baptists, embarked upon a new phase of building what may be defined as the *second great institutionalization of the African American church*. The 1750s and the 1850s saw the establishment of, first, independent or at least relatively autonomous black Baptist congregation; and second, regional associations, and even, arguably, efforts at national organization of black Baptists. While separate black congregations during the antebellum era in non-slave areas enjoyed a great degree of autonomy from white control, independent congregations in the Southern and slave states faced severe restrictions on their liberties.

With the coming of the Civil War and the gradual defeat of the Confederacy, former slaves could more freely establish their own institutions and connect more openly with their siblings from non-slave areas of the country. In other words, this second institutionalization of the African American church, flowering during the 1860–1920 period, witnessed black Baptists, more boldly and definitively separating institutionally from their white counterparts. Black Baptist congregations in the Civil War and postwar eras arose in a number of ways: groups of people from various religious backgrounds organized new congregations; blacks seceded from racially mixed (but segregated) churches; blacks remained in locales with rights to the church property as whites seceded to form new white churches; or some combination of the above. Generally, it seems the separation of black and white memberships was relatively amicable. Though some blacks and whites hesitated, the impossibility of people practicing two very different approaches to Christianity under the same roof, so to speak, soon

---

[18] Ibid., 9.

became quite apparent to both parties. Whites, though often expressing some sense of genuine concern for African Americans, could not accept the idea that their ex-slaves should be their equal brothers and sisters—even in the house of the Lord. Just as most Southern whites had seen no disconnect between enslavement and Christianity before emancipation, they now found no contradiction between racial supremacy and Christianity after the war.

Liberated from slavery, blacks could no longer tolerate racial discrimination and segregation in the house of God now that they had tasted a fuller measure of freedom. And, to underscore a point made earlier, the issue of race was not merely a social and political matter. Blacks fundamentally rejected any version of the gospel that would endorse and enforce "caste Christianity"; they would countenance no membership where belief in the fatherhood (parenthood) of God remained severed from the practice of the brotherhood (siblinghood) of humanity.

These African American Baptists, like other black Christians with vindicated faith, established congregations and moved in quickly to found regional associations, both intra- and inter-state.[19] By 1870, a number of state Baptist conventions had already emerged, including bodies in Virginia, North Carolina, and South Carolina. There were general conventions encompassing a range of activities; soon appearing, however, were associations and conventions focused on specific activities, such as Sunday schools, foreign or overseas missions, and domestic mission work. On another level, Baptists throughout the nation in light of the liberating developments of the Civil War and post-Civil War years eagerly moved toward national unity. It is important to note that there were many auxiliaries, conventions, and societies founded and operated by women Baptists in connection and/or cooperation with these generally male-led

---

[19] In addition to Fitts's text cited earlier, details on the organization of black Baptist organizations are outlined in James M. Washington, *Frustrated Fellowship: The Black Baptist Quest for Social Power* (Macon, GA: Mercer University Press, 1986); Martin, *Black Baptists and African Missions*, pays some attention to institutional organization, particularly as it relates to the pursuit of African missions; additionally, the vital dimension of women's participation in Baptist organizational life and history can be found in Evelyn Higginbotham, *Righteous Discontent: The Women's Movement in the Black Baptist Church, 1880–1920* (Cambridge: Harvard University Press, 1993).

organizations.[20] Although it would take about three decades beyond the Civil War to institute a truly enduring national organization of black Baptists, serious efforts were made along the way and ultimately with quicker success (e.g., the National Baptist Convention in 1895) than that achieved by the mainly white Northern Baptists (originally the Northern Baptist Convention founded in 1907,[21] that is, if we measure national unity by a body covering the broad range of activities.

Of course, this second institutionalization of black Baptists had the assistance of Northern whites and blacks and some Southern whites. The antebellum period and Civil War occasioned tensions and divisions among some white-controlled church bodies, including the family of mainly white Baptists. Yet, this same period saw the greater cooperation and joining together of black Baptist forces. As Southern black Baptists formed their institutions, they often did so with the indispensable assistance of others, mainly white Northern groups such as the American Baptist Home Mission Society. These groups provided valuable assistance in a number of ways, including church construction and support of educational institutions. Although white Southerners faced their own financial challenges as a result of the war, some nonetheless provided a great deal of needed support to black churches, as well. Northern blacks and longtime free blacks in the South also provided valuable aid to their ex-enslaved siblings. Indeed, the quest to uplift the race contributed mightily to the push toward national unity, witnessed as early as the 1860s with the expansion into the South of groups such as the Consolidated American Baptist Missionary Convention and the Northern and Southwestern Baptist Convention. To be sure, there were occasional sectional and class tensions within various black groups, yet their commitment to spread the Gospel and uplift the race helped produce the eventually successful national solidarity of these Baptists.

As indicated already, black Baptists and other Christians emerged from slavery and slave society with the conviction that they had a special commission from God to spread the Christian faith and uplift the race within the US and around the world. The minutes and reports regarding

---

[20] See Armstrong's chapter in this volume for more information to this point.

[21] See a brief overview of Baptists in the US, including the American Baptist Churches, formerly Northern Baptist Convention, at American Baptist Churches, "Our History," http://www.abc-usa.org/what_we_believe/our-history/ (accessed 25 September 2013).

local black churches, associations, societies, and conventions express strongly the commitment and determination of these Baptists to make their God-commanded contribution to Christianity and world civilization. First, their constitutions, covenants, and statements of faith, whether originated by them or brought with them from white-controlled and other settings, revealed a strong emphasis on Christian piety and the proper formation and operation of churches. We also see these emphases in the minutes of their meetings. For example, in the *Eighth Annual Session of the Colored Missionary Baptist Convention of Alabama*—a meeting held in Mobile, Alabama, in November 1875—on the second day of the meeting, an elder moved the formation of committees to address Sunday schools, mission work, temperance, and printing. The Committee on Church Complaints made a report accepted by the general assembly that the Monday Street Church had been improperly organized, that its name be stricken from the list of convention churches, and that the elder responsible for bringing the congregation into the convention be required to account for this error. On the third day of the convention, the committee and the body made decisions about other churches, some of which were in acceptable standing and some not. Interestingly, a certain Elder N. G. Scurlock made a motion regarding the convention's support of the formation of a national convention of African American Baptists and also moved for a theological school for the training of clergy to be established in the state "in order that we may be able to defend ourselves against 'popery'."[22]

This same session indicates evidence of interdenominational, intra-denominational, and interracial cooperation. For instance, Elder R. Ramsey from Meridian, Mississippi, addressed the convention bearing a letter requesting that Alabama Baptists and those of his state unite in "fraternal cooperation" and that they establish a school that, like the recommendation from Elder Scurlock, would prepare men (presumably) for the Christian ministry. Elder Ramsey noted that some white Baptists in Mississippi had provided support to his Baptist association's fund for education. Elder W. G. Strong of the African Methodist Episcopal Zion Church in a letter to the delegates welcomed the convention (to the city of Mobile, apparently)

---

[22] Minutes, *The Eighth Annual Session of the Colored Missionary Baptist Convention of Alabama*, meeting in Mobile, AL, 17–24 November 1875, 6, http://archive.org/details/minutesofeightha00colo (accessed 27 September 2013).

and asked God's blessings on their deliberations. Finally, very noteworthy, the Methodist elder also seemed to be inviting Baptist ministers to preach in his church, given his statement, "It will afford me great pleasure to have my pulpit supplied by members of your body on Sabbath next."[23]

Granted, these minutes represent only one Baptist state convention for a period of a couple of days in 1875. However, the above points regarding the Alabama Convention are similar to those that appear prior to and after 1875 in the records of many local churches, associations, societies, and conventions. These black Baptists, whose faith in the liberating activity of God on their behalf had been vindicated by the emancipation and results of the Civil War, were serious about the teachings and ideals of their faith, their Baptist identity, the proper organization and execution of church work, the multi-faceted issues and challenges that confronted them in the church and the world, the need to build strong institutions, some measure of cooperation with white Christians and receipt of assistance from them, and the willingness to combine their commitment to Baptist particularity with the universality of the Christian faith. Were there black Baptists who did not wholeheartedly share the above-referenced sentiments? Yes, some black Baptists on the basis of their understanding of the tradition eschewed organized mission societies and were not as openly receptive to non-Baptist religious associations as these Alabama conventioneers appear to be. However, this Alabama group very accurately represents the consensus of African American Baptists, North and South, male and female, during this era.

Not surprisingly, therefore, many black Baptist individuals, including many born in slavery because of, and motivated by, this vindicated faith became prominent pastors, Baptist church historians, teachers and professors, lawyers, and physicians, governmental office holders. In addition, they became founders of educational institutions, banks, insurance companies, fraternal organizations, founders and editors of newspaper, and pursued many other paths that led to success and public service. Moreover, what often appears most prominently in their writings, speeches, and in comments from others about these men and women is not their quest for

---

[23] Ibid.

personal success and glory but a deep sense of service to God, race, and humanity.[24]

Conclusion

The above discussion outlines, from a contemporaneous worldview, the reality of a vindicated faith for African American Christians, including Baptists, during the Civil War and postwar eras. The intent has been to demonstrate that blacks emerged from slavery with a firm conviction that God had liberated them from slavery and that through the postwar decades, even in the midst of all the trials and tribulations that the race faced, black Baptists and other Christians still held on to the conviction that the God who had liberated them had a special mandate for them in human history. Furthermore, they built and augmented black Baptist institutions locally, regionally, statewide, and nationally in large part based on this vindicated faith.

It is unlikely that this one essay has fully captured the fullness of African American Baptist activities and thinking during the period under consideration. Hopefully, however, it has made some fruitful demonstration that, far from experiencing the Civil War and even the collapse of Reconstruction as an occasion for a religion of Lost Cause, African American Baptists instead held on to the convictions that God was still acting in history to liberate them spiritually and temporally and that the Emancipation Proclamation and Civil War had vindicated such a faith.

---

[24] See Charles Octavius Boothe, *The Cyclopedia of Colored Baptists of Alabama: Their Life and Their Work* (Birmingham: Alabama Press, 1895). A number of black Baptists compiled histories and encyclopedias of religious leaders and institutions during the late 19th and early 20th centuries; see, for example, A. W. Pegues, *Our Baptist Ministers and Schools* (Springfield, MA: Wiley and Sons, 1892).

2

North Carolina's Black Baptists and the Predicament of Emancipation

Charles F. Irons

The white pastor at Abbot's Creek Baptist Church near High Point, North Carolina, conducted an especially successful revival in September 1870. He and his assistants preached for ten days, at the end of which twenty-eight persons were ready to confess faith in Christ and to join the church. The pastor was so exhausted after preaching so many consecutive sermons that F. M. Jordan, another elder in the church, did the actual baptisms at the conclusion of the protracted meeting. Jordan immersed not only twenty-six whites but also Minerva Wood and Lucinda Clinard, two "colored" women.[1] By their decision to submit to the discipline of Abbot's Creek Baptist Church, Wood and Clinard confounded just about every rule historians have laid out to understand the decisions of freedpeople during the postwar period. Most importantly, they appear to have moved in the wrong direction—into a white-dominated church instead of out of one, from a position of ostensible autonomy to one of ecclesial subordination to whites.

Historians have emphasized the quest for racial autonomy as the defining characteristic of African American life during Reconstruction, especially within churches, and have marginalized accounts like those of Wood and Clinard. Eric Foner and Steven Hahn represent well the guild's emphasis on self-rule when they describe black-controlled churches as the most enduring achievements of Reconstruction.[2] Foner, Hahn, and others have depicted black churches as the most visible signs of black aspiration and the key theaters for community self-empowerment. As Evelyn Brooks

---

[1] Minutes, September 1870, Abbot's Creek Baptist Church, North Carolina Baptist Historical Society (NCBHS) Church Records Microfilm (CRMF) 363.

[2] Eric Foner, *Reconstruction: America's Unfinished Revolution, 1863–1877* (New York City: Harper & Row, 1988) 88; Steven Hahn, *A Nation under Our Feet: Black Political Struggles in the Rural South from Slavery to the Great Migration* (Cambridge: Belknap Press of Harvard University Press, 2003) 230.

Higginbotham puts it, "In the decades following Reconstruction, the church's autonomy and financial strength made it the most logical institution for the pursuit of racial self-help."[3] In more specialized treatments of the process through which black Southerners left white-controlled churches after the war, William Montgomery, Katherine Dvorak, and others have also crafted a narrative of increasing autonomy and have treated independent black churches as the essential postwar ligaments of African American politics and culture. "So vitally important was the church, in fact," Montgomery wrote, "that it is difficult to imagine how the black community in the post-Civil War South could have developed as well as it did without it."[4] In their valorization of black agency and institution-building, these scholars echo generations of African American churchmen and scholars, authors such as J. A. Whitted and C. F. Graves, who emphasized the organizational "progress" of black Protestants. In his work on the immediate postwar period, for instance, Graves devoted one chapter to Shaw University and another to the state convention.[5] For historians, the meta-narrative is one of insistent African American demands for autonomy, and the exceptional cases are the ones in which black Southerners deferred independence willingly.

---

[3] Evelyn Brooks Higginbotham, *Righteous Discontent: The Women's Movement in the Black Baptist Church, 1880–1920* (Cambridge: Harvard University Press, 1993) 5.

[4] William E. Montgomery, *Under Their Own Vine and Fig Tree: The African American Church in the South, 1865–1900* (Baton Rouge: Louisiana State University Press, 1993) xii; Matthew J. Z. Harper, *Living in God's Time: African American Faith and Politics in Post-Emancipation North Carolina* (PhD diss., University of North Carolina at Chapel Hill, 2009); Canter Brown, Jr., and Larry Eugene Rivers, *For a Great and Grand Purpose: The Beginnings of the AMEZ Church in Florida, 1864–1905* (Gainesville: University Press of Florida, 2004); Katherine Dvorak, *An African American Exodus: The Segregation of Southern Churches* (Brooklyn: Carlson Publishing, 1991); Sandy Dwayne Martin, *For God and Race: The Religious and Political Leadership of AMEZ Bishop James Walker Hood* (Columbia: University of South Carolina Press, 1997).

[5] J. A. Whitted, *A History of the Negro Baptists of North Carolina* (Raleigh, NC: Edwards and Broughton Printing Co., 1908) 75–111, http://docsouth.unc.edu/church/whitted/whitted.html; and Charles F. Graves, *The Story of the Negro Baptists of North Carolina, 1620–1955* (informally published, 1955) 17–23.

When historians emphasize freedpeople's quest for autonomy, ecclesiastical and otherwise, they valorize the determined actions of men and women of color to stand up to white oppression. The unfortunate corollary of this position is that scholars also therefore characterize (either explicitly or implicitly) black Southerners who did *not* hasten to join black-controlled churches or pursue independent black politics as treacherous, weak, or damaged. Leon Litwack, for instance, cites the "old slave habits" that prohibited some men and women from exercising their freedom, and Hahn is so disturbed by the idea that any freedperson would hesitate to join an independent black church that he explains away the delays he find in the documentary record by citing logistical reasons (the difficulty of acquiring a place to worship, of finding an educated minister, etc.).[6]

The number of black worshippers who remained in white-controlled churches—or, like Wood and Clinard, who joined them—was not trivial, nor can it be explained away by practical considerations. Roughly one-third of the black Protestants who had worshipped in biracial churches before the war remained in those same churches through 1867, or two years after Appomattox. Across the former Confederacy, tens of thousands of freedpeople remained in white-controlled churches until 1870, and a small percentage remained until their deaths. Black Baptists approximated this broader pattern. There were just over 50,000 black Baptists in full membership in Virginia in 1860, for example, and that state's General Association calculated that 28,000 had departed by 1867 (leaving approximately 44 percent).[7] Among those African American Baptists who left quickly in the Old Dominion were those who had worshipped in large, highly organized, semi-independent congregations before the war. In

[6] Leon Litwack, *Been in the Storm So Long: The Aftermath of Slavery* (New York City: Alfred A. Knopf, 1979) 451; Hahn, *A Nation under Our Feet*, 231.

[7] *Minutes of the Baptist General Association of Virginia ... 1867* (Richmond, VA: Dispatch Steam Power Presses, 1867) 56. Methodist proportions were roughly the same (31.5 percent of the pre-war totally of 171,857 colored members remained in 1867). *Minutes of the Annual Conferences of the Methodist Episcopal Church, South, for the Year 1860* (Nashville: Southern Methodist Publishing House, 1861) 293; *Minutes of the Annual Conferences of the Methodist Episcopal Church, South, for the Year 1867* (Nashville: Southern Methodist Publishing House, 1870) 196. Please note that the Methodist Episcopal Church, South, figures included a small number of black members of conferences in states that remained loyal to the Union.

August 1865, representatives from seven thriving, urban churches epitomized this trend when they met in Richmond, formally declared their independence from white oversight, and formed the Colored Shiloh Baptist Association. These churches averaged well over one thousand members apiece, with a range from 200 (Third Baptist Church, Petersburg) to 3,474 (First African Church, Richmond), so the wholesale withdrawal of their members made up a significant proportion of the early departures.[8] The story was much the same in the Georgia Association of Baptists (representing Baptists in the northwest portion of the state, including Augusta). In that body, five enormous, semi-independent congregations of black Baptists departed immediately, giving the association a 55 percent loss of black members by 1866. Those in other Georgia Association congregations were much slower to leave, however, to the extent that 2,046 men and women still remained in 1875.[9]

The North Carolina State Convention did not publish aggregate membership records prior to, during, or immediately following the war, making it difficult to estimate exactly how quickly black members left white-controlled churches in the state. Compounding the difficulty, Primitive and Freewill churches made up a relatively high proportion of Tarheel Baptists (one-fifth, based on 1847 figures), and these congregations did not publish composite membership records either.[10] Fragmentary evidence from associations suggests that the number of black Baptists who remained in white-dominated churches for several years after the war was higher in the Old Pine State than elsewhere, most likely because North Carolina did not boast any of the large, semi-independent congregations like those that had formed the Colored Shiloh Association so soon after the armistice. For instance, in 1867, the Chowan Association retained 1,726 of the 3,175 black members listed from 1861 (54 percent); the Cape Fear Association increased the number of black members from 656 in 1860 to 708 in 1867 (a gain of 8 percent); and the Raleigh Association still held onto 818 of its 883

---

[8] *Minutes and Proceedings of the Colored Shiloh Baptist association of Virginia ... 1865* (Richmond, VA: Republic Book and Job Office, 1865) 4.

[9] Daniel Stowell, *Rebuilding Zion: The Religious Reconstruction of the South, 1863–1877* (New York City: Oxford University Press, 1998) 82–3.

[10] For a discussion of these statistical problems, see Maloy A. Huggins, *A History of North Carolina Baptists, 1727–1932* (Raleigh, NC: General Board of the Baptist State Convention, 1967) 259–61, 282–3.

antebellum black members in 1867 (93 percent).[11] The fact that the Cape Fear Association actually gained members underscores the fact that the drive for autonomous worship was not universal among black Baptists (or at least not immediately universal after the war). It also suggests that depicting freedpeople who failed to join a black-controlled church immediately following the war as deficient, damaged, or unaware of their racial self-interest may not be the most helpful way to understand Reconstruction.

Some scholars have wrestled with the fact that the numbers do not always add up to an immediate mass exodus. In the main, historians have assumed, in Hahn's words, that black Southerners who did not leave white-controlled churches immediately must simply have lacked the "opportunities and resources" to do so.[12] Derek Chang is also reluctant to believe that anyone who had lived through slavery would be willing to remain in spiritual fellowship with the men and women who had defended their enslavement any longer than absolutely necessary. He acknowledges that some black Southerners remained in white-controlled churches but emphasizes that freedpeople shared a desire "to establish autonomous institutions through which to craft their post-Emancipation lives." Citing the very real struggles that black ecclesiastical pioneers faced when striking out on their own, he suggests that "financial hardship often proved to be a formidable obstacle to fully realizing this sacred and secular freedom."[13] Daniel Stowell and Paul Harvey have offered the most nuanced depictions of black Protestants in the postwar period and have left the most room for diverse perspectives on ecclesiastical independence within black communities. Harvey has been especially attentive to the ongoing and often paradoxical relations between black and white Baptists after emancipation; this essay is not an attempt to refute Harvey's findings in *Redeeming the South* or *Freedom's Coming* so much

---

[11] *Minutes of the Sixty-First Annual Session of the Chowan Baptist Association ... 1867* (Raleigh, NC: Hufham & Hughes, 1867); *Minutes of the Annual Session of the Cape Fear Association ... 1867* (Raleigh, NC: Mills & Hughes, 1867); *Minutes of the Sixty-Second Annual Session of the Raleigh Baptist Association ...1867* (Raleigh, NC: Biblical Recorder Publishing Co., 1867).

[12] Hahn, *Nation under Our Feet*, 231.

[13] Derek Chang, *Citizens of a Christian Nation: Evangelical Missions and the Problem of Race in the Nineteenth Century* (Philadelphia: University of Pennsylvania Press, 2010) 45, 46; see also pages 47, 184.

as it is an effort look more closely at the years directly following the war's conclusion.[14]

It may be that Wood, Clinard, and other black Southerners who voluntarily remained in fellowship with whites have just as much to teach about Southern religious history as do Henry McNeal Turner, James Walker Hood, and other famous African American religious and political leaders of Reconstruction. Indeed, their counterexample suggests a different way of understanding freedpeople's postwar possibilities, ecclesiastical and otherwise. Emancipation was a predicament, in the same way that Vincent Brown and others have described enslavement as a predicament.[15] Escape from the house of bondage was sweet, but militant white Southerners and white Northerners who were unwilling to experiment with redistributive justice or to garrison the subjugated South with sufficient strength guaranteed that men and women of color entered freedom with few allies or resources.[16] In this light, it is more helpful to see building autonomous churches as the most popular strategy, rather than the only strategy, for black Protestants to find security, self-worth, and belonging in a changed world. Those black Southerners who remained in or joined white-controlled churches were seeking shelter from the same storm.

---

[14] Stowell, *Rebuilding Zion*, especially chapter 4; and Paul Harvey, *Redeeming the South: Religious Cultures and Racial Identities among Southern Baptists, 1865–1925* (Chapel Hill: University of North Carolina Press, 1997); and *Freedom's Coming: Religious Culture and the Shaping of the South from the Civil War through the Civil Rights Era* (Chapel Hill: University of North Carolina Press, 2005). Scholars who have carried out local or regional studies of particular denominations have also been more willing to acknowledge divisions among black Southerners about how to respond to emancipation and have been less intent on a relentless narrative of autonomy. The best example is Reginald Hildebrand, *The Times were Strange and Stirring: Methodist Preachers and the Crisis of Emancipation* (Durham, NC: Duke University Press, 1995). For Baptists in particular, see Bruce T. Gourley, *Diverging Loyalties: Baptists in Middle Georgia during the Civil War* (Macon, GA: Mercer University Press, 2011).

[15] Vincent Brown, "Social Death and Political Life in the Study of Slavery," *American Historical Review* 114.5 (2009): 1231–49.

[16] For a recent work stressing the desperation of North Carolinians following the war, see Gregory F. Downs, *Declarations of Dependence: The Long Reconstruction of Popular Politics in the South, 1861–1908* (Chapel Hill: University of North Carolina Press, 2011).

The central argument of this essay is therefore that, despite the relative rapidity and thoroughness of racial separation in the churches, freedpeople by no means agreed that racial separation was necessarily the best option for them to pursue—especially in the first, confusing years after emancipation. Some of the variation was geographic; northern missionaries, strong local leaders, Union soldiers, or agents of the Freedmen's Bureau could accelerate the formation of autonomous black churches in communities in which they operated and/or in territories they occupied. However, scholars have made too much of these patterns and have overlooked the extent to which black churchgoers within the very same congregations pursued divergent postwar courses. Even when pioneers formed independent black-controlled churches in their neighborhoods, some black churchgoers chose to remain in white-controlled congregations when others left. Beyond demonstrating the fact of black Baptists' ambivalence about separation, this essay also initiates an exploration of some of the reasons people of color might have chosen to remain in white-controlled churches. The promise of patronage or church property doubtless attracted some black churchgoers, while others sought security or acted on a commitment to Christian unity. In the end, these possible reasons for remaining in fellowship with whites played out in intensely personal ways. The decision was private, and most black Baptists who sat out the initial exodus subsequently left white-controlled churches one individual or household at a time.

Most of the accounts that follow come from the minute books of white-controlled congregations that had black members when white Southerners led their states out of the Union. African American Baptists in North Carolina did not begin to organize on the state level until 1867, and most associations did not begin meeting or publishing minutes until at least 1870. The Old Eastern Baptist Association—centered on James City—began earlier in 1865, but it is unclear whether members of this group published minutes of their first annual meetings. Black Baptists formed the Goose Creek and Cedar Grove Associations in 1869 and produced under their auspices some of the first black-authored Baptist records for the state.[17] These African American sources are of real historical value, for in them, black Southerners declared for the world their motivations for forming

---

[17] Whitted, *History of the Negro Baptists*; early minutes from Goose Creek and Cedar Grove are available at the NCBHS.

separate churches. The minutes of the Zion Colored Baptist Association from its founding meeting in 1873 are illustrative of the limitations of the sources. Most importantly, like almost all extant sources, the founders of Zion did not begin documenting their ideas until several years after slavery ended, skipping over the half-decade when outcomes were most uncertain and when the debate within black communities was most vigorous. Moreover, Zion's patriarchs spoke primarily for those who had already exited white-controlled churches, and they worked from within a narrative of separation fairly well established by the early 1870s. Indeed, in his founding sermon about God equipping Moses to lead the Israelites out of bondage in Egypt, Elder J. W. Davis assumed that separation was normative.[18] Despite the racist assumptions many white clerks harbored, historians can nonetheless glean from documents they authored phase of black ecclesiastical life not fully captured by black churchmen.[19] The month-by-month accounts they left behind constitute an excellent window into the lives of both those black Baptists who left *and* those who stayed put.

A majority of black Baptists did attempt to form their own churches within two years of the war's conclusion. The fact that hundreds of thousands of black churchgoers of every denomination left relatively quickly affirms both the broad outlines of historians' narrative of separation and also indicates that African American churchgoers had the freedom to leave white-controlled churches if they so chose. One way in which freedpeople sought relief from centuries of race-based exploitation was clearly to worship "under their own vine and fig tree" and away from white oversight. Sometimes, black members began to form new churches even before the war concluded. Harry Cowan, the storied "Father of Black Baptists in North Carolina," helped to organize Cedar Grove Baptist Church in Mocksville in 1862.[20] Cowan organized more black-controlled churches, the vast majority of which came out of preexisting biracial congregations, in the year after the

---

[18] *Minutes, Constitution, Rules of Decorum, and Declaration of Principles of the Zion Colored Association, Compiled by T. J. Polk* (Wadesboro: N. Knight & Son, 1873) 1. Davis chose as his text Exodus 4:15.

[19] The North Carolina Baptist Historical Society houses its extensive archives at Wake Forest University. The findings in this essay are based on a close reading of the records of over sixty congregations.

[20] On Cowan, see Whitted, *History of the Negro Baptists*; Cedar Grove [B] (Mocksville) Vertical File, NCBHS.

war. He helped to organize Salisbury's First Calvary Baptist Church in 1866, for example, and Chapel Hill's Mount Zion Baptist Church in 1867.[21] In almost all cases, it appears that black Southerners who withdrew from white-controlled churches took the initiative to do so. In August 1866, for instance, after participating in a protracted meeting with their white coreligionists, people of color in Perquimans County requested permission from the voting white members to form their own congregation. Accordingly, whites in the Bethel Baptist Church passed an order "granting letters of dismission to our colored brethren and sisters to organize a church to themselves."[22]

In the aggregate, two persons left a white-controlled church within two years for each individual who remained. The dividing lines between those who left quickly and those who decided not to move out of their antebellum churches were messy, indeed. There were some broad patterns, sketched briefly below, which suggest important geographic fault lines. In the main, however, the variation was most pronounced *within* individual churches. Men and women who worshipped in the same communities with the same external constraints and same alternatives read the tea leaves differently; while they doubtless shared a sense of solidarity looking out from slavery, they did not reach the same conclusions about how best to maximize their safety and happiness in the postwar world.

Union soldiers, chaplains, and aid workers reshaped the ecclesiastical geography of the Southern states. Daniel Fountain has written about how freedpeople in contraband camps or otherwise behind Union lines enjoyed a measure of security denied their enslaved brethren and about how they began organizing faith communities even before the war was over. In his account, black Southerners who had converted before the war enjoyed new influence among their peers in the moment when emancipation seemed to vindicate their hope in God's deliverance.[23] While black believers doubtless

---

[21] First Calvary [B] (Salisbury) and Mount Zion [B] Chapel Hill, Vertical Files, NCBHS. There is some dispute about the date for Mount Zion; some sources cite 1865.

[22] August 1866, Bethel Baptist Church (Perquimans Co.) NCBHS, CRMF, 151.

[23] Daniel L. Fountain, *Slavery, Civil War, and Salvation: African American Slaves and Christianity, 1830–1870* (Baton Rouge: Louisiana State University Press, 2010).

preached from a position of new strength after the Union officials and freedpeople together made ending slavery a war aim, this rhetorical boost is not the only explanation for why African American believers (Baptist and otherwise) experienced organizational success behind Union lines. Demographics mattered as well. In January 1865, the Freedman's Bureau tallied 10,782 freedpeople as residents of New Bern and its environs, more than anywhere else in North Carolina. Black Baptist leaders operating in precisely this area formed the "Old Eastern," the state's first black-controlled Baptist association.[24] Demographics could work in the opposite direction as well. The few black Baptists in Western North Carolina had a harder time getting critical mass for independent institutions, and mountaineers of color did not leave white churches until they did so *en masse*, forming the New Covenant Association in 1873.[25]

Black and white missionaries who traveled on the coattails of the Union army helped to create a correlation between Union occupation and ecclesiastical separation when they urged freedpeople to leave Confederate-controlled churches. In Wilmington, North Carolina, William H. Hunter, chaplain of a regiment of United State Colored Troops, arrived with soldiers following the fall of Fort Fisher in the late winter of 1865. The first Sunday after the capture of Wilmington, he preached in the Front Street Methodist Church to an ecstatic reception—and subsequently urged the 1,600 black members of the congregation affiliated with the Methodist Episcopal Church, South to seize control of the church and bring it into the African Methodist Episcopal (AME) Fold.[26] Ministers from African Methodist Episcopal Zion (AMEZ) were even more active in North Carolina than were their rivals in the AME. David Cecleski has shown how blacks behind the lines in the eastern part of the state began during the war to welcome

---

[24] Patricia Click, *Time Full of Trial: The Roanoke Island Freedman's Colony, 1862–1867* (Chapel Hill: University of North Carolina Press, 2000) 11.

[25] Mark S. Sexton, *The Chalice and the Covenant: A History of the New Covenant Baptist Association, 1868–1975* (Winston-Salem NC: Hunter Publishing Co., 1976) 1–8.

[26] See L. S. Burkhead, "History of the Difficulties of the Pastorate of the Front Street Methodist Church, Wilmington, N.C., For the Year 1865," *An Annual Publication of Historical Papers [of the Trinity College Historical Society]*, series 8 (1908–9): 35–118; and for the most influential account of the event in the secondary literature, see Litwack, *Been in the Storm*, 465–6.

AMEZ missionaries and to try to wrest black Methodists from white-controlled churches.[27] Baptists also sent organizers into the occupied South; the American Missionary Association's first missionary in North Carolina was in "little Washington" in late 1864, schooling about two hundred and planning to form a black-controlled church before being driven off by Confederates.[28]After the war, Union soldiers continued to create space for independent organizing. Goldsboro, one of the key nodes on the North Carolina railway system and one of four administrative centers for the Freedman's Bureau in that state, not coincidentally became the hub of black Baptist organizing after the war. Representatives from independent black Baptist churches organized the Educational and Missionary Convention of North Carolina there in 1867.[29]

The dichotomy between separation in parts of the state that experienced Union occupation (whether eastern parts during the war or transportation and administrative hubs after the war) versus persistence in the interior breaks down so frequently that it is best understood as a tendency rather than a rule. Indeed, within the same congregations, when the surrounding political/ecclesial context was constant, men and women reached different conclusions about whether or when to leave white-controlled churches. The themes of choice and variation more accurately capture the black experience in the immediate postwar period than the theme of separation. Historical actors did not always exercise choice in a way that led to autonomy or even in ways consistent with their self-interest.[30]

A few African American Baptists enshrined their decision to remain in white-controlled churches in the documentary record, giving voice to the

---

[27] David Cecleski, *The Fire of Freedom: Abraham Galloway & the Slaves' Civil War* (Chapel Hill: University of North Carolina Press, 2012).

[28] *Twenty-Third Annual Report of the American Baptist Home Mission Society* (New York: ABHMS Mission Rooms, 1865) 49.

[29] Whitted, *History of the Negro Baptists*, 34.

[30] The discussion above was particularly influenced by John C. Rodrigue, "Black Agency after Slavery," in Thomas J. Brown, ed., *Reconstruction: New Perspectives on the Postbellum United States* (New York City: Oxford University Press, 2006) 40–65; Peter A. Coclanis, "Captivity of a Generation: Review of *Generations of Captivity*," *William and Mary Quarterly* 61. 3 (2004): 544–5; Walter Johnson, "On Agency," *Journal of Social History* 37.1 (2003): 113–24; and Laura M. Ahern, "Language and Agency," *Annual Review of Anthropology* 30 (2001): 109–37.

thousands who remained on church rolls but who left little testimony to their reason or doing so. In late August 1869, for instance, whites in a Robeson County Baptist church tried to exclude an African American woman, referred to only as "Fanny Freedwoman," for the offense of joining another church. The records do not indicate whether she had been visiting another church, staying home on Sunday, or making moves to join another congregation, but they do record Fanny's determined effort to stay in the white-controlled congregation. At the September meeting, whites noted to their surprise that Fanny "was present and desired to remain with this Church" and therefore decided that she should therefore be "retained in full fellowship."[31] Even though she had already paid the social cost of leaving, Fanny chose to proclaim her primary allegiance to the white-controlled church. Black church members spoke corporately in Orange County's Antioch Baptist Church when they indicated their desire to remain as full members in a situation similar to Fanny's. Whites wondered what blacks would do in fall 1867 after they resolved that every church member, regardless of race, needed to contribute to the upkeep of the church and the pastor's salary. Enslaved members had offered their "widow's mite" often enough in the antebellum period but had not been required to pay towards the pastor's salary or any other expenses. Speaking unequivocally after whites made universal contributions mandatory, "the Colored Brethring [sic] proposed to continue their membership with this church, and thereby agreed to aid in all church expenses."[32]

A similarly well-documented instance of black ambivalence of whether or not to form or join independent churches happened in North Carolina's capital city, where plenty of Northern interlopers sought to convince black churchgoers in general and black Baptists in particular to leave white-controlled churches. Shaw University founder and American Missionary Association missionary Henry Martin Tupper was not able to convince appreciable numbers of black Baptists to leave the city's first church after his arrival in late 1865. In his efforts to separate black Baptists from the white church, Tupper pulled out all of the stops. According to his own tally, in

---

[31] August and September, 1869, Antioch Baptist Church (Robeson Co.) NCBHS, CRMF, 625.

[32] September and October, 1867, Antioch Baptist Church (Orange Co.) NCBHS, CRMF, 732.

October and November of 1865 alone, Tupper met with 137 black families and preached thirteen sermons to freedpeople. A regiment of colored troops in the capital city even got in on the act, donating funds to the purchase of a building that Tupper intended to function as both a school and a church. Even though they enjoyed financial support and encouragement from Northern whites and blacks, however, blacks in that city's First Baptist Church kept their affiliation with the city's leading white Baptists, led by proslavery ideologue Thomas Skinner. Raleigh blacks did not leave their home congregation *en masse* until 5 June 1868, when they formed the "First Colored Baptist Church" and stood "at the door" of their parent congregation demanding for the whites to ratify their decision .[33]

Even the surprising examples above, of Raleigh's First Colored Baptist Church and Orange County's Antioch Baptist Church, give a false sense of racial solidarity because of the way in which black members ultimately acted in concert. But in scores of white-controlled churches black members did not agree on whether or when to separate and did not coordinate their actions. In Wendell, North Carolina's Hephzibah Baptist Church, for instance, whites "agreed that the church grant her colored members a letter in a body and constitute them into a separate church" in 1866. Most, but not all, African Americans took their white brethren up on the offer and straightway founded Good Hope Baptist Church. The number of black members on Hephzibah's rolls fell from 200 in 1867 to 26 in 1870 (there were no reports from 1868 or 1869), as most black members went to the new congregation. After 1870, more African Americans joined (or rejoined—the minutes do not reveal which) Hephzibah, and the total number of people of color in that congregation rebounded back up to 44 by 1872,[34] indicating that African American residents of Wendell were dealing with the spiritual challenges of Reconstruction in different ways.

---

[33] For a recent account of Tupper's rebuff, see Chang, *Citizens of a Christian Nation*, 107. For a much older account, see Whitted, *History of the Negro Baptists*, 14–15. There is a brief account of this episode in W. Glenn Jonas, Jr., *Nurturing the Vision: First Baptist Church, Raleigh, 1812–2012* (Macon, GA: Mercer University Press, 2012) 134–5.

[34] "History of Good Hope Baptist Church," in Claude R. Trotter, ed., *History of the Wake Baptist Association* (Raleigh, NC: Irving-Swain Press, 1976); *Minutes of the Sixty-Second, Sixty-Fifth, and Sixty-Seventh Annual Sessions of the Raleigh Baptist*

The members of Cashie Baptist Church in Windsor, North Carolina, provided an exceptionally clear example of how members of the same community of believers could evaluate differently the advantages and disadvantages of joining an all-black church. Even though they had the option of doing so promptly after the war, most delayed going to a fully independent black church for years. Moreover, those who left did so in a piecemeal fashion. Blacks and whites had worshipped together at Cashie for almost a century by the time the Civil War began in 1861. The faithful in the thriving church had an intimate view of the fighting; the Union army took nearby Edenton in early 1862, and a Confederate ironclad built nearby gave the Confederate navy some of its greatest maritime success. All the while, the clerk recorded a steady stream of new enslaved and free black persons joining the church. A few black residents of the eastern North Carolina town made a profession of faith in 1863. Groups of twos and threes gave way to small crowds by 1864, and the clerk then marveled at the astounding rate at which enslaved men and women began to pour into the congregation in the closing months of the war. In the calendar year before Appomattox, the awed scribe noted that his church had received by baptism, "one hundred and ten" new members, "nearly all colored."[35]

Once the Union army had finally overcome Confederate resistance and made emancipation a reality by the force of arms, the black converts within Cashie responded equivocally. Whites discussed in December 1865 "the sentiments of the Church relative to selling the Old Cashie Church and grounds over the bridge to the coloured members for a house to be used by them as a place of divine worship and a diposit for their dead." Whites did not record a vote on this proposition, but an offhand comment in the minutes over a year later makes it seem as if they accepted it. What the separate black congregation meant ecclesiastically is less clear. Whites may have continued to count the blacks who worshipped in their old building as members of their congregation. (Baptists routinely counted persons who worshipped at different services as part of the same congregation.) Alternatively, they may have reckoned those worshipping over the bridge as a separate congregation. What is certain, though, is that black members

---

Association ... 1867, 1870, and 1872 (Raleigh, NC: Edwards & Broughton, 1867, 1870, 1872).

[35] May, 1865, Cashie Baptist Church, NCBHS, CRMF, 649.

debated among themselves the best place to worship for the next *ten years*, a remarkably long "settling out" period for this ecclesial transition.[36]

Blacks in Cashie simply could not decide on whether to remain in the white-controlled church. Again, it is not clear whether whites retained oversight only of the black members who continued to worship with them, or also of the black Baptists worshipping over the river. Either way, the white clerk documented in entry after entry his colored coreligionists' uncertainty about what to do. Instead of dismissing all of the black members at once to form the new congregation, the clerk recorded more than a dozen different dismissions of black members, a few family members at a time, over the next ten years. There was no "mass movement" from Cashie, only a series of individual tipping points. Thus, Molly Ferguson (colored) asked for and received her letter of dismission in November 1866. A larger group, mainly the Bond, Ruffin, and Speller families, took their letters in August 1867. Most of the Smallwood clan left in October of that year. The Smithwick and Miller families left in July 1868, and the very large (twelve persons) Cooper family left in December. More members of the Bond family followed in January 1869, with smaller groups (not always obviously clustered around families) leaving every few months afterwards. By May 1875, there were still nineteen colored members on the rolls, despite the dismission of more than a hundred souls in the previous decade.[37]

Black North Carolinians in other parts of the state also exercised independent judgment about whether or not to join a black congregation. In Norlina, close to the Virginia line in the Piedmont, Brown's Baptist Church boasted hundreds of black members before the war. While some had died, moved away, or been excluded for disciplinary reasons, 341 different African American men and women had become members of the church since 1846. In October 1867, already more than two years after Appomattox, some members of this piedmont community made their first bid for spiritual independence. Thirty-four African American members of the congregation received letters of dismission "that they mite constitute a col. church in the neighborhood of Mr. W. K. Kenney." The vast majority of black Baptists at Brown's, however, stayed put. As was the case in Cashie, many miles away,

---

[36] December, 1865, March, 1867, Cashie Baptist Church.

[37] November, 1866, August and October, 1867, July and December, 1868, January, August, October, 1869, August, 1870, Cashie Baptist Church.

the remaining one hundred or so members left in small groups over the next twenty years. New African American members even continued to be added to the rolls for a few more years, including six in July 1868. However, a large group of eight or more departed in 1875 and three more in 1883, until there were only five left in 1885.[38]

In both Durham County's Cedar Fork Baptist Church and Clayton First Baptist Church, whites attempted to understand how their African American coreligionists were responding to emancipation and recorded the varied choices black Baptists made during Reconstruction. In March 1868, whites in Cedar Fork Baptist Church devoted time during their monthly conference to asking each "coloured member" one-by-one exactly what he or she wanted to do. Three individuals took the opportunity to ask for letters of dismission to other, presumably black-controlled, churches. Seventeen people failed to show up for the conversation, and the whites determined that these people had decided to leave the church and excluded them (although one of the women subsequently appeared and successfully petitioned to be added back to the rolls in good standing!). Five people (later six, counting the restored member) elected to continue as members in good standing of the white-controlled church.[39] The situation was much the same in Clayton First Baptist Church (originally Johnston Liberty Church), where whites called the question in June 1870, asking all members of color to "let it be known whether they wish to remain with us or not." In their investigation, whites discovered both that they had been doing a poor job keeping tabs of their black membership and also that more black members wanted to remain in fellowship with them than they had imagined. A shocking number of the names on the roll, twenty-four, turned out to belong to persons who had died during the previous decade. "Many others could not be accounted for at all or were known to have left the neighborhood." In the end, though, despite white members' evident neglect of the African

[38] The 1846 Roster of Colored Members contains 341 names and was continually updated, making it a beautiful snapshot of a community in transition. See also October, 1867 and July, 1868, Brown's Baptist Church (Warren Co.) NCBHS, CRMF, 239.

[39] March, 1868, Cedar Rock Baptist Church (Durham Co.) NCBHS, CRMF, 321.

Americans who worshipped with them, twenty-one reiterated their desire to remain in the church and did so in good standing.[40]

Although rare, there were even churches like Skewarkey and Spring Green Primitive Baptist Churches in Martin County, in which black accessions outpaced black departures for many years following the war. One of the elders who served these churches for decades, Cushing Biggs Hassell, kept a tally of every baptism he performed, organized both by date and by congregation. While Hassell's numbering system is inconsistent (he sometimes numbered the occasions on which he baptized, at other times the number of individuals he baptized), it is nonetheless thorough. Thirty-one African Americans attended Skewarkey in 1860, according to a roster the clerk compiled in January of that year, including eleven men and twenty women. In July 1866, it appeared that the men and women remaining from this antebellum core were on the cusp of forming a new, black-controlled congregation. Hassell noted in his diary that "A proposition was also submitted to the consideration of conference in regard to giving the colored members a dismission so as to form a separate church to themselves. And all were given till the succeeding meeting to consider of it and report their conclusions." Hassell did not record the result of this discussion in his diary, nor did the church members record a resolution in their minutes. There is no doubt, though, in light of the subsequent flood of black residents of Martin County into the church that blacks and whites agreed not to form a separate congregation for blacks. Between this discussion in summer 1866 and 1880, Hassell baptized just over one hundred individuals. At least forty-nine of those who submitted to being dunked under the water by Hassell's hand were African American, designated variously as "col'd," "negro," or "colored" in his notes. The ratio of black to white baptisms remained roughly even all the way through to the end of Hassell's ministry. On 11 October 1879, at Leggett's Bridge, he administered the sacrament to "Lucinda Culifer, Winifred Whitaker white, Patty Jones, Esther Reddick, Lila Lathan col'd." Some of the churches at which Hassell preached did not record *any* black accessions after the war, but one—Spring Garden Primitive Baptist—kept pace with Skewarkey. The minister identified twenty-three of

---

[40] June and July 1870, Clayton First Baptist Church (Johnston Co.) NCBHS, CRMF, 187.

seventy-six persons baptized from the commencement of the war through 1879 (and evenly spaced at one or two per year) as "colored".[41]

Mainstream historians have been so fixated on the narrative of black autonomy that calling attention to counter-currents within black churches and black communities is itself a useful corrective to the literature. The reasons why so many men and women hesitated before taking the step to autonomy, however, remain evasive. Ultimately, the panoply of explanations that appear in the historical record is instructive in its very variety. Within the same congregation, there might be aged members, especially women, reluctant to make a change late in life; aspiring church builders hoping to acquire property by staying in fellowship with whites just a little while longer; freedmen seeking high-status leadership positions approved by whites or dependent for employment upon white patrons; devout souls loathe to break the unity of the congregation; and individuals with a host of other specific longings that they thought might be best fulfilled by staying the course. The survey of possible explanations below, then, is not weighted; the point is that black Southerners had individual agendas that diverged from one another. This heterogeneity of aspiration among black churchgoers recalls the furious discussion Eddie Glaude, Jr., touched off in 2010 with his contention "the black church is dead."[42] In the nineteenth century, black Protestants proved to be just as divided as their contemporary successors.

In Brown, Cashie, and elsewhere, some men and women deemed the disruption of their lives that changing churches would entail too great to ever make a move. Hixie Merrit, one of those who stuck with Hephzibah (near Raleigh) rather than co-found Good Hope, stayed with the white church until she died in 1912 at the ripe old age of 101, the last black

---

[41] January, 1860 Roster, Skewarkey Primitive Baptist Church (Martin Co.) NCBHS, CRMF, 814; Cushing Biggs Hassell Diary, 7 July 1866, Folder 14 and List of Baptisms, Folder 28, in the Cushing Biggs Hassell Papers, #00810, Southern Historical Collection, Louis Round Wilson Special Collections Library, University of North Carolina at Chapel Hill (SHC).

[42] Glaude's broadside first appeared in the *Huffington Post*, but scholars picked up the thread and elaborated an extensive online dialogue in *Religious Dispatches*, "The Black Church is Dead: Long Live the Black Church," http://www.religiondispatches.org/archive/atheologies/2331/updated_with_response __the_black_church_is_dead_long_live_the_black_church.

member.[43] Merrit was fifty-three at the time of emancipation and had perhaps been in the church for decades. At least one of the final five black members of Brown's Baptist Church fit Merrit's demographic closely. Marlin Allen, born in 1814, was the oldest of the five black women remaining in the Norlina Church in 1885.[44] Unless seen as a proxy for a potentially vulnerable station in life, however, advanced age does not appear to have been a useful predictor of who decided to stay in—or even join—a white-controlled church.

Minerva Wood and Lucinda Clinard, the two women who joined Abbott's Creek Baptist Church in 1870, are two cases that belie the stereotype of aging women remaining in white-dominated orbits. The two women were neighbors and surely knew one another well. Wood, at thirty years old when she joined, was the older of the two women. She was either the sister or wife of John Wood, five years her junior, who was the head of her household. Wood and Clinard both did household labor, although Wood worked in her own home while Clinard worked as a domestic servant. Eighteen-year-old Clinard might have been working for the Roper family, with whom she lived, or for someone further afield. Neither Wood nor Clinard owned any property. While neither of the two was particularly vulnerable as a result of their advanced age, there were other possible markers of vulnerability that may help to explain why Clinard, at least, was interested in seeking the support of whites. The enumerator marked Clinard as "deaf, dumb, blind, insane, or idiotic" in the census, an impossibly broad (and often-abused) designation that nonetheless intimates that Clinard may have been close to the margins of the community.[45] Among the women of color who elected to remain in white-controlled churches number some others in what might be classified as vulnerable positions. Harriett Barbee, for instance, who stayed in Cedar Fork Baptist Church, found herself in 1870 at the age of 24 heading a household that included a four-year-old and two two-year-old twins, as well as a fourteen-year-old and a twenty-one-

---

[43] "History of Good Hope" and "Hixie Merritt.Find a Grave Memorial" (# 32120171), www.findagrave.com.

[44] See not only the 1885 roster in the church records but also Allen's entry in the federal census: Year: *1900*; Census Place: *Sandy Creek, Warren, North Carolina*; Roll: *1222*; Page: *13A*; Enumeration District: *0098*; FHL microfilm: *1241222*.

[45] Year: *1870*; Census Place: *Abbotts Creek, Forsyth, North Carolina*; Roll: *M593_1137*; Page: *298B*; Image: *8*; Family History Library Film: *552636*.

year old. Intriguingly, the enumerator listed Barbee as "Black" but all of her children (and other members of the household) as "Mulatto." Based on the local geography, various scenarios are possible. The father of her children may have been one next-door neighbor, a twenty-five-year-old mulatto man named Jack Barbee. Or it could have been her neighbor on the other side, a forty-one-year-old white man named Simpson Barbee.[46]

Most black women who remained in white-controlled churches, though, had no special vulnerability. It is possible, though far from certain based on the limited evidence that women may have been more likely than men to remain in white-controlled churches. After all, they could not hope for ordained leadership roles within either the white or the black churches and therefore might not have had the same incentive to leave; moreover, they might have had even a greater need for white patronage than did black men. In the final analysis, the impetus behind Wood and Clinard joining Abbot's Creek—or Allen (along with Matilda Watson, Nancy Green, Lucy Brown, and Leatha Hawkins) staying in Brown's Baptist, for that matter—remains hidden. Regardless, their tragically typical biographies are reminders that it was a course within the realm of possibility for all freedpeople.[47]

Some black Baptists probably stayed long enough to retain the goodwill of whites in hopes of gaining assistance in keeping their place of worship or in finding another one. Historians have documented the interracialism that characterized much of Southern church life throughout the nineteenth century, including the negotiated process through which whites helped blacks set up independent churches.[48] Blacks who patiently waited until their

---

[46] July 1870, Cedar Fork Baptist Church. Year: *1870*; Census Place: *Patterson, Orange, North Carolina*; Roll: *M593_1153*; Page: *325B*; Image: *656*; Family History Library Film: *552652*.

[47] For an opposing argument, one emphasizing the key role women played in organizing separate churches and black postwar politics in general, see Elsa Barkley Brown, "Negotiating and Transforming the Public Sphere: African American Political Life in the Transition from Slavery to Freedom," *Public Culture* 7 (Fall 1994): 107–46.

[48] For the antebellum period, see, for example, Randolph Scully, *Religion and the Making of Nat Turner's Virginia: Baptist Community and Conflict* (Charlottesville: University of Virginia Press, 2008); Erskine Clarke, *Dwelling Place: A Plantation Epic* (New Haven: Yale University Press, 2005); Sylvia Frey and Betty Wood, *Come Shouting to Zion: African American Protestantism in the American South and British Caribbean to 1830* (Chapel Hill: University of North Carolina Press, 1998); Mechal

white Baptist brethren were ready to set them off sometimes won tangible rewards. In one sample of thirty-seven black Baptist churches in North Carolina founded in 1868 or earlier, for instance, white Baptists donated the land on which ten of the congregations built their churches.[49] Black Baptists who left in haste could not hope for this kind of largesse, which might explain why blacks in communities like Bear Creek Baptist Church in Chatham County waited until whites asked them what they wanted before mentioning the possibility of independence. In August 1867, over two years after emancipation, a committee of white congregants approached the colored members of that congregation. Only then did the whites learn that "there was a place selected or had been selected by the colored Brethren at Gils Old Field and the colored Brethren wished this church to appoint a committee to help organize a church at the above named place."[50]

In Orange County, the black members of Mount Moriah (Baptist) Church appear to have stayed in fellowship with whites precisely in hopes of keeping access to a favorite meeting place. The church did not keep accurate enough membership rolls to document precisely the ebb and flow of black members into and out of the church after emancipation, but a critical mass

---

Sobel, *The World They Made Together: Black and White Values in Eighteenth-Century Virginia* (Princeton: Princeton University Press, 1987); John B. Boles, ed., *Masters and Slaves in the House of the Lord: Race and Religion in the American South, 1740–1840* (Lexington: University Press of Kentucky, 1988). For the postwar period, see Chang, *Citizens of a Christian Nation*; Harvey, *Freedom's Coming* and *Redeeming the South*; and Edward J. Blum, *Reforging the White Republic: Race, Religion, and American Nationalism, 1865–1898* (Baton Rouge: Louisiana State University Press, 2005).

[49] This sample is drawn principally from M. W. Williams and George W. Watkins, *Who's Who Among North Carolina Negro Baptists: With a Brief History of Negro Baptist Organizations* (n.p., 1940); Trotter, *History of the Wake Baptist Association*; and *The Centennial Celebration of the Middle District Missionary Baptist Association, 1871–1971* (Wilmington: n.p., 1971) but it is supplemented by a variety of newspaper articles and programs from the vertical files housed in the North Carolina Baptist Historical Society in Winston-Salem, North Carolina, viz., "Cedar Grove dedicates new edifice," *Winston-Salem Chronicle*, 6 August 1998; "New beginning for Negro worship emerges," *Goldsboro News Argus*, 26 April 1985; "First Calvary," *The Salisbury Post*, 21 July 2001; "Nazareth Baptist Church Founded Here in 1867," *Asheville Times*, 15 December 1993.

[50] August 1867, Bear Creek Baptist Church, NCBHS, CRMF, 315.

of black members does not appear to have stayed in for at least five years. At some point—the record is not clear—the black members may have begun to worship at a different time in the same building even while insisting that they desired to remain in fellowship with the white members and to submit to their discipline. In April 1870, whites and blacks made the separate arrangement official and set a course to eventual independence. The whites resolved that the "colored Brethren were allowed the privilege of worshipping as heretofore on the evenings of the second Sabbath in each month until they shall have organized themselves into a separate church." Black members took their time, however; not until September 1871 did a Brother Patterson ask white congregants "for permission or rather letters of dismission for the purpose of organizing a church of their own." The church did not resolve this question at its January 1872 meeting and let it ride for another whole year. Black members were still technically part of the white church, still subject to their discipline and still worshipping in the same building in 1873. That February, white congregants finally took action and did so in a manner that revealed the probable reason why the church's "colored members" had not pressed too hard for separation. In the same resolution, they agreed "1st that this church is no longer responsible for the conduct of the colored brethren who were once members of this church but left for the purpose of organizing a separate church" and "2nd that they can not [sic] longer hold their meeting in this house." As black members must have known all along, separation had a price.[51]

Some black Baptists also found exciting leadership possibilities within white churches that may have been an incentive to stay. After emancipation, black class leaders who had flourished informally despite post-Nat Turner (1831) prohibitions on ordained black ministers came into the open. Within individual congregations, whites tapped for more formal roles those who were already pastoring their peers. One of the reasons that whites in Cashie Baptist Church were able to retain so many African American families in good standing is that Emanuel, a black member, claimed pastoral responsibility for freedpeople within the church. Among his many duties, Emanuel carried the requests of black members who wanted to leave before

---

[51] April 1870, September, 1871, January, 1872, February, 1873, Mount Moriah Church Records, #04669, SHC.

the all-white voting body.[52] Whites in Orange County's Antioch Baptist Church ordained one of their own, Ned Stroud, to the deaconate and to a similar role as Emanuel on 11 July 1868, long after most black Baptists had left white-controlled churches. Stroud, who was first named in the records in August 1866, supervised the discipline of black members, kept an accurate roll, etc.—tasks that required him to work closely with the white leaders of the church. Stroud stayed in the church for five years after his ordination. Not until September 1873, when he received permission to take seventeen other black members of the church out with him to form a new congregation, did he formally break with his white coreligionists.[53] In Mount Moriah (Baptist) Church, whites ordained Calvin Hackney an Elder and allowed him to take the lead in some situations when doing so did not imply spiritual authority over whites. For example, on one Sunday in May 1868, "there being no white candidates [for baptism,] Elder Calvin Hackney (Col) after examining the candidates administered the ordinance."[54] A few black Baptist leaders even earned positions on the extra-congregational level as well. North Carolina black Baptist pioneer, L. W. Boon—co-founder of the state convention in 1867 and missionary to the northeastern portion of the state—enjoyed the confidence and patronage of white Baptist leaders, who commissioned him in 1866 as special missionary to black Carolinians.[55]

In addition to prestige, some black Baptists found material rewards in remaining in fellowship with whites. Elder Cushing Biggs Hassell, the white minister who carefully recorded every baptism he performed, also documented some of these patronage relationships. Hassell, to be clear, shared the same white supremacist assumptions as did most white Southerners at this time. When black and white Republicans put in place Republican judges and allowed both blacks and whites in the courthouse in October 1868, Hassell lamented there was such a "a motley crew in the Court House, a disgrace to civilization, because of negro rule." Nonetheless, Hassell gave preferential treatment to some black residents of Martin County, especially those prominent in one of the churches he served. The

---

[52] Emanuel first appears in this capacity in October 1867, Cashie Baptist Church.

[53] August 1866, July 1868, February, May, June, and July 1869, July and September 1873, Antioch Baptist Church (Orange County).

[54] May 1868, Mount Moriah Church Records.

[55] *Minutes of the ... Chowan Baptist Association ... 1866*, 9, 12.

best examples are Miles Rogers and Bennett Burgess. On 10 August 1867, whites in Skewankey Primitive Baptist Church gave these two men—"one had been a slave & the other was always free. Both seemed to be sound in the faith and their deportment was good"—license to preach in public. Both Rogers and Bennett appear again in Hassell's notes about his ecclesiastical life but, very significantly, they are among the few black North Carolinians who also appear in his record of financial affairs. On 18 October 1867, "He rented to Miles Rogers colored the Warren Biggs tract." On 17 September 1868, he hired Burgess for the job of "putting some pillars under warehouse." The only black men in Hassell's postwar diary with a more prominent profile than Rogers and Burgess were Boland Hyman and Harmon Whitley. Hyman aided Hassell's son in agricultural work, and Whitley worked alongside a hired white clerk in his general store. While it is not possible to be completely certain about Hyman's church membership, he did attend a Baptist Union meeting with the Hassell family in March 1869, and Hassell officiated at his wedding in January 1870. Whitley appears to have died prematurely, and Hassell baptized into membership his widow into Skewarkey Primitive Baptist Church in August 1870.[56]

Hassell never stated explicitly that he favored Rogers, Bennett, Hyman, or Whitley *because of* their affiliation with a Baptist church, but it is remarkable that almost all of the black men with whom he came to do business were also his fellow believers. The extent to which these men remained in one of Hassell's churches in hopes of capturing precisely this kind of patronage, or whether this patronage was an unsought fringe benefit, is impossible to determine. Marie Gordon Rice, a white Virginia Presbyterian, claimed in her reminiscences that the only black member of her church had his material interests in mind when deciding where to worship. She recounted what Matilda Robertson, the man's wife, told him when he was worried about having nice enough clothes in which to be buried: "'Look hyeh, Parker,' she said, 'you de onlies' coloured Democrat in de Aspenwal precinck an de onlies' coloured member o' Roanoke Church, an' you boun' to be laid out decent. Don't you talk 'bout dyin' ont wel I steps down to Miz. Rice's and axes her for a swoud.'" According to Rice, "Uncle

---

[56] Hassell Diary, 6 October 1868, 10 August 1867, 18 October 1867, 17 September 1868, and 29 March 1869, List of Baptisms, and List of Marriages, Cushing Biggs Hassell Papers.

Parker postponed his demise, and 'lo! like Miss Betsy, outlived his 'swoud', often wearing it as he sat in solitary state in the 'white folks' church', the one coloured member who had refused to leave."[57] If Rice is to be trusted as an informant, some churchgoers considered their self-interest when thinking about whether to attend a black- or white-controlled church.

Some black Baptists may have been long suffering with white-controlled congregations because they believed that their faith commanded them to esteem the authority of the local church higher than their own inclinations. While direct black testimony about the value of church unity over individual preference is scarce, there are two patterns of behavior that are consistent with this explanation. First, black Baptists who stayed continued to submit to church discipline. For the antebellum period, some scholars have seen the process through which white church members monitored and sanctioned black members' behavior as a mechanism of racial control only masquerading as a spiritually efficacious practice. When black Baptists continued to subject themselves to this oversight after emancipation, though, they affirmed the spiritual value of church discipline. Second, when they did leave—either individually or corporately—most black Baptists displayed an extreme sensitivity to good order and to collegial relations with whites. Ironically, on their way out, these men and women gave testimony to the strength and nature of the bonds in which their white coreligionists had held them.

When black Baptists remained in a white-controlled church, they gave members of that church permission to police their behavior. This cession represented an intrusion upon their private lives so profound that it strongly suggests black Baptists considered the work of their coreligionists in keeping them faithful to God's law profitable to their souls. Virtually every church in this study recorded in their minute books the work of trying to hold members of both races accountable to Christian standards of moral conduct. Church members tried to get one another to repent of sins and amend their lives, preferring to keep their brethren in fellowship when possible. With particularly scandalous offenses or unrepentant sin, however, members excluded one another from the church if and until the offender was ready to repent and return to the fold. Members of Mocksville's Bear Creek Baptist

---

[57] "Reminisces of Marie Gordon (Pryor) Rice" [1920s], #MSS 5:1 R3652:1, Virginia Historical Society, Richmond, VA.

Church were typical. In one full session in January 1866, the whites who controlled the disciplinary process excluded two white men from the church for drunkenness, one of whom was disorderly while intoxicated and the other abusive of his wife. They also excluded "negro Frank and negro Nan," for reportedly "carrying an insane negro Boy in to the woods & Leaving him to perish with hunger." Frank and Nan did not simply take this harsh judgment as an excuse to escape white oversight. Instead, they fought to clear their name and to remain members of the white-controlled church, successfully convincing white Baptists to reverse their judgment two months later.[58] Baptists of color had routinely submitted to white-controlled discipline before the Civil War, but doing so afterward emancipation assumes a new meaning. When people like Jim Darden of Hertford County's Buckhorn Baptist Church "came forward and asked to be restored to fellowship, confessing his sins," he was affirming the importance of his unequal, biracial community—even in the face of black-controlled options nearby.[59]

Some black members signaled their contempt for white ecclesiastical authority by leaving without permission to worship independently, an offense whites rewarded with excommunication. Six black men and women were still worshipping in Raft Swamp Baptist Church in Robeson County in 1868, but an undisclosed number left precipitously as soon as the shooting stopped in the Civil War. White congregants immediately sanctioned those who went out, presumably to start their own churches, resolving "all the Black members that have left with out leaf [leave] air to be excluded."[60] A minority of black members in Buckhorn Baptist Church fled during the war, probably seeking freedom rather than a new church, and received an identical sanction. White leaders "agreed that the names of the coloured members be called and those that have left voluntarily their homes and church be and is hereby unanimously expelled."[61]

---

[58] January–March 1866, Bear Creek Baptist Church (Davie County) NCBHS, CRMF, 46.

[59] May 1869, Buckhorn Baptist Church (Hertford County) NCBHS, CRMF, 188.

[60] July,1865, Raft Swamp Baptist Church (Robeson County) NCBHS, CRMF, 45.

[61] June 1864, Buckhorn Baptist Church.

Most African American individuals who sought to leave a white-controlled congregation, especially after the war, displayed more deference to white ecclesiastical authority than did the people from Raft Swamp or Buckhorn Baptist Churches. The mechanism through which those who left as individuals deferred to white control was by seeking letters of "dismission" proving that they were members in good standing before leaving a church. At Badin Baptist Church, for example, before Rebecca—who was still with the church in April 1871—finally decided to leave, she asked permission, and the white members resolved that "Sister Rebecca (Col) have a letter of dismission."[62] These operations were matters of course for both whites and blacks. One Cumberland County church, for example, in January 1869 noted that "a letter of dismission was ordered for sister Catherine McDuffie also for Jane McDaniel (col)."[63] White-led Buckhorn Baptist Church issued letters of dismission to their black coreligionists on at least eight occasions between 1867 and 1871, as their mixed-race community gradually unraveled.[64] Black Baptists' insistence on maintaining good order probably restricted somewhat the pace of black withdrawal.

Blacks in Rockingham, North Carolina, demonstrated a similar commitment to working carefully with whites when withdrawing but did so as a group. After remaining in fellowship for four years after 1865, they only moved out in June 1869 with the full blessing and support of their white brethren. The white-controlled church, then known as Dockey's Baptist Church, reported the following in its minutes:

> After preaching on Saturday the ministers and Church proceeded to the dismission in regular order of all the colored members amounting to the number of fifty-one or two and without adjournment constituted the same into a regular Baptist Church and this Church was called THE HOLLY GROVE BAPTIST CHURCH. The new church appointing Washington Dockery and Richmond Covington, deacons, was then dismissed from the White Church to start the organization of their own church.[65]

---

[62] April 1871, Badin Baptist Church (Stanly County) NCBHS, CRMF, 214.

[63] January 1869, Beaver Dam Baptist Church (Cumberland County) NCBHS, CRMF, 753.

[64] May 1867, June 1869, March, May, August, and September 1870, May and October 1871, Buckhorn Baptist Church.

[65] Holly Grove [B] (Rockingham) Vertical File, NCBHS.

Significantly, black Baptists demonstrated this sensitivity to white ecclesiastical prerogatives even after they had established new churches. North Carolina black Baptists invited white associational leaders to help them organize their state convention in 1867, for instance, an act of deference and goodwill noted with pleasure by the secular press.[66] A congregation of black Baptists in Chapel Hill wrote to the Sandy Creek Association in early 1867. This association had provided oversight to most of its members when they had been part of white-dominated churches. The African American Carolinians asked the assembled churchmen for advice on the most fundamental questions of church organization, clearly seeking goodwill and affirmation from the white denominational leaders rather than guidance. They asked whether they were allowed to have a black minister, sought for confirmation whether segregated worship was acceptable, and inquired whether it was appropriate for them to join one of the emerging all-black associations.[67] Black Baptists in other locales also tried to maintain interracial relations after separation. The black membership in Anson County's Blackwood Chapel Baptist Church increased modestly from nine to ten in the three years following the Civil War. Sixteenth October 1868 is the last time these ten appear in the minutes, after which they apparently joined an all-black congregation. If the white church historian of the late nineteenth century is to be believed, however, "In later years, sometimes the aged ones would return and worship with us."[68]

In conclusion, black Baptists weighed many different factors when deciding with which church to affiliate in the postwar period, and they sometimes decided based on their individual circumstances to act counter to what scholars have perceived as their racial self-interest. Some freedpeople decided to stay in white-controlled churches and to submit to spiritual censure by whites for many years after emancipation, even after many of their coreligionists left to form black-controlled churches. Scholars agree that black churches were the most important black institutions to emerge from Reconstruction but have overstated the unanimity with which black Southerners embraced them looking out from slavery. The modest

---

[66] "Quite a pleasing event," *Raleigh Register*, 25 October 1867.

[67] *Minutes of the ... Sandy Creek Baptist Association... 1867* (Raleigh, NC: Biblical Recorder Publishing Co., 1867) 11.

[68] The white chronicler was Jewell Ray Berta Robbings, Blackwood Chapel Baptist Church, NCBHS, CRMF, 1031.

contribution of this essay is to recapture some of the contingency and uncertainty of the period immediately following emancipation, to show that not all black Baptists pursued ecclesiastical independence immediately, and to explore some of the possible reasons why some remained under white authority for a season. If true for the ecclesiastical realm, this conclusion might have implications for how scholars think about black politics as well during the critical Reconstruction era.

3

From Cary to Colley:

The Ethiopian Factor in the Formation of the Baptist Foreign Mission Convention[1]

Eric Michael Washington

At the third annual session of the National Baptist Convention, USA (NBC-USA) held in Boston in September 1897, President E. C. Morris gave his annual address in which he remarked on the progress of the work of the convention and offered encouragement to press on to greater works. In the course of his address, Morris spent a good deal of time speaking of foreign missions. This should have come to no one's surprise in the audience as Morris had served as the president of the Baptist Foreign Mission Convention (BFMC) in 1894 only one year prior to the consolidation of the BFMC with the American National Baptist Convention, and the National Baptist Educational Convention creating the NBC-USA.[2] Founded in 1880, the BFMC was the first national convention of African American Baptists. At the time of this annual session of the NBC-USA, the work of foreign missions had fallen on hard times, to say the least. The Foreign Mission Board had only one missionary in the African field, R. A. Jackson in South Africa, and the claim on that one missionary was, according to Morris, by "the finger of God."[3] Toward the end of his report on foreign missions, Morris exclaimed, "It will hardly be denied that the work of giving

---

[1] A portion of the research for this chapter was funded by a grant from the Calvin Center for Christian Scholarship.
[2] See Table VII in E. A. Freeman, *The Epoch of Negro Baptists and the Foreign Mission Board* (Kansas City: The Central Seminary Press, 1953. Reprint, New York: Arno Press, 1980) 278.
[3] E. C. Morris, "Negro Baptists Retrospective and Prospective," in *Sermons, Addresses, and Reminiscences* by E. C. Morris (Nashville: National Baptist Publishing Board, 1901. Reprint, Nashville: Townsend Press, 1993) 80.

the Gospel to the heathen in Africa lies nearer the heart of our people than any of the special objects of our Convention."[4]

This punctuating statement by Morris offers scholars of African American Baptists a window into one of their primary commitments at the turn of the twentieth century—sending missionaries to Africa. In his work on the Foreign Mission Board of the NBC-USA, late Baptist pastor and scholar E. A. Freeman asserted that foreign missions prompted the formation of the NBC-USA.[5] Another Baptist pastor and historian Leroy Fitts writes that African American Baptist interests in foreign missions predates that of home missions.[6] This raises two important questions, however. Was this a commitment solely based on obedience to the Great Commission (Matt. 28:18–20), or did it include social, political, and economic concerns? How did African American Baptists conceptualize and frame this commitment?[7]

Although African American Baptists founded the BFMC in 1880, this essay argues that African American Baptist commitment to African missions stretches as far back as 1815. In that year African American and white members of the First Baptist Church in Richmond organized the Richmond African Baptist Missionary Society that helped to send Lott Cary and Collin Teague, the first American-born missionaries to Africa in 1821. This mission work continued moderately throughout the nineteenth century through the work of the American Baptist Missionary Convention (ABMC) founded in 1840 and through post-Civil War African American Baptist state conventions, particularly in Virginia, North Carolina, and South Carolina, and culminated in the founding of the BFMC. African American Baptists conceptualized their commitment to African missions within the theology of Ethiopianism articulated by missionaries such as Lott Cary and William Colley.

---

[4] Morris, "Negro Baptists Retrospective and Prospective," 80.

[5] Freeman, *Epoch of Negro Baptists*, 2.

[6] Leroy Fitts, *A History of Black Baptists* (Nashville: Boardman Press, 1985) 109.

[7] The Great Commission refers to statements by Jesus Christ recorded in all four Gospels and the Book of Acts given to his disciples after his resurrection commanding them, and by extension the entire Church to preach the gospel to all nations.

Historians and other scholars have pinpointed the prevalence of Ethiopianism in motivating African American missions and emigration. Wilson Moses has done illuminating work on the Ethiopianism of Alexander Crummell, Episcopalian priest and missionary to Liberia. Hollis Lynch's biography of the West Indian-born Edward Blyden is still regarded as the best biography on the late Presbyterian missionary to Liberia and highlights his Ethiopianism as well. In a similar vein, a number of historians have written on the Ethiopianism of the outspoken African Methodist bishop, Henry M. Turner.[8] While these scholars have provided valuable information on the Ethiopianism of specific missionaries to Africa, this essay provides a newer scholarly focus by *tracing* the development of African American Baptist *articulation* of Ethiopianism and how that development affected the *application* of Ethiopianism to African missions, thereby providing an analytical framework of the significance of the concept of Ethiopianism as African American Baptists applied it to the African mission field.[9] By tracing African American Baptist Ethiopianism from Lott Cary to William Colley, this essay concludes that there was an unbroken framing of African missions within Ethiopianism demonstrating that, much like Crummell, Blyden, and Turner, some Baptists also affirmed Ethiopianism's claims. This essay also illustrates the importance of mission work in the forging of African American Baptist national unity in the late nineteenth century; however fragile it was. Finally, Ethiopianism provided African American Baptists a theological basis for racial uplift both at home and on the continent of Africa, as many African American Baptist leaders strongly

---

[8] See Wilson J. Moses, *Alexander Crummell: A Study of Civilization and Discontent* (New York City: Oxford University Press, 1989); Hollis Lynch, *Edward Wilmot Blyden: Pan-Negro Patriot, 1832–1912* (London: Oxford University Press, 1967); A couple of works focusing on Turner's Ethiopianism, in part, are J. M. Chirenje, *Ethiopianism and Afro-Americans in Southern Africa, 1883–1916* (Baton Rouge: Louisiana State University Press, 1987); and James T. Campbell, *Songs of Zion: The African Methodist Episcopal Church in the United States and South Africa* (Chapel Hill: University of North Carolina Press, 1998).

[9] See Walter L. Williams, *Black Americans and the Evangelization of Africa 1877–1900* (Madison: University of Wisconsin Press, 1982); Sylvia M. Jacobs, ed., *Black Americans and the Missionary Movement in Africa* (Westport: Greenwood Press, 1982).

desired to steer their own course as it pertained to African missions and because they distrusted white Baptist mission work in Africa.[10]

In his classic text *The Golden Age of Black Nationalism*, eminent historian Wilson Moses defines Ethiopianism as "the effort of the English-speaking black or African person to view his past enslavement and present cultural dependency in terms of the broader history of civilization."[11] Although this definition aids in understanding the intellectual grappling Christian persons of African descent undertook at this time and even their attempt to historicize their experiences, it fails to root Ethiopianism within their understanding of God's providence, the scriptures, and biblical prophecy. In brief, Moses secularized a nuanced theology.

In later work, however, Moses analyzes the thought of late eighteenth-century Christian African writers of the Atlantic World, among whom were Phillis Wheatley, Jupiter Hammon, and Olaudah Equiano.[12] In this work, Moses treats previous theological texts within an Afro-Christian understanding of suffering and hope that focuses on the concept of the "fortunate fall."[13] He commits little space to dealing with Ethiopianism precisely; rather, he chooses to think of it synonymously as the fortunate fall theology. Although appreciative of Moses' work in this area, there is room to distinguish the doctrine of the fortunate fall and Ethiopianism, although there are obvious similarities across both theologies.

The theology of Ethiopianism can be traced back to the late eighteenth century in the British Atlantic World as free African Christians ruminated on what God had intended in his providence as he had ordained their

---

[10] Evelyn Brooks Higginbotham summarizes African American Baptist denominationalism during the late 19th century and into the early 20th century as fostering racial consciousness and racial uplift. See *Righteous Discontent: The Women's Movement in the Black Baptist Church, 1880–1920* (Cambridge: Harvard University Press, 1993) 4–7.

[11] Wilson J. Moses, *The Golden Age of Black Nationalism, 1850–1925* (New York City: Oxford University Press, 1978) 160–1.

[12] Wilson Jeremiah Moses, *The Wings of Ethiopia: Studies in African American Life and Letters* (Ames: Iowa State University Press, 1990) 141–58.

[13] See Moses, *The Wings of Ethiopia*, 142. Moses traces the doctrine of the Fortunate Fall to ancient Christianity in which theologians viewed the Fall of Adam in terms of it bringing salvation to humanity through the Incarnation of Jesus Christ and his death, burial, and resurrection.

enslavement. It could be understood as a Christian African theological modification of the "Providential Design" theology of American Protestants such as that of Ezra Stiles and Samuel Hopkins.[14] Writers like Olaudah Equiano articulated that God's purpose in his enslavement, in part, was to save his soul; but it was also to carry the gospel and civilization back to Africa.[15] In the preface to his narrative, Equiano writes:

> By the horrors of that [slave] trade was I first torn away from all the tender connexions that were naturally dear to my heart; but these, through the mysterious ways of Providence, I ought to regard as infinitely more than compensated by the introduction I have thence obtained to the knowledge of the Christian religion, and of a nation which, by its liberal sentiments, its humanity, the glorious freedom of its government, and its proficiency in arts and sciences, has exalted the dignity of human nature.[16]

Although the fortunate fall doctrine helps Christians to understand God's decrees regarding humanity's fall into sin and their redemption on a more universal plane, this proto-Ethiopianist understanding of Equiano is grounded in his immediate context of enslavement, freedom, and the future of Africans in the Atlantic World. Equiano's proto-Ethiopianism also incorporates political and economic realities, which can be subsumed under the general heading of "civilization." For example, toward the end of the narrative, Equiano found himself involved in the humanitarian scheme to repatriate the "poor blacks" of London to West Africa in order to found a Christian colony, which would eventually become Sierra Leone.[17]

---

[14] "Providential Design" refers to the thinking of Reformed Protestants like Stiles and Hopkins that God had determined to have Africans enslaved and brought to America within an all-encompassing belief that God's design in this providential occurrence was for Africans to receive the gospel of Christ, set be free from slavery, and then return to Africa to preach the gospel and spread "civilization." In short, slavery had a redemptive purpose for Africans and Africa alike.

[15] This is evident in various parts of Equiano's narrative. He identifies himself as "a particular favourite of Heaven." See Olaudah Equiano, *The Interesting Narrative of the Life of Olaudah Equiano*, edited by Robert Allison. Second Edition (Boston: Bedford-St. Martin's, 2007) 43.

[16] Equiano, *Interesting Narrative*, 41.

[17] Equiano, *Interesting Narrative*, 206–10. Owing to some problems Equiano had with some of the organizers of the scheme, Equiano never returned to Africa.

As an addendum to Moses' more secular definition of Ethiopianism, religious historian Albert Raboteau offers a more sensitive and accurate description of Ethiopianism as expressed by nineteenth-century African American Christians. He writes, "Nineteenth-century blacks needed to reclaim for themselves a civilized African past in order to refute the charge that they were inherently inferior."[18] According to Raboteau, this was done with their application of Psalm 69:31, "Princes shall come out of Egypt, and Ethiopia shall soon stretch forth her hands unto God."

The most renowned of African American Baptist missionaries during the Early Republic period was Lott Cary, missionary to Liberia. As early as 1835, Ralph Gurley wrote a sketch biography of Carey as an appendage to his main biography of Jehudi Ashmun, the first governor of Liberia. In 1837, James Braxton Taylor, the pastor of Second Baptist Church of Richmond, Virginia, published a brief biography solely on Cary.[19] The purpose for Taylor's biography was to use Cary's extraordinary story to encourage other African American men to enter the African mission field. Without a doubt, Cary is recognized as the father of American missions to Africa. Taylor held to the providential design theology regarding African Americans and African missions, as did other Evangelicals during this time. He believed that African Americans should be the primary people traveling to Africa to spread the gospel and to aid in the uplift of Africa. For Taylor, the preaching of the gospel in Africa with the bringing of Western civilization were twin ways in which "civilized nations" could atone for the "degradation and misery" they had brought to Africa. Taylor saw the clear intent of providence in having African Americans as primary agents of this endeavor of evangelism and atonement. He writes, "Though white men may and ought to enter this field, yet the indication of Providence, thus far, have been in favor of making our colored brethren the chief instruments of this labor of love."[20]

---

[18] Albert J. Raboteau, *Fire in the Bones: Reflections on African American Religious History* (Boston: Beacon Press, 1995) 43.

[19] Ralph Randolph Gurley, *Life of Jehudi Ashmun, late Colonial Agent in Liberia With an appendix, containing extracts from his journal and other writings; with a brief sketch of the life of the Rev. Lott Cary* (Washington: James C. Dunn, 1835).

[20] James Braxton Taylor, *Biography of Elder Lott Cary, Late Missionary to Africa* (Baltimore: Armstrong and Berry, 1837). Reprinted in *The African Preachers* (Harrisonburg: Sprinkle Publications, 1998) 9–10.

Into the twentieth century, African American church historians began to write of Cary's life and career. African American Baptist pastor and professor Miles Mark Fisher wrote an essay published in 1922 detailing Cary's ministry, followed by historian Lewis G. Jordan in 1930, a pastor and the former corresponding secretary of the Foreign Mission Board of the NBC-USA, who drew heavily from Taylor's biography. In 1970, historian William Poe published an article on Cary's life and mission, followed by the 1993 work by Leroy Fitts.[21] More recent work has highlighted Cary's life and work within the larger narrative of African American and white cooperation in Virginia in the formation of Liberia, notably historian Marie Tyler-McGraw's *An African Republic* published in 2007.[22]

According to the historiography, little is known about Lott Cary's childhood. Scholars have discovered that Cary was born a slave in Charles City County, Virginia, circa 1780 on the estate of William A. Christian. Cary's father was a Baptist, and although his mother did not hold membership in any church she did appear to be a Christian. Cary moved to Richmond in 1804, where his master hired him out to work at a tobacco warehouse. While working at the warehouse Cary was an unconverted drunkard who laced his conversation with profanity. Such behavior characterized his life for three years when in 1807, on the cusp of a defining moment, Cary attended a worship service at First Baptist Church of Richmond where he heard Rev. John Courtney preach from the gospel of John on Jesus and Nicodemus. Through this sermon on the necessity of the new birth in Christ, Cary then knew his terrible, sinful condition, which led

---

[21] Taylor, *Biography*; Miles Mark Fisher, "Lott Cary, the Colonizing Missionary," *Journal of Negro History* 7 (October 1922): 380–418; Jordan, *Negro Baptist*; William A. Poe, "Lott Carey: Man of Purchased Freedom," *Church History* 39.1 (March 1970): 49–61, http://www.jstor.org/stable/3163213 (accessed 19 June 2009); Leroy Fitts, *The Lott Carey Legacy of African American Missions* (Baltimore: Gateway Press, 1994). This is work by Fitts is a revision of his 1978 work published by Judson Press, *Lott Carey: The First Black Missionary to Africa*.

[22] Marie Tyler McGraw, *An African Republic: Black and White Virginians in the Making of Liberia* (Chapel Hill: University of North Carolina Press, 2007). Prior to her book, Tyler-McGraw published a solid article that offers much to the previous work on Cary. See Marie Tyler McGraw "Richmond Free Blacks and African Colonization, 1816–1832," *Journal of American Studies* 21 (1987): 207–24.

to his conversion as a Christian. That year, Courtney baptized Cary and he subsequently became a member of First Baptist Church.[23]

After receiving baptism and holding membership in the First Baptist Church of Richmond, Cary had an intense desire to learn how to read the passage of scripture that led to his conviction of sin and his conversion to Jesus Christ. Yearning to read the passage for himself, Cary purchased a Bible and commenced to teach himself to read, starting with John 3. With the help of fellow warehouse workers he later learned to write. According to Fitts, "It is significant that Carey's literary education began in his young adult life concomitant with his conversion experience." Around this time as well, Cary began to preach the gospel to other African Americans, both slave and free, in Richmond and its environs. After giving evidence of his spiritual gift, Cary was soon licensed to preach by First Baptist Church. In the aftermath of his licensure, Cary spent each Sunday preaching on plantations surrounding Richmond. Cary would preach as far South as Norfolk and as far East as Lynchburg. As a licensed Baptist preacher, Cary had a growing desire to improve his mind by reading, which he did voraciously, even using his spare time at the warehouse to read.[24]

During this time as well, Cary became more useful at the warehouse and he began to accumulate money. He received promotions on the job and his boss gave him extra money and extra tobacco for him to sell. Owing to his thrift and industry, Cary purchased his freedom and that of his two children for $850 in 1813. As a freeman, Cary received a regular salary that increased over time. At the time of his manumission, Cary was undoubtedly

---

[23] Taylor, *Biography*, 11–2; Fisher, "Lott Cary," 381–2; Jordan, *Negro Baptist*, 12; Poe, "Lott Carey," 49–50; Fitts, *Lott Carey*, 3–5. Just recently there has been a small debate regarding whether Cary was converted at the time he heard Courtney's sermon on the new birth or if he was converted earlier. See Perry Thomas, *From Slave to Governor: The Unlikely Life of Lott Cary* (Mobile, AL: Parson Place Press, 2010) 24. Thomas's book is a historical novel that he claims is based on solid research including the note that Cary was converted by hearing another sermon by Courtney. Thomas fails to indicate what primary source he gleaned this from. For the sake of this work, the prevailing consensus from the historiography will be accepted.

[24] Taylor, *Biography*, 13–4; Fisher, "Lott Cary," 382, 384; Jordan, *Negro Baptist*, 12; Fitts, *Lott Carey*, 13–4.

a widower, but he married again in 1815 and became an able provider for his family.[25]

As Cary continued to be a devoted, Christian family man, his usefulness in the church grew. Because of Cary's preaching and influence in Richmond's African American community, he was also, in the words of Fisher, "instrumental in awakening among his Colored brethren in the city of Richmond a lively interest on behalf of the spiritual condition of Africa." According to Fisher, William Crane, a deacon at First Baptist Church, was the major organizer of a night school for free African Americans housed in the meeting house of First Baptist Church. Through his night school, Crane engaged his students, including Cary and Colin Teague, about African missions. Teague, who was also a freeman, was a fellow preacher in First Baptist Church and was a close friend of Cary's who would also leave for West Africa in January 1821. Crane was successful in igniting a fire within Cary and Teague's bosoms.[26]

Deacon Crane's encouragement of Carey and Teague to take an interest in African missions occurred at a time when American Baptists began to organize and engage in foreign missions work. American Baptist interest in foreign missions was influenced by English Baptists and the mission work of William Carey in India, who began his work there in 1795. According to Jacobs, the missionary zeal of English Baptists owed itself to the Evangelical revival of the eighteenth century.[27] The English Particular Baptists had organized the Baptist Missionary Society three years prior in London. William Straughton, pastor of First Baptist Church in Philadelphia, was knowledgeable of the activities of the English Particular Baptists; he was English, and he had been present at the founding of the Baptist Missionary

---

[25] Taylor, *Biography*, 15; Fisher, "Lott Cary," 383; Jordan, *Negro Baptist*, 13; Fitts, *Lott Carey*, 15.

[26] Taylor, *Biography*, 15–6; Fisher, "Lott Cary," 384–5; Jordan, *Negro Baptist*, 13; Poe, "Lott Carey," 50; Fitts, *Lott Carey*, 8. Fisher erroneously wrote that the school was in the African Baptist Church, but African Baptists organized in 1841. See the website of First African Baptist Church of Richmond, "About Us" http://www.firstafricanbaptist.org/page.php?id-2.

[27] Sylvia M. Jacobs, "The Historical Role of Afro-Americans in American Missionary Efforts in Africa," in *Black Americans and the Missionary Movement*, ed. Sylvia Jacobs (Westwood: Greenwood Press, 1982) 5. Jacobs also agrees that American Baptist mission movement emerged from the English effort, 7.

Society. Baptists in America were noticeably excited about Carey's mission. Along with reading Carey's letters from the mission field, they also gave their financial support to the endeavor as well as prayed for the success of the mission. English Baptist missionaries, en route to India, stayed in America and spoke in Baptist churches. When American Congregationalists founded the American Board of Commissioners for Foreign Missions in 1810, Baptists once again gave their money.[28]

The impetus for American Baptists to organize for foreign missions resulted from a rather remarkable turn within Congregationalist ranks. American Board missionaries Adoniram Judson and Luther Rice became convinced of baptism by immersion during their journey to India in 1813. Judson and Rice decided to resign their posts with the American Board believing it would be disingenuous for them to receive support from a Congregationalist organization, and they set out to seek support from American Baptists. Judson and his wife stayed in Burma, and Rice returned to America to solicit funds from the Baptists. When Baptists in Boston caught wind of this surprising news, they founded a local missionary society even before Rice returned to the United States.[29]

It was through the Boston Baptists and Luther Rice that American Baptists organized nationally. At the behest of the leaders of the Boston Baptist community, Rice traveled through the mid-Atlantic states and through the South to gauge the level of interest Baptists had in supporting foreign missions. Rice and the Boston Baptists found the interest great, and it was Rice's idea that all of the Baptist Associations send delegates to a meeting to organize the interest in foreign missions. At a meeting in May 1814 in Philadelphia, American Baptists organized the General Missionary Convention of the Baptist Denomination in the United States for Foreign Missions, which was also known as the General Convention or the Triennial Convention. The convention elected Richard Furman, pastor of First Baptist Church of Charleston, as the president. Imbued by this new missionary zeal among Baptists, Crane began to influence African Americans toward the prospect of African missions.[30]

---

[28] Torbet, *History*, 248–9; McBeth, *Heritage*, 343, 345.
[29] Torbet, *History*, 249; McBeth, *Heritage*, 345.
[30] Torbet, *History*, 249–50; McBeth, *Heritage*, 346.

Along with an awakening among Baptists to engage in foreign missions, the colonization movement had organized formally at the end of 1816 after decades of interest and various endeavors. According to Franklin, colonization sentiments date back to 1714, but the idea of transporting free Africans back to Africa failed to die, as Samuel Hopkins and Ezra Stiles, two Protestant ministers, during the Age of Revolution were interested in sending Christian Africans back to Africa to colonize and evangelize Africans. According to Poe, supporters of colonization believed that free African American Christians "would be a means of spreading Christianity and civilization" to Africa.[31]

The plans that Stiles and Hopkins had for sending Christian Africans back to their homeland failed, but it aroused interest among some within the free African American community in New England. One such freeman was Paul Cuffee, an entrepreneur and ship owner who provided a ship to thirty-eight free African Americans who sailed to West Africa in 1815. Cuffee worked with interested white Americans who would become the founding members of the American Colonization Society, including Bushrod Washington and Robert Finley.[32]

Following the formal colonization of Sierra Leone by Great Britain in 1787, Evangelical Christians founded the American Colonization Society in 1816 to facilitate African American repatriation to Africa. Just as Americans such as Stiles and Hopkins viewed colonization as a means to spread the gospel to West Africans, so did the British. According to Lamin Sanneh, the period from 1787 to 1893 was a period "that created a hospitable

---

[31] John Hope Franklin and Alfred A. Moss, *From Slavery to Freedom: A History of African Americans*, 8th ed., (New York: Alfred A. Knopf, 2006) 187–8. See also Peter Duignan and L. H. Gann, *The United States and Africa: A History* (London: Cambridge University Press, 1984) 81–2; Poe, "Lott Carey," 49 Lamin Sanneh, *West African Christianity: The Religious Impact* (Maryknoll, NY: Orbis Books, 1983) 90. Sanneh mentions Ezra Stiles specifically also as an American interested in colonization as well as that the African American founded African Union of Newport, Rhode Island, which was founded in 1780.

[32] Franklin and Moss, *From Slavery to Freedom*, 188; Duignan and Gann, *United States and Africa*, 82. There is a discrepancy in the year that Cuffee transported these thirty-eight persons. Franklin lists 1815, but Duignan and Gann list 1816 as the year that corresponds directly with the founding of the American Colonization Society. See Poe, "Lott Carey," 49.

environment for the diffusion of Christianity" and it was an "era of promise."[33] Among the free African community in Britain were staunch supporters of colonization, the most renowned of whom were Ottobah Cugoano and Equiano. Cugoano, a vociferous opponent of both the African slave trade and slavery, desired to return to West Africa as a missionary; and his writings inspired African Americans to follow suit more so than Equiano's narrative and his controversialist writings published in British newspapers.[34]

It is within this context of American Baptist interest and subsequent organization for foreign missions that Cary, Crane, and Teague joined forces to found the Richmond African Baptist Missionary Society in 1815.[35] Crane used his night school to inform students of the spiritual condition of Africa, which proved enough to motivate Cary and others. Owing to the social situation in Virginia that precluded African Americans from outwardly leading organizations in civil society, Crane had to assume the offices of president and corresponding secretary of the new missionary society. Remarkably, both slaves and former slaves sacrificed for the cause of sending the gospel to Africa. This society contributed $100 to $150 per year to African missions for several years after its founding. What also makes the founding of the Richmond African Baptist Missionary Society unique is that it was the first organization established by African Americans within the context of a racially integrated church.[36]

As mentioned above, the Triennial Convention came into existence to support foreign missions, but the first missionary it supported was in Burma. It was through the Richmond African Baptist Missionary Society that the Triennial Convention came to have an interest in African missions. At its meeting in Philadelphia in 1817, the Triennial Convention heard a report from William Crane, the corresponding secretary of the Richmond African Baptist Missionary Society, urging it to form a board for African missions. The leaders of the convention viewed the wishes of the Richmond society as a providential leading to interest itself in African missions, and they believed that free African American Baptists should go back to Africa to preach the

---

[33] Sanneh, *West African Christianity*, 53.

[34] Sanneh, *West African Christianity*, 55–6.

[35] Poe makes this assertion as well. See Poe, "Lott Carey," 51.

[36] Taylor, *Biography*, 15–6; Fisher, "Lott Cary," 384–5; Jordan, *Negro Baptist*, 13; Fitts, *History*, 45; Fitts, *Lott Carey*, 8.

gospel. Because of these factors, the Triennial Convention established a board to facilitate missions work in Africa, which made the convention the first American Christian denomination to sponsor foreign missions work in Africa. One more dynamic this decision produced was a vital connection between white Northern Baptists and African American Baptists in Richmond and throughout Virginia.[37]

The formation of the Richmond African Baptist Missionary Society proved to be a watershed moment, as it sparked more African American interest in African missions. African American Baptists from Philadelphia to Petersburg, Virginia, formed their own respective missionary societies, while those in North Carolina and Georgia contributed money to the cause of African missions in 1816 and in 1817. It is apparent that African American Baptists, whether slave or free, believed in the necessity of sending the gospel to Africa.[38]

Once African American Baptists in Richmond broke ground in founding a missionary society specifically to provide the gospel to Africans, the next question would be, "Who will go?" White Baptists held that it would be much better for free African Americans to serve as missionaries in Africa. William Crane believed this as well, and according to Fisher, it was Crane's idea to have Cary seek to become a missionary through the Triennial Convention and an agent through the American Colonization Society. Cary, too, had a strong desire to travel to Africa and preach and found a colony even though Cary had achieved material prosperity and a solid reputation in Richmond among African Americans and whites. According to Taylor, a man asked Cary how he could even consider leaving such a prosperous and comfortable life in Richmond to preach the gospel in Africa, and Cary responded, "I am an African, and in this country, however meritorious my conduct, and respectable my character, I cannot receive the credit due to either. I wish to go to a country where I shall be estimated by my merits, and not by my complexion; and I feel bound to labor for my suffering race."[39]

Judging from this statement, it appears that Cary was a race man, who wanted a better life for himself and his family. He sought to escape from the racism that pervaded Virginia, where a free man of color could never

---

[37] Fisher, "Lott Cary," 385–6; Fitts, *Lott Carey*, 8–9.

[38] Fisher, "Lott Cary," 386.

[39] Taylor, *Biography*, 17.

experience true civil and social equality. Fisher, however, related that Crane embellished upon Cary's sentiments. Using a piece of evidence that reveals Cary speaking to Crane about going to Africa for himself to preach the gospel, Fisher argued that Cary may have never expressed such sentiments. However Jordan and Fitts include the above quote in their writings, and both view it as Cary making a vivid statement on being racially conscious as well as being a good Christian. The majority view from the historiography on Cary is that he did articulate a keen sense of his own African identity, and he believed the gospel of Jesus Christ would be the only remedy to lift up his people on the African continent. This sentiment was definitely an Ethiopian one.[40]

Other than Crane's encouragement and Cary's own compulsion, Taylor and Jordan asserted that the triggering effect for both Cary and Collin Teague to immigrate to Africa in 1821 was their reading of the journal of Mills and Burgess, who explored the west coast of Africa for the American Colonization Society. This journal appeared in 1819, and in this journal, there were published letters from repatriated Africans residing in Sierra Leone inviting African Americans to join them. The existence of such a journal provides evidence in support of the argument that Cary possessed a certain degree of race consciousness.[41]

A letter from William Crane to O. B. Brown, a member of the board of managers of the American Colonization Society and a board member of the Triennial Convention, was the means by which Cary and Teague became affiliated with both bodies. Jordan included an excerpt from the letter dated 28 March 1819, which informs Brown that Cary and Teague desire to know how to become missionaries to West Africa. In it, Crane provides valuable glimpses into the comfortable and prosperous life that Cary was willing to forego for the sake of the gospel and human dignity. According to Crane, by the age of forty Cary owned a house just "below Richmond." He was the chief manager of laborers at the tobacco warehouse where he was also in charge of "receiving, marking, and shipping tobacco," and received a nice salary of $700 per year. Crane also indicates that both Cary and Teague wanted to be affiliated with the Colonization Society and

---

[40] Taylor, *Biography*, 17; Fisher, "Lott Cary," 389; Jordan, *Negro Baptist*, 14; Fitts, *Lott Carey*, 9–10.

[41] Taylor, *Biography*, 17–8; Jordan, *Negro Baptist*, 14.

go to Sierra Leone. In addition, they both desired to spread the gospel to their African brethren and, according to Crane's letter, they wanted to live in a place "where their color will be no disparagement to their usefulness." This statement reads very similar to the one stated by Cary mentioned above. Cary's motivation can be viewed as a mix of Christian commitment to preach the gospel in a foreign field, a belief that free persons of color should lead the charge to evangelizing and civilizing Africa, and that American racism's sting can only be escaped if free persons of color emigrate to Africa. This mix is foundational to the more mature articulation of Ethiopianism by African American Baptists later in the century. After receipt of this letter the Colonization Society received Cary and Teague as emigrants, and the Triennial Convention commissioned them as missionaries. They left for Africa in January of 1821.[42]

After being received by the Triennial Convention and the American Colonization Society, Cary and Teague spent all of 1820 studying in preparation for their ministries. Before leaving for the mission field, First Baptist Church ordained them into the gospel ministry. According to Fisher, despite their sponsorship from the former organizations, Cary and Teague were very much missionaries of the Richmond African Baptist Missionary Society, which contributed the most money in support of these two men and their families. Fisher reported that the Richmond society had given $483.25 to the Triennial Convention toward the cause of African missions since 1817. Fitts writes that when Cary and his party left for Africa in January 1821 the Richmond society gave $700 for the mission while the Triennial Convention gave $200, and $100 worth of books. Before the party embarked upon their journey, Cary gave a stirring farewell sermon at First Baptist in Richmond, and the party organized itself into a church as well. They left from Norfolk en route to Sierra Leone on 23 January 1821. The formal movement toward African missions by African Americans had begun.[43]

While the 1815 founding of the Richmond African Baptist Missionary Society proved to be a watershed moment in African American Baptist

---

[42] Taylor, *Biography*, 18–21; Fisher, "Lott Cary," 387–8; Jordan, *Negro Baptist*, 14–6; Fitts, *Lott Carey*, 11–2.

[43] Taylor, *Biography*, 23–4; Fisher, "Lott Cary," 390–2; Jordan, *Negro Baptist*, 16–8; Poe, "Lott Carey," 50–1; Fitts, *Lott Carey*, 14.

missionary and church history as it led to Lott Cary's historic presence in West Africa, it was during the 1830s that the Cooperative Movement commenced among African American Baptists in the east and Midwest. It is within this context that the American Baptist Missionary Convention (ABMC) came into existence in 1840. The Cooperative Movement denotes the activities and efforts of African American Baptist churches forging local and regional associations and conventions. This movement lasted until the founding of the NBC-USA in, 1895. What characterizes this movement is African American Baptist *initiative* and *social consciousness* because associations in Ohio, Illinois, and Michigan were all against slavery, but they also had missionary zeal as they focused on planting local churches in their respective areas. Only the ABMC sent missionaries to West Africa during the early period, and eventually state conventions in Virginia and North and South Carolina would send missionaries to West Africa. As the first African American Baptist associations grounded themselves throughout the Midwest, progressive-minded African American Baptist leaders in the east organized for missions with an abolitionist bent. The churches in the east were members of predominately white Baptist Associations; therefore, their intent was to organize on a regional basis rather than a local one.[44]

The ABMC was the first regional convention founded by African American Baptists, but its founding was rather humble. At its organization in New York City, only three churches were members: Abyssinian Baptist in New York City, Zion Baptist also of New York City, and Union Baptist in Philadelphia. Membership eventually grew as churches from Washington, DC, to Boston, and throughout the Midwest joined the convention as well, the latter consenting to membership at the behest of Rev. John Berry Meachum of St. Louis, Missouri. Led by Rev. Sampson White, then pastor of Abyssinian Baptist Church who served as the first moderator of the convention, the ABMC boldly demanded a gospel application to social justice as they strongly repudiated the practice of American slavery in the

---

[44] See James Melvin Washington, *Frustrated Fellowship: The Black Baptist Quest for Social Power* (Macon, GA: Mercer University Press, 2004) 38–9. Washington asserts that the founding of the ABMC along with other regional conventions founded in the 1860s led directly to the formation of the BFMC and eventually the NBC-USA. Once African American Baptists organized regionally, the momentum carried through the antebellum period and into subsequent periods of American history.

1850s, going so far as to exclude slave-owning ministers from its membership. By 1858, White and other key leaders of the convention encouraged member churches to withdraw from their white controlled associations owing to prejudice.[45]

According to the late scholar of the African American Church James Melvin Washington, the impetus for the formation of the ABMC was two-fold: the lack of attention on African missions by the Triennial Convention and the lack of strength toward abolitionism on the part of white Baptists. The convention committed itself to African missions primarily, but it was concerned with "domestic" issues such as planting churches, caring for ministers' widows, and temperance. Rev. Jeremiah Asher, though an abolitionist, was interested in creating what Washington calls "a black Christian civilization in Africa." He believed that the gospel preached in Africa to Africans would remedy the slave trade and slavery itself.[46] Though Washington failed to apply the term "Ethiopian," Asher's thought was clearly Ethiopian as discussed below.

The constitution of the ABMC reveals a strong emphasis on missions work following in the footsteps of the American Baptist Home Missions Society (ABHMS) of the Triennial Convention. According to Article 2 of the Constitution of the ABMC:

> It shall be the object of this convention to propagate the gospel of Christ, and to advance the interests of his kingdom, by supplying vacant churches when requested; by sending ministers into destitute regions within our reach; and by planting and building up churches, whenever a favorable opportunity

---

[45] Fitts, *History*, 67; Washington, *Frustrated Fellowship*, 39, 41; Bobby J. Lovett, *A Black Man's Dream: The Story of R. H. Boyd, the First One Hundred Years* (Nashville: Mega Corporation, 1993) 6. See also J. H. Jackson, *A Story of Activism: A History of the National Baptist Convention U. S. A. Inc.* (Nashville: Townsend Press, 1980) 25, 27. It is interesting that an African American Baptist Convention would have to make a statement barring slave-owning ministers from having membership. There are two intertwined reasons for this: first, the membership of the convention was open to whites from the South; and second, in the wake of the split among Baptists in 1845 owing to slavery, the leaders of the ABMC believed it needed to make its position clear thereby siding with the Northern Baptists.

[46] Washington, *Frustrated Fellowship*, 39–41.

offers. This convention shall in no case interfere with the internal regulation of the churches or associations.[47]

Such a design on the part of the convention demonstrates at least two concerns: first, it was unconvinced that the ABHMS put forth enough energy to plant African American Baptist churches; and second, the object of the convention reveals the need for African American Baptists to organize their own work for their people *without interference*. Although this became the case with the founding of the convention, the leaders still maintained fraternal relations with the leading men of the Triennial Convention.

The ABMC was concerned with foreign missions work as well, especially work in West Africa. Fitts offers this interesting statement regarding ABMC priorities: "To be sure, the foreign mission motif was the dominant reason for the organization of the American Baptist Missionary Convention."[48] Although the convention would eventually support African missions, it began with an interest in planting churches in the east; therefore, Fitts has overstated the ABMC's emphasis on African missions. However, with this interest in foreign mission during this time, it can be understood that the ABMC attempted to enlarge the African missions work first begun with the Richmond African Baptist Missionary Society in 1815 that the Triennial Convention helped to facilitate. It is obvious that Africa never became a priority for the Triennial Convention, as these Northern African Americans believed that they needed to launch their own missions work there.

Although the ABMC formed in 1840, the first record of it sponsoring a missionary to Africa is in 1858. The minutes of its annual session of 1858 include a section entitled, "Rules for a Christian Teacher," which reads like a type of commissioning, or charge, addressed to William J. Barnett, who was "[u]nder the patronage" of the ABMC.[49] He was to "keep" himself "unspotted from the world," to teach in Jesus' name as far as he would go in Sierra Leone, to report to the corresponding secretary regarding his work

---

[47] Ninth Annual Report of the American Baptist Missionary Convention, 12; See also Jordan, *Negro Baptist*, 31. Jordan published the extant reports of this convention.

[48] Fitts, *History*, 67.

[49] Report of the Seventeenth and Eighteenth Anniversaries of the ABMC, 19.

there, and to report the number of conversions and baptisms that occurred.[50] Furthermore, in the report is a notification detailing the farewell and commissioning service for Barnett, who was a member of the Temne ethnic group from Sierra Leone. The service occurred on 9 September 1857, at Concord Baptist Church in Brooklyn, New York. The report also states that he departed from New York City on September 23 returning to Sierra Leone as the "religious instructor" sponsored by the ABMC. After a stop in London, he disembarked in Freetown, Sierra Leone, in the middle of November 1857. At the meeting, the convention leaders implored the well-wishers to pray that Barnett would "be instrumental in turning pagan Africa from idols to serve the living God."[51]

At the next annual session of the ABMC, the Board offered a rather detailed update regarding its West African mission work. Jeremiah Asher, Corresponding Secretary of the Board, penned the report, which stated that Barnett was busy preaching the gospel "to the untutored heathen, in order to prepare the way of civilization."[52] Asher clarified what he meant by *civilization*. He and the ABMC believed that the gospel was "the only effectual remedy for the traffic in human flesh on the shores of Africa."[53] In these words is a clear statement of the Ethiopian spirit implied thus far in the convention's readiness to support an African born man as a missionary to Sierra Leone in 1857. Here, in 1859 as free African Americans in the United States fought and protested to end slavery, but witnessed an intransigent and paranoid South and a largely compliant North, members of the convention viewed the support of a missionary in West Africa as serving two ends: one, to save souls from eternal perdition; and two, to save souls from temporal yet horrible perdition in slavery.

It is clear from the report that the ABMC conceptualized its West African mission work within Ethiopianism. The convention had directed its zeal toward bringing the gospel to the people in Sierra Leone in order to plant new Baptist churches, but also to fight against the remnants of the slave trade and slavery. For the ABMC, this defined in part what civilization

---

[50] Ibid.

[51] Ibid., 20.

[52] Report of the Nineteenth Anniversary of the ABMC, 17.

[53] Ibid., 18.

meant. As Asher ended this report, he left the convention with these words written through the lens of Ethiopianism:

> Now dear Brethren, we submit this whole matter to your careful and prayerful consideration. We wish you to look at it in the light of eternity, and with reference to the judgment, when the assembled heathen of Africa, in the language of Sierra Leone, in a plea for the spread of the gospel among the heathen of Africa, said "Now if we refuse to tell them of a Savior's love, they will then say to us, 'Now you been seen us going to hell, and never told us.'"[54]

In the language and sentiment of mid-century Ethiopianism, Asher positioned African American Christians as the primary ones who possessed the spiritual, cultural, and relational wherewithal to succeed in this mission to Africa.

As the ABMC met for the twentieth year, the United States was torn in two by slavery. The turbulent decade of the 1850s ended with the hanging of John Brown, who attempted to end slavery through violent means. During a year that would witness the Union broken by South Carolina's secession in December, part of the attention of the members of the ABMC turned their gaze to Africa. The precarious future of Africans in the United States in 1860 made the idea of African eternal and temporal redemption even more urgent, particularly considering their belief that the gospel alone could save African souls from both the wrath of God and the wrath of the slave system.

Although the ABMC still maintained its fledgling work in Sierra Leone, William Walker wrote a letter that made a strident appeal to remember Africa. In his circular letter that the convention published in its anniversary report of 1860, Walker called for members of the ABMC to look beyond their own personal salvation in order to realize that others were in need of salvation. Specifically, he called for his fellow members of the convention to remember that the redemption of Africa was a prevalent issue. He wrote, "Africa, benighted Africa appeals to you!"[55] He called for the members to support the work in Africa to bring "light, knowledge, and civilization" to Africa.

---

[54] Ibid., 20–1; Jordan, *Negro Baptists*, 58.
[55] Report of the Twentieth Anniversary of the ABMC, 26–7.

On the eve of the Civil War, the ABMC struggled to remember Africa. This is significant because free African Americans had seen their freedoms curtailed owing to the 1850 Fugitive Slave Act, which put them at risk even in so-called free states, followed by the Dred Scott decision of 1857, which effectively nationalized slavery. As a result of these two federal acts, free states were no longer havens free of slavery. In the midst of the darkness of slavery, Walker called African Americans to remember that their mission in the world was to bring the gospel and civilization to Africa. They looked to a powerful God, whose gospel they believed would solve the social ills of the day. The gospel would penetrate the hearts of men, thus destroying the besetting sin of slavery and racial hatred. This was clearly an Ethiopian call on the eve of the Civil War.

As the Civil War ended and freedom came to approximately four million slaves, a new era of church planting and denomination-building emerged for African Americans, especially in the South. During the 1860s, African American Baptists throughout the South founded independent churches and organized district associations and state conventions. This "exodus," as described by late National Baptist Convention chronicler E. L. Thomas, consisted of churches that had been separate branches of white churches, or under white supervision, seizing their opportunity to achieve ecclesiastical freedom.[56] From the numerous district associations founded in the 1860s and 1870s came state conventions. It is within a few important state conventions that the missionary spirit of African American Baptists remained alive. The missionary endeavors of these few conventions are the link between Lott Cary's enterprise in the 1820s and the founding of the BFMC in 1880 that led to the formation of the NBC-USA in 1895.

Founded in 1868, the Virginia Baptist State Convention (VBSC) would emerge as the leading African American Baptist state convention as it pertained to African missions. It was in 1874 that this convention established a Foreign Mission Board. During its sixth annual session in May 1874, the convention called for a special committee "to nominate twelve to compose the Board of Foreign Missions."[57] The committee subsequently

---

[56] E. L. Thomas, *A History of the National Baptist Convention: The Programs, Personalities, and Power Base* (Nashville: Townsend Press, 1999) xiii.

[57] Minutes of the VBSC held in Liberty, VA, 13, 14, 15, 16, and 17 May 1874, 20.

approved a motion to locate the Foreign Missionary Board in Richmond.[58] There is no indication of why the convention decided to compose a Foreign Missionary Board at this time. It is difficult to speculate why the VBSC would commence its own African missions work during the 1870s. Judging from the immediate political context, Reconstruction had failed to usher in a just and equitable society for African Americans in the South. This led to a sense of independency among African Americans, especially among the elite to organize their own means toward uplift. For African American Baptists this context provided fodder for a renewed call for African missions as a means of both African American uplift and African uplift.

Although the VBSC organized a Foreign Missionary Board, there was no missionary activity until 1878. At the annual session of that year, Friday morning, 10 May, "Bro. Sol. Cosby was called out, who made some remarks, expressing his willingness to go to Africa, under the direction of this Convention."[59] After Cosby's statement regarding his candidacy to venture to Africa as a missionary, convention delegates W. J. Barnett, M. T. Lewis, and W. H. Brooks, presented "the claims of African missions."[60] The name W. J. Barnett is important, as this is the same Barnett who served as a missionary under the ABMC during the 1850s. This was an historic moment in African American Baptist history, demonstrating that a state convention just a decade into its history had the wherewithal and vision to send its own man to Africa as a missionary. Although four years had passed since the convention organized a Foreign Missionary Board, it is obvious that the board was at work attempting to pinpoint a suitable person to serve.

The former point is substantiated by President Wells of the convention, who gave a stirring address to the convention in 1878. In his address, Wells stated: "After diligent search and patient waiting a young man is found that is willing to go to Africa to preach the gospel as a missionary—his name is Solomon Cosby; he was educated at the Richmond Institute, to preach, and he is willing to labor at the above named place under the auspices of this Convention."[61] This president's excitement is evident in this address about the prospects of the convention sending its first

---

[58] Ibid., 21.

[59] Minutes of the VBSC held in Portsmouth, VA., 8 9, 10, 11, 12 May 1878, 16.

[60] Ibid., 7.

[61] Ibid., 30.

missionary to Africa. The "above named place" was Dahomey in what is now Nigeria.

Although the organization of state conventions directly spurred the movement toward the BFMC, the social and political climate of the 1870s particularly in the South, also renewed African American interests in evangelizing Africa through emigration schemes and Ethiopianism was still an adequate theological framework within which to articulate and apply these interests. During the 1870s, African Americans in the South engaged in honest discussions regarding their place in the United States. Not even a generation removed from slavery Southern African Americans had grown frustrated over the lack of progress they saw regarding gaining full equality in the land of their birth. Such states as South Carolina and Georgia, for example, had witnessed the rise of African American political power as African American voters elected scores of African American men to serve at all levels of government. With the Compromise of 1877, African Americans in the South saw their hopes dashed. As a result, African American Southerners contemplated the real potential of emigration out of the US to Africa and the Caribbean.

Just as there was a connection between African American emigration to Africa and missions work in the 1820s, there was also a link between African American emigration to Africa and state convention mission work during the 1870s. In 1877, African American Baptists in South Carolina organized the Baptist Educational, Missionary, and Sunday-School Convention (BEMSSC). Its historic inaugural session, held in May of that year, reveals the high level of commitment that African American Baptists in South Carolina had towards African missions. A resolution was made in effect to ask for the aid of white Baptists in South Carolina to help them in organizing and funding their efforts in both home and foreign missions. Even though this was the first annual session, the leaders concluded that foreign missions were something that had to be undertaken by them.[62] In an address to the convention, the president, Rev. I. P. Brockenton, chastised South Carolina Baptists for failing to do anything of note to send home and foreign missionaries into the field. As this was the first session of a state

---

[62] Minutes of the Baptist Educational, Missionary and Sunday School Convention of South Carolina (BEMSCC) 2–4 May 1877 held at Sumter, SC, 9.

convention, Brockenton must have referred to the paltry efforts of individual churches and district associations.[63]

During its second annual session, the BEMSSC addressed the issue of foreign missions with more clarity and zeal demonstrating that the leadership was busy directing the efforts of the convention toward increased foreign mission activity. The Committee on Missions reported to the convention that it should begin working in both home and foreign missions.[64] There is an urgent tone to the report, and the minutes reflect that an "animated discussion ensued" following the report, which was unanimously accepted.[65] There can only be conjecture as to whether the "animated discussion" centered on foreign missions. However the events in the immediate aftermath suggest reason to believe that the convention discussed foreign missions at some length.

Reflecting that this convention was quite aware of what was astir among African American South Carolinians, Rev. J. S. Daniel offered prayer for Africa and a resolution regarding the possibility of foreign mission work in Africa, to pray for Africa for five minutes, and the safe arrival of persons on the *Azor* on its way to Monrovia. This is an interesting entry into the minutes demonstrating that this convention saw an opportunity to engage in African missions work owing to the emigration of African American South Carolinians. The African American South Carolinians aboard the *Azor* were involved in a venture of the Liberian Exodus Joint Stock Steamship Company led by Martin Delany and others in Charleston. Unlike the Cary mission, those aboard the *Azor* traveled to Liberia under the auspices of an African American initiative.[66]

Attached to the minutes is an open letter to the convention members by Corresponding Secretary E. M. Brawley, titled, "South Carolina and Africa for Jesus."[67] This letter served as an update regarding the convention's plans to sponsor a missionary to Africa, an issue that was left unclear during

---

[63] Ibid., 17.

[64] Minutes of the Second Anniversary of the Baptist Educational, Missionary and Sunday School Convention of South Carolina, 1–5 May 1878 held at Orangeburg, SC, 15.

[65] Ibid., 15.

[66] Ibid., 19–20. See also Edwin Redkey, *Black Exodus: Black Nationalism and Back-to-Africa Movements, 1890–1910* (New Haven: Yale University Press, 1969) 22.

[67] Minutes, BEMSSC, Orangeburg, 24.

the annual meeting in May. Brawley reported both that the convention had commissioned home missionaries and decided to send a missionary to Africa. The unnamed missionary was expected to sail to Africa within a few months.[68]

At the second meeting of the BEMSSC the board of managers' report clarifies these points in the minutes regarding foreign missions. Although a foreign missionary had yet to be commissioned, they believed that God commanded the Church to conduct foreign mission work in all "heathen lands." Africa drew their particular attention and focus due to the lack of consideration given to Africa by white Baptists, and the convention determined to send at least one missionary to Africa, which they acknowledged as the land of their forefathers. At present, there were only two Baptist missionaries in Africa, both of whom were affiliated with the Southern Baptist Convention (SBC), which according to the board, was reason enough to arouse the interest of the 71,000 African American Baptists in South Carolina. As this section of the report closed, the board linked its desire to send a missionary to Africa with the emigration movement in South Carolina. The sailing of the *Azor* from Charleston en route to Monrovia, Liberia, on 21 April was orchestrated by the Shiloh Baptist Church. This venture was so hastily planned that the group of eighty church members set sail without calling a pastor. Eager to support this endeavor, the board proposed sending a missionary-pastor to Liberia, thus heralding the beginning of the convention's foreign mission work.[69]

The next annual session of the BEMSSC of South Carolina signified further progress toward sending a missionary to Africa. By this meeting, the convention had organized a separate committee specifically on African missions indicating the importance of this movement with the convention. The Committee on African Missions reported the commissioning of H. N. Bouey as missionary to Liberia who, according to the previous year's minutes, had been one of four home missionaries. Notably, the lack of attention given by white American Baptists instigated the urgency of African American Baptists in South Carolina to send a missionary to Africa.

---

[68] Ibid.

[69] First Annual Report of the Board of Managers of the Baptist Educational, Missionary, and Sunday-School Convention of South Carolina, 1 May 1878, v–vi. Redkey writes that Christians specifically were a prominent group that desired to emigrate. See Redkey, *Black Exodus*, 9.

Minutes also state that the secretary read letters from Bouey while en route, indicating that he was of good spirits and health and realized "the importance and magnitude of the work before him." The minutes also state that the convention prayed for its work in Africa.[70]

The board of managers' report offers more specifics on Bouey's commissioning as the convention's first missionary to Africa. In its section on African Missions, the board states that on 14 August 1878, the convention commissioned Harrison N. Bouey as missionary-pastor to lead the Shiloh Baptist Church in Liberia. He sailed from New York City in April 1879 to Monrovia.[71] With the commissioning of H. N. Bouey by the South Carolina convention, African American Baptists had successfully sent its second missionary to Africa in the space of two years. This alone is remarkable during this time period, but this particular commissioning wedded missionary work and the renewal of African American emigration during a challenging period for African Americans, especially Southern African Americans.

During the same year that the South Carolina convention commissioned Bouey as a missionary-pastor to Liberia, the Baptist State Convention of North Carolina commissioned its first missionary, as well. Preserved in the minutes of its annual session of 1880, the convention highlighted African missions. For example, the convention heard from Rev. J. A. Mundy of the white Baptist church of Warrenton, and he spoke on the subject of Foreign Missions. The missionary J. O. Hayes had returned from his mission field to address the convention. He stated that his heart was committed to foreign mission work, especially work in Africa. The corresponding secretary, J. O. Crosby, mentioned that, through visiting various churches and associations in the state, North Carolina African American Baptists had a strong commitment to foreign missions, especially the evangelization of Africa. Owing to this, Cosby was confident that African American Baptists in the state could support their one missionary in Africa.[72]

---

[70] Minutes of the Third Anniversary of the Baptist Educational, Missionary, and Sunday-School Convention of South Carolina, May 1879, 11–2.

[71] Second Annual Report of the Board of Managers of the Baptist Educational, Missionary, and Sunday-School Convention of South Carolina, May 1879, 2.

[72] Minutes of the 14th Annual Session of the Baptist State Convention of North Carolina in Warrenton, NC, 20–23 October 1880, 6, 13–4.

In rehearsing the activities of these three state conventions in the late 1870s, it is clear that from an historical perspective that a fresh movement was afoot among Southern African American Baptists. Historians of National Baptist history agree that the commissioning of Cosby of Virginia, Bouey of South Carolina, and Hayes of North Carolina as missionaries to Africa helped develop a vision of cooperation among African American Baptists in the enterprise of African missions specifically.[73] According to historian Sandy Martin, the Virginians sparked discussions of cooperation among African American Baptists beginning in 1879 through their former Southern Baptist missionary, William W. Colley, who was also a Virginian. Other writers such as E. L. Thomas boldly wrote that Colley's work in this arena "create[d] the nucleus for our beginning." As mentioned above, William W. Colley served as a missionary in West Africa representing the SBC.[74] Colley was born in Prince Edward County on 12 February 1847 of Scottish, American Indian, and African descent. With this multi-racial heritage, Colley self-identified as an African American. In 1875, Colley began his four-year tenure as a missionary under the auspices of the Foreign Mission Board of the SBC. Colley assisted a white missionary from Mississippi, named W. J. David; they worked together among the Yoruba in Nigeria. While there, he became upset over the treatment of Africans by white missionaries. To remedy this racist treatment, he became convinced that there needed to be more African American missionaries in the African field, which is a strong Ethiopian sentiment.[75]

---

[73] The work of Sandy D. Martin is important in crystallizing the activities of the state conventions as leading to the foundation of the BFMC. See Sandy D. Martin, *Black Baptists and African Missions: The Origins of a Movement 1880–1915* (Macon, GA: Mercer University Press, 1989.

[74] According to Eddie Stepp, the Foreign Mission Board of the Southern Baptist Convention commissioned African American missionaries from its founding in the 1840s. See Eddie Stepp, "Interpreting a Forgotten Mission: African American Missionaries of the Southern Baptist Convention in Liberia, West Africa 1846–1860," (unpublished dissertation, Baylor University, 1999).

[75] Freeman, *Epoch of Negro Baptists*, 69–70; Jackson, *A Story of Activism*, 33; Martin, *Black Baptists*, 49. See also Jordan, *Negro Baptist*, 99–100; William A. Harvey, *Bridges of Faith Across the Seas: The Story of the Foreign Mission Board National Baptist Convention, USA, Inc.* (Philadelphia: Foreign Mission Board National Baptist Convention, USA, Inc., 1989) 22–3; Fitts, *History*, 114; Martin, *Black Baptists*, 49–50; Thomas, *National Baptist Convention*, 1–2.

Returning to Virginia with this general disposition, Colley met with the leaders of the Virginia state convention and with African American Baptist leaders from Washington, DC. Jackson places moderate significance to Colley's meeting the Virginians and rightly recognizes that the Virginians had been the leaders of African American mission interest in Africa going back to the formation of the Richmond African Missionary Baptist Society in 1815 and the work and legacy of Lott Cary. Freeman posits that the Virginia Baptists "employed" Colley to stir interest for foreign missions among African American Baptists. Martin, however, takes this argument further. According to Martin, it was collaboration between Colley and the Virginians that prompted Colley's tour of the Southern states primarily to survey the interest of forming a national missionary convention. Martin states that "it was quite obvious that the BFMC to a great extent represents an outgrowth of the Virginia Baptist State Convention." Martin supports this argument by stating that since it was the Virginia convention's goal to "evangelize and" uplift "their racial kin," it realized that great amounts of funds were necessary, which it was unable to raise itself. Thus, a convention of churches would solve the financial concern. Because of this, Colley embarked on his most momentous tour. In addition to what Martin asserts regarding the Virginians' motivations, other historians have remarked on Colley's personal motivations. Jordan wrote of the personal motivation of Colley as "a never failing faith in God and a desire to be of greater service to the Master." He also explained that Colley had a great desire to revive "the Colored Baptists to a greater love for God and Africa."[76] This statement by Jordan further evinces Colley's Ethiopian vision of African American Baptist missions work in Africa, not merely as missionaries serving in white conventions but also serving in African American ones.

To elaborate on the above point, it is clear that the major motivation for this campaign was two-fold: first, African Americans needed to direct their own course regarding sending their own missionaries to Africa; and second, African Americans perceived themselves as possessing a unique qualification to be missionaries in Africa in order to eradicate racism on the

---

[76] Jackson, *A Story of Activism*, 32–3; Freeman, *Epoch of Negro Baptists*, 70; Martin, *Black Baptists*, 53–4. Even within the ranks of the Virginia Baptists, the Richmond African Baptist Missionary Society was most influential in sending Colley on his tour. See also Jordan, *Negro*, 99–100.

mission field. African American Baptist leaders in Virginia believed that this was the time to seize the opportunity to forge a new national convention to enlarge their own desires regarding African missions.[77]

Colley's tour and engagements with Southern African American Baptist leaders was successful, and there was strong interest in forming a new national missionary convention. According to Freeman, Colley impressed upon the brethren their responsibility to share the gospel with their African kin. These leaders heeded Colley's appeals. In May 1880, Colley gave a positive report of his travels to the Virginia convention, and it gave support to Colley to initiate the formation of the new convention. Colley planned a meeting to be held in November of 1880 in Montgomery, Alabama, for all African American Baptists interested in forming the new convention.

As previously mentioned, the formation of the BFMC in November 1880 is considered to be the beginning of the NBC-USA. Lewis Jordan unequivocally holds that the birth of the NBC-USA was in Montgomery, Alabama.[78] In Jordan's collection of primary sources, he provides a complete copy of the constitution of the BFMC. Its preamble is important to note as it gives testimony to what had been arguably the driving force attempting to unify African Americans Baptists nationally:

> Whereas it becomes necessary and is our duty to extend our Christian influence to advance the kingdom of Christ and as Africa Missions claims our most profound attention and feeling that we are most sacredly called to do work in this field and elsewhere abroad, therefore, we the representatives from the various churches, Sunday schools, and societies of the Baptist denomination in the United States, do solemnly organize ourselves in a Convention for the above named object.[79]

According to the founding document of the BFMC and implicitly the NBC-USA, the purpose of the convention was to organize to send missionaries to Africa for the sake of spreading the gospel and tacitly to civilize Africans. This purpose was an Ethiopian one, as it articulated both spiritual and temporal concerns framed within the perception that African American Baptists are particularly fitted for this task.

---

[77] Martin, *Black Baptists*, 49–50.
[78] Jordan, *Negro Baptists*, 99.
[79] Jordan, *Negro Baptists*, 154–5.

When Lott Cary waved farewell to friends and well-wishers as the brig *Nautilus* drifted from Norfolk into the vast Atlantic Ocean he had no idea that his voyage and missionary work in Liberia would reverberate all the way at the end of the nineteenth century. When President Morris of the NBC-USA remarked that foreign missions was dear to the hearts of his fellow National Baptists, he referred back to the legacy of Lott Cary. What is interesting is that, at the same annual session of the NBC-USA that Morris spoke those aforementioned words, a group of delegates from the east coast, including Cary's home state of Virginia, decided to cut ties with the convention to organize one that focused solely on foreign missions. Kindling the spirit of Lott Cary, this group would form the Lott Carey Baptist Foreign Mission Convention in December 1897. At the inaugural session of the Lott Carey Convention C. S. Brown, the first president of the convention boldly proclaimed the task of foreign missions was "divinely imposed upon the Churches."[80] Although the NBC-USA had branched out into other objects such as publishing, a group of stalwarts including members from the state of Virginia desired to maintain continuity with the past work of the BFMC and the Richmond Baptist Missionary Society.

From Lott Cary to W. W. Colley, African American Baptists conceptualized their desire to evangelize Africa within the theology of Ethiopianism. At the heart of Ethiopianism was a belief that God had decreed the redemption of Africa and included in that decree was the enslavement, emancipation, and emigration of persons of African descent in the United States of America. With Cary, there was distinct cooperation with white Baptists; but with the ABMC there arose a spirit within a company of Northern free African American Baptists to initiate their own movement to send missionaries to Africa. This movement spread to Southern African American Baptists in the South Atlantic region in the late 1870s. It would be African American Baptists from the South that would spearhead the movement founded in the first African American Baptist national convention in 1880. Although Ethiopianism is a theology, it

---

[80] C. S. Brown, "Why the Lott Carey Convention Was Organized" in Lott Carey Baptist Foreign Mission Convention, *Lott Carey Baptist Foreign Mission Convention, The Convention of Distinction: Fifty-Five Years of Ceaseless Service to Others* (Washington, DC: Lott Carey Baptist Foreign Mission Convention, 1953) 8. This is a reprint of a speech given by Brown in 1926 in which he reiterated points given in his speech at the first annual session of the Lott Carey Convention in 1898.

included a spirit of independence among African American Baptists, even a Pan-African inspired nationalism. A type of African American nationalism continued to pervade the NBC-USA, as it established a publishing board for an official literature by and for African Americans and expanded its African mission fields to include Central and Southern Africa.

4

Annie Walker Armstrong, Nannie Helen Burroughs, and Cooperation among Baptist Women of the South across Racial Divides

April C. Armstrong

After the Woman's Convention (WC), Auxiliary to the National Baptist Convention (NBC), met in 1936, its corresponding secretary, Nannie Helen Burroughs, wrote to Kathleen Mallory, her counterpart in the Woman's Missionary Union (WMU), Auxiliary to the Southern Baptist Convention (SBC). She wanted to thank Mallory for visiting their meeting: "Your visit did as much for us in 1936 as Miss Annie W. Armstrong's visit did in 1900. It set the music of good will and Christian cooperation ringing anew in our hearts."[1] Mallory wrote back saying that she appreciated being compared to Armstrong, although she knew that she could never truly be said to be as helpful as Armstrong had been to the WC, "especially as I know how genuinely you appreciate her."[2] Armstrong's relationship with Burroughs was well known among WMU leaders during the women's lifetimes, and it is still a part of biographies the WMU has recently published about both women in its *WMU Heritage Series*, a series that includes only three biographies—those of Burroughs, Charlotte "Lottie" Digges Moon, a missionary to China in whose honor the SBC receives an offering each Christmas, and Armstrong, who led the WMU in its early years and in

---

[1] Burroughs is probably referring to Armstrong's 1901 visit. There are no records suggesting Armstrong was present at the formation of the WC in 1900. As discussed below, Armstrong was in Indian Territory at that time. Nannie Helen Burroughs, Washington, DC, to Kathleen Mallory, Birmingham, Alabama, 18 September 1936, Nannie Helen Burroughs Papers, Manuscript Room, Library of Congress, Washington, DC.

[2] Kathleen Mallory, Birmingham, Alabama, to Nannie Helen Burroughs, Washington, DC, 21 September 1936, Nannie Helen Burroughs Papers, Manuscript Room, Library of Congress, Washington, DC.

whose honor the SBC takes an offering each Easter.[3] In preparing this manuscript, I mentioned the WMU's biography of Burroughs to a colleague, who expressed discomfort over the idea that an organization originally composed of white Baptist women in the South would attempt to "claim" the black advocate of African American equality and opportunity as a part of their heritage. This is but one example indicating how, among scholars of African American women's religious history, there are few (if any) who demonstrate an awareness of what Mallory knew about Armstrong's assistance in the formation of the WC or in other matters related to race relations in the American South, or how her relationship with Burroughs served as a catalyst to shape the activities of both women within their respective organizations.

Most of what has been written on Burroughs tends to focus on her efforts for racial uplift through the school she founded in 1909, the National Training School for Women and Girls in Washington, DC (now the Nannie Helen Burroughs School), but in general, Burroughs has not figured prominently in scholarship on African American reformers until recently.[4]

---

[3] See Cathy Butler, *The Story of Lottie Moon*, WMU Heritage Series (Birmingham, AL: Woman's Missionary Union, 2004); idem, *The Story of Annie Armstrong*, WMU Heritage Series (Birmingham, AL: Woman's Missionary Union, 2004); Sondra Washington, *The Story of Nannie Helen Burroughs*, WMU Heritage Series (Birmingham, AL: Woman's Missionary Union, 2006).

[4] There is limited discussion of her work with the WC in most of the following sources, and rarely is there any mention of the broader Baptist circles in which she circulated. See L. H. Hammond, *In the Vanguard of a Race* (New York: Council of Women for Home Missions and Missionary Education Movement of the United States and Canada, 1922); Earl L. Harrison, *The Dream and the Dreamer: An Abbreviated Story of the Life of Dr. Nannie Helen Burroughs and Nannie Helen Burroughs School at Washington, D.C.* (Washington, DC: Nannie H. Burroughs Literature Foundation, 1956); Karen A. Johnson, *Uplifting the Women and the Race: The Educational Philosophies and Social Activism of Anna Julia Cooper and Nannie Helen Burroughs*, Garland Studies in African American History and Culture, ed. Graham Russell Hodges (New York: Garland Publishing, 2000); Audrey Thomas McCluskey, "We Specialize in the Wholly Impossible': Black Women School Founders and Their Mission," *Signs* 22. 2 (Winter 1997): 403–26; William Pickens, *Nannie Burroughs and the School of the Three B's* (New York: n.p., 1921); Traki L. Taylor, "'Womanhood Glorified': Nannie Helen Burroughs and the National

Sharon Harley's 1996 article in *The Journal of Negro History* accused the scholarly community of exercising its own form of discrimination in determining "who were the black intellectuals and race leaders" and excluding others on the basis of "class, gender, and even skin color."[5] Harley may be right about discrimination, although perhaps on other grounds. If they are looking for a woman who defiantly shattered glass ceilings and crusaded for female ordination, scholars will not find her in Burroughs, and there might be a bit of ideological bias with regard to whom scholars of African American women's religious history choose to study. Yet she is not wholly unexamined, even as a social activist. The works of Evelyn Brooks Higginbotham and Barbara Savage address Burroughs's social and religious activism in a way that allows readers to gain an appreciation for the complexity of her thought, including some of the seeming paradoxes of her activities—at once independent of and subordinate to the male authority structure of the NBC and being an outspoken proponent of both the inherent equality of all races and of keeping the races "pure" and separate.[6]

Some of the picture is still missing, however. In *Righteous Discontent*, Higginbotham mentions Armstrong in passing, saying her 1901 visit to the WC annual meeting was evidence of "the new spirit of cooperation that emanated from southern white church women."[7] In a book of more than three hundred pages, Higginbotham devoted only two paragraphs to the WC's relationship with the WMU. Scholarship like hers and that of Anthea D. Butler on the relationship between Bible reading and the formation of the WC strongly imply that white Baptist women in the South do not have much to do with the history of black Baptist women, while many Northern

---

Training School for Women and Girls, Inc., 1909–1961," *Journal of African American History* 87 (Autumn 2002): 390–402.

[5] Sharon Harley, "Nannie Helen Burroughs: 'The Black Goddess of Liberty,'" *Journal of Negro History* 81.1–4 (Winter–Autumn 1996): 62.

[6] See Evelyn Brooks Barnett [Higginbotham], "Nannie Burroughs and the Education of Black Women," in *The Afro-American Woman: Struggles and Images*, ed. Sharon Harley and Rosalyn Terborg-Penn (Baltimore: Black Classic Press, 1997) 97–108; idem, *Righteous Discontent: The Women's Movement in the Black Baptist Church, 1880–1920* (Cambridge: Harvard University Press, 1993); Barbara Savage, *Your Spirits Walk Beside Us: The Politics of Black Religion* (Cambridge: Harvard University Press, 2008) 163–204.

[7] Higginbotham, *Righteous Discontent*, 197.

white Baptist women are recorded as having had close and extensive relationships with their black counterparts.[8] More recently, Savage has written about Burroughs's relationship with WMU leader Una Roberts Lawrence in the 1930s, but how Burroughs might have become acquainted with the WMU leadership remains somewhat a mystery beyond the general relationship that existed between the NBC and the SBC.[9]

Few scholars have examined Armstrong other than those appointed by the WMU or the SBC. The SBC's own publications claim that Armstrong played a large role in the formation of the WC, in addition to participating in various projects meant to aid African Americans in Baltimore for many years before and after the organization was operational. Armstrong and Burroughs acted as representatives for their respective women's groups, and through their relationship, they acted as liaisons between black and white Baptists in the South, respectively. Armstrong, who had met with Burroughs in the late nineteenth century to plan the organization of the WC, continued to help Burroughs behind the scenes for years after Burroughs had begun her work as corresponding secretary. After Armstrong left her position as corresponding secretary of the WMU, advocacy for African American causes largely left the WMU for at least a decade, evidence for just how crucial Armstrong was to these efforts.[10] These accounts are lacking in detail, however, because they focus primarily on Armstrong's work with the SBC.[11]

---

[8] See Anthea D. Butler, "Only a Woman Would Do: Bible Reading and African American Women's Organizing Work," in *Women and Religion in the African Diaspora*, ed. R. Marie Griffith and Barbara Diane Savage (Baltimore: Johns Hopkins University Press, 2006) 155–78. Butler's only mention of white women in the South appears on page 161, where she describes the difference between the egalitarian northern white missionary Joanna P. Moore and "most white people who lived in the areas where she conducted her missionary work." See also Higginbotham's chapter in *Righteous Discontent* titled "Unlikely Sisterhood."

[9] Barbara Diane Savage, *Your Spirits Walk beside Us*, 175–8.

[10] Catherine B. Allen, *A Century to Celebrate: History of Woman's Missionary Union* (Baltimore: Woman's Missionary Union, 1987) 241–5.

[11] See Butler, *The Story of Annie Armstrong*, 94–99, 121, Elizabeth Marshall Evans, *Annie Armstrong*, ed. Nan F. Weeks (Birmingham: Woman's Missionary Union, 1963) 31, 115, and Bobbie Sorrill, *Annie Armstrong: Dreamer in Action* (Nashville: Broadman Press, 1984) 138–41, 180–83, 245. The one exception is Henry Y. Warnock's "Prophets of Change: Some Southern Baptist Leaders and the Problem of Race, 1900–1921," *Baptist History and Heritage* 7.3 (1972): 172–83,

Yet without the relationship between Armstrong and Burroughs, an important part of this story is missing that would illuminate the roles of both of their respective organizations. Overall, Armstrong did play a significant role in the formation of the WC and worked closely with Burroughs, but due to the nature of the work Armstrong did, the way in which the WMU and the WC publicly discussed that work, as well as the fact that Armstrong's contributions run counter to most scholarly intuition about white Baptist women in the American South, it has yet to be examined in the field of American religious history. The story is surprising and complicates the accepted narrative about the women of the NBC and the SBC in the late nineteenth and early twentieth centuries. What is known about the story of Armstrong and Burroughs can teach the scholarly community something about the circumstances under which the WC was formed, as well as how the WMU addressed race relations during this period—and, indeed, the WMU did address race relations at the time, although they saw it as a religious, rather than political, issue.

Annie Walker Armstrong was born in Baltimore on 11 July 1850, a little less than twenty-nine years before the birth of Nannie Helen Burroughs in Orange, Virginia, in May 1879. Armstrong would live in Baltimore her entire life. She was the descendent of two wealthy Maryland families, although her parents experienced financial problems, and her father's death in 1852 served to worsen the situation. However, relatives most likely aided Armstrong's newly widowed mother and siblings. Armstrong grew up in a downtown home with black servants. The family attended Baltimore's Seventh Baptist Church until the construction of Eutaw Place Baptist Church in 1871. In contrast to the women at Seventh Baptist, women at Eutaw Place were very active in the church's ministries. They formed an organization of women from various Baptist churches in Baltimore, Woman's Mission to Woman, in the same year as the church's founding. Armstrong's mother was active in this society, which may have had an

---

which attempts to answer the question of what the effects were of Armstrong's work with African Americans. He devoted only two paragraphs to her in a larger article dealing with the SBC as a whole on the subject of race, and consulted only a few letters she wrote in 1901 as source material. Based on these, Warnock concluded that despite Armstrong's passion, "It cannot be recorded that in the early twentieth century much was ever achieved in the area of [WMU] women's work [with African Americans]" (Ibid., 177).

impact on Armstrong's view of the importance of women in the church. In 1878, Eutaw Place appointed home and foreign missions committees, with both male and female members, which was highly unusual for the time. Armstrong's older sister, Alice, was a member of the committee on foreign missions. Armstrong does not appear to have been involved in mission activities herself until she heard a speech in November 1880 about the plight of the Native Americans who had recently been forcibly removed to Indian Territory (now Oklahoma). She was on a committee that included members of both black and white Baptist churches in Baltimore that worked to sew and send clothing to children at a school for Native American children in the Creek Nation, Indian Territory (present-day Wetumka, Oklahoma). Armstrong distinguished herself as a leader during this project, and the Southern Baptist churches involved in it elected her president of a new organization, the Woman's Baptist Home Mission Society of Maryland (WBHMS). In this capacity, Armstrong began to make contact with figures such as Isaac Taylor Tichenor, the corresponding secretary of the SBC's Home Mission Board, and was quickly gaining influence in the SBC.

In 1884, the SBC held its annual meeting in Baltimore, and the WBHMS planned and hosted a gathering of women from every missionary society in the SBC in conjunction with the convention's meeting. At this gathering, the women agreed to meet every year at the time and city where the SBC meeting was being held. When they met in Richmond in 1888, the WBHMS voted to form a national organization, the Executive Committee of the Woman's Mission Societies (which would soon change its name to the WMU), and they elected Armstrong as their first corresponding secretary. This organization, unlike similar organizations in other denominations or among Northern Baptists, would not send its own missionaries. It would simply act as an aid to the existing mission boards of the SBC.[12]

Forming the WMU was controversial, and the shape it took was a reflection of those controversies. Although as early as 1872 male leaders in the SBC had been encouraging the women to organize via its annual "Report on Women's Work," not all of the men were pleased with the idea. In 1885, the SBC voted to amend its constitution, substituting the word "brethren" for "members" and excluding women from all official business,

---

[12] Sorrill, *Annie Armstrong*, 19–40, 47, 57–79.

although women had attended and participated in the SBC meetings prior to that time.[13] It is perhaps telling that the women rarely held their annual meetings in a Baptist church even into the twentieth century, instead finding Presbyterian or Methodist churches more willing to allow them the use of their buildings.[14] One woman involved in the early efforts to organize the WMU wrote that SBC pastors were very discouraging when women asked to meet in their churches and that the discussions of the WMU at the SBC's meetings at that time frustrated her so much, "I would say to my dear husband that I thought—or was afraid—that the best of men had great big streaks of the old heathen in them."[15] However, in 1921, she took comfort in the thought that "the dear brethren have overcome the great fears and awful apprehensions of the dreadful things the women would do if backed with a little authority..."[16]

Catherine B. Allen offers three reasons why the men of the SBC were so resistant to the WMU. First, they viewed outside organizations as a threat to church autonomy. (Baptist polity is congregational—the decisions of organizations like the SBC are not binding on individual churches, and membership and the level of involvement in any convention or association is determined by local churches.) Second, they feared that women would seek to become preachers if allowed to organize. "[S]uch an independent organization," a committee of the Baptist General Association of Virginia reported, "naturally tends toward a violation of the divine interdict against women's becoming a public religious teacher and leader—a speaker before mixed assemblies, a platform declaimer, a pulpit proclaimer, street preacher, lyceum lecturer, stump orator." Third, there was a fear that women's organizations would erode the culture of the South. After all, it was the North that had developed these organizations in the first place. "Our

---

[13] Southern Baptist Convention, *Annuals*, 1872–1885. See also Allen, *A Century to Celebrate*, 27–40.

[14] Woman's Missionary Union, *Annuals*, 1889–1910. It is perhaps also telling that the WMU published its own annual minutes and reports, separate from any SBC publications (See also Allen, *A Century to Celebrate*, 39).

[15] [Lucinda Beckley] Williams, *Golden Years: An Autobiography* (Dallas: Baptist Standard, 1921) 117.

[16] Williams, *Golden Years*, 108.

women," they said, did not want it. Anybody who said otherwise did not understand what a true Southern woman ought to want.[17]

In order to ease the men's anxieties, the women insisted that they wanted an organization that would not send its own missionaries but would work to help the SBC under the authority of their local church bodies. They would show their commitment to not speaking to mixed audiences by not allowing men to attend their meetings. Theirs would not be like the women's missions organizations of the North. Although many were still suspicious of them, the women managed to get enough male support to begin their experiment. In large part because they were quickly successful in raising large amounts of money for the deeply indebted mission boards, the WMU earned a permanent home among the agencies of the SBC.[18] In 1895, Armstrong reported that "by its amiable and proper conduct," the WMU had become "entirely welcome in the family circle, where at first some of the members looked askance and shook solemn heads in warning at the awful things which this youngster was to perpetuate—disintegrating churches and other seismic performances." The two organizations were not independent. "We are ... at work for and in the church."[19]

Perhaps because she lived in Baltimore, a city with a large population of African Americans on the northern edge of the South that had been ambivalent during the Civil War, or because of her relationship with her own household servants, or because of her previous work with the women of black Baptist churches in clothing children in Indian Territory, Armstrong quickly began to demonstrate an interest in African Americans. This is evident in her work as the WMU's corresponding secretary and as the WBHMS president, a position she still held throughout her service as a WMU officer. At the 1890 WMU meeting, her report on the activities of the WBHMS states that they had begun working with African Americans.[20] With the exception of 1892, reports of the activities of the WBHMS at the annual WMU meetings would include reference to this work each year until 1904. Beginning in 1892, the WBHMS established industrial schools and

---

[17] Allen, *A Century to Celebrate*, 30–31.

[18] Ibid., 37–42.

[19] Annie Walker Armstrong, Report of Corresponding Secretary, Woman's Missionary Union, *Annual*, 1895, 10.

[20] Woman's Missionary Union, *Annual*, 1890, 21.

"Mothers' Meetings" for black women in Baltimore.[21] The WMU's Committee on Plan of Work for 1892 had urged, "That without fail we gather our colored women and teach them by precept and example the way of the Lord,"[22] but the minutes from their meeting in 1893 suggest that only the WBHMS women in Baltimore, under Armstrong's leadership, took action. In 1892, Armstrong had also partnered with black pastors in Baltimore to establish an orphanage for black children.[23] Armstrong's report as the WMU corresponding secretary admonished the women of other regions that they needed to take up such projects, as well. Her rationale gives some indication of her motivation:

> The need for this work is imperative and immediate. If Protestants do not seek to help them, Romanists will. They are laying broad their foundations through sisterhoods, colored priests, industrial schools, and unlimited money, ultimately to secure control of the colored vote. Ought we to be less anxious to secure salvation for their immortal souls? Mothers' Meetings and Sewing Schools have proved successful agencies to interest, aid and instruct the colored women and children. Patriotism and religion cry aloud for this effort.[24]

The WMU shared Armstrong's belief that the best way to aid African Americans was through conversion to Protestant Christianity (preferably Baptist Christianity). The women of the WMU at large, however, were not eager to embrace the model Baltimore had given them, despite a widespread prejudice against Roman Catholics and a perceived threat that Catholics would take over America through black converts. It was difficult for the women of the Deep South to view African Americans as people whose struggles should trouble them. Armstrong would continue to plead for them to change their minds in numerous ways. She published a series of tracts

---

[21] Woman's Missionary Union, *Annual*, 1893, 31.

[22] Woman's Missionary Union, *Annual*, 1892, 26.

[23] Sorrill, *Annie Armstrong*, 123.

[24] Annie Walker Armstrong, Report of the Corresponding Secretary, Woman's Missionary Union, *Annual*, 1893, 14. Armstrong's Baltimore had long been home to a substantial community of black Catholics, and Armstrong's "sisterhoods" may have been a reference to Baltimore's Oblate Sisters of Providence, an order of African American nuns. See Diane Batts Morrow, *Persons of Color and Religious at the Same Time: The Oblate Sisters of Providence, 1828–1860* (Chapel Hill: University of North Carolina Press, 2002).

aimed at arousing interest in the plight of African Americans in the South, occasionally inviting prominent African American leaders to be guest authors, including Virginia Broughton and Booker T. Washington. One pastor submitted a manuscript stating that black people could not be helped, which she refused to print.[25] Armstrong appealed to the missionary zeal that motivated the WMU women by reporting on evangelistic efforts in Africa. She believed that African Americans would be the best missionaries to the continent of their origins. Hopes for a "Christian Africa" could only be realized through "Christian America."[26] Armstrong also believed that it was the responsibility of Southern Baptist women to reach African American women for conversion. At the 1894 meeting of the WMU in Dallas, she brought up Baltimore's Bible classes, missionary societies, "Mothers' Meetings," and industrial schools as examples of useful endeavors proven to be effective in African American communities: "Living with them' and really sympathizing with them as others not similarly situated cannot do, let us take up this work just to our hands and do it 'In His Name,'"[27] she urged. Armstrong had become something of an expert on African Americans in the WMU's estimation, and the women asked for extra time so that they could hear more from her about the "Mothers' Meetings for Colored Women in Baltimore."[28]

Despite the women's professed interest, in 1895, Maryland was still the only state reporting work with African Americans. Armstrong did not despair; the formation of the NBC that year meant easier contact with leadership of black Baptists, and "There are signs of a growing readiness to help in holding meetings with them," she said. "We are coming closer together where the Lord can bless us." Industrial schools and "Mothers' Meetings" had grown in Baltimore. The conference at Fortress Monroe (a meeting of Northern and Southern white Baptists) had led to an agreement that not only meant the two groups would both work with black Baptists but

---

[25] Allen, *A Century to Celebrate*, 242.

[26] See Annie Armstrong, Report of Corresponding Secretary, Woman's Missionary Union, *Annual*, 1894, 10.

[27] Annie Armstrong, Report of Corresponding Secretary, Woman's Missionary Union, *Annual*, 1894, 14.

[28] Woman's Missionary Union, *Annual*, 1894, 30–31.

that they would not interfere with each other.[29] Armstrong quoted an African American woman as having said in response, "Nothing so good as this has come to us since the emancipation." Armstrong felt that Southern Baptists would be better workers than their counterparts in the North, urging the women to take action on their own because "we are the people appointed of God to do this ..., as our life long acquaintance with the race and daily contact furnish us with the most favorable opportunities. There may be more romance in it to those at a distance; there are larger possibilities in it to us."[30]

Armstrong became more firmly convinced that white women of the South were better equipped to help African Americans than their Northern counterparts after addressing the Woman's Congress on Baptist Day at the Exposition in Atlanta that year. Her address was titled "Woman's Work in the Evangelization of the Homes of the Colored People." Mary G. Burdette, the Woman's Home Mission Society in the North's corresponding secretary, spoke also. Armstrong reported that Burdette "acknowledged" the way she had gone about these ministries in Baltimore "as the ideal."[31] Later, Armstrong would express frustration that Burdette continued to accept donations from black Baptist women's missionary societies for the northern organization. She met with Burdette to discuss, among other "Southern" methods she felt would be of greater good than what Burdette was doing, the possibility of encouraging black women to keep their money for their own NBC, which was the way the WMU handled the matter. Reflecting on the matter later, Armstrong stated that "she acknowledged that the plans which I suggested were good, but I do not think she considers them feasible."[32]

---

[29] This essentially established territorial boundaries for Northern and Southern Baptists because there had been significant conflict over which group had a right to do what and where. See H. Leon McBeth, *The Baptist Heritage: Four Centuries of Baptist Witness* (Nashville: Broadman Press, 1987) 430–2.

[30] Annie Walker Armstrong, Report of Corresponding Secretary, Woman's Missionary Union, *Annual*, 1895, 12.

[31] Annie Walker Armstrong, Report of Corresponding Secretary, Woman's Missionary Union, *Annual*, 1896, 15.

[32] Annie Walker Armstrong, Baltimore, Maryland, to J. M. Frost, Nashville, Tennessee, 2 July 1897, in *Rescue the Perishing: Selected Correspondence of Annie W. Armstrong*, ed. Keith Harper (Macon, GA: Mercer University Press, 2004) 345.

For Armstrong, "helping" African Americans was a paternalistic form of evangelism. One can view her dislike of Burdette's willingness to accept donations from black Baptists as both reflective of her paternal attitudes (whites should be the patrons of blacks, not vice versa) and her desire for black Baptists to have an independent organization. "Help" meant both material missions with an aim toward conversion, as evidenced in the "Mother's Meetings" and sewing and industrial educational programs, and aiding the black Baptists of the South in forming organizations that would work toward similar goals. Many black Baptists would have shared Armstrong's desire to increase their ranks through evangelism, and many felt they should have an organization independent of white Baptists. Despite these collaborative efforts with black Baptists in the South, Armstrong had some rather condescending attitudes toward them. Armstrong looked upon the American institution of slavery with some approbation, feeling that the fact that slavery had meant so many Africans had become Christians under Christian masters had been one of many "wonderful manifestations of God's power." In her estimation, "The Colored People are not yet fully developed as Christians, and in their development I believe we must aid."[33] Armstrong did not attempt to achieve racial justice through civil rights, nor did she push to integrate her racially segregated denomination. Her writings and speeches suggest that she felt her goals would be best achieved without recourse to the government. African American Baptists in the Jim Crow South generally seem to have thought otherwise, as Burroughs's relationship with Armstrong illustrates.

Burroughs's mother had taken her to Washington, DC, when Burroughs was five years old in order to secure for her a better educational future. Washington's school system was segregated, but the black schools were good and received funding comparable to white schools in the area. She had graduated from Washington's M Street High School with honors in 1896 and wanted to become a science teacher. Failure to find work in the area was a severe discouragement for her, but she settled on a job in Philadelphia as associate editor at the *Christian Banner*, a Baptist newspaper. She then took a civil service examination and, believing that her high score

---

[33] Annie Walker Armstrong, Baltimore, Maryland, to J. M. Frost, Nashville, Tennessee, 11 October 1901, James Marion Frost Papers, Southern Baptist Historical Library and Archive, Nashville, Tennessee.

would help her get a new job as a clerk, she returned to Washington but found no one willing to hire "colored clerks." After doing janitorial work in an office building, she found work as the assistant to Lewis G. Jordan, the corresponding secretary of the NBC's Home Mission Board.[34] African American Baptist women had attempted to organize nationally prior to the formation of the NBC in 1895, but they met with little success. Like the SBC of just a few years earlier, male leaders of the newly formed NBC also resisted efforts for women's organization at the national level.[35] It was time to take a new approach. In December 1896, Jordan visited Armstrong, saying he hoped the NBC could develop an organization for women. He wanted to bring a "colored woman from Washington" to Baltimore to discuss the possibility with Armstrong and seek her advice, as Armstrong had already provided an example of successfully navigating such a difficult path. Jordan asked Burroughs to write to Armstrong about the prospect.[36] Armstrong was eager to help, as she wrote to R. J. Willingham, the corresponding secretary of the SBC's Foreign Mission Board, about Jordan's plan and Burroughs's letter. "[A]n immense amount of good can be performed—not only in developing the colored women here at home, but in doing work in Africa—if we can get the colored women organized as missionary workers."[37]

In January 1897, Armstrong met with Jordan and Burroughs. She invited G. R. Waller, a pastor of one of Baltimore's black Baptist churches, and two women from the Standing Committee on Work among the Colored People in the WBHMS, referred to in her letter to J. M. Frost reporting on this meeting as Mrs. W. J. Brown and Mrs. W. J. E. Cox, to join the discussion. During the four-hour meeting, the group developed a plan for starting a missions organization for women within the NBC. First, they decided, they would need to develop interest among the women. Armstrong would begin preparing a women's column for Jordan's *Afro-American Herald*, and the publication would also print a sample constitution and bylaws for Women's Mission Societies (taken from the WMU's version

---

[34] Easter, *Nannie Helen Burroughs*, 25–27.

[35] Higginbotham, *Righteous Discontent*, 155.

[36] Sorrill, *Annie Armstrong*, 139.

[37] Annie Walker Armstrong, Baltimore, Maryland, to R. J. Willingham, Nashville, Tennessee, 6 January 1897, in *Rescue the Perishing*, 340. See also Allen, *A Century to Celebrate*, 243; and Sorrill, *Annie Armstrong*, 139.

of such documents). Development of local societies would make it easier to start a national organization. The team placed Martha Clark, an African American woman with whom Armstrong had worked in Baltimore during the previous 14 years, in charge of answering correspondence from women wanting to start these local groups. Burroughs would try to arouse interest among the NBC women of Washington. As would be their method throughout their relationship, the white women would try to keep a low profile. "I am sure, for many reasons, it is better for us to be working out of sight and trying to fit the colored people to do their own work," Armstrong explained. "When the time comes, I shall of course try and get the ladies in the different States to show the colored women in the various communities how to organize Women's Mission Societies."[38]

At the WMU meeting in 1897, Armstrong reported that Jordan had visited her and that he was attempting to gain the interest of the NBC women in organizing mission societies. She also continued to point to the success of the work of the Baltimore women in the industrial schools and "Mothers' Meetings," encouraging the other women to begin similar projects.[39] Word of the WMU had gotten out among the African American Baptist women, and several attended the annual meeting in Wilmington, North Carolina. The WMU passed a resolution thanking "the colored sisters who attended our sessions—trusting that these evidences of good feeling ... may stimulate us to greater efforts on their behalf."[40] While the only efforts seemed to be taking place in Baltimore, there was growth in North Carolina, and "We believe quietly, but effectively, good is being done."[41] It is probable that Armstrong or Burroughs encouraged the African American women in Wilmington to attend so they could learn more about women's mission societies.

Armstrong continued to receive visits from leaders of the NBC. Jordan was an especially frequent visitor.[42] Burroughs may have accompanied him,

---

[38] Annie Walker Armstrong, Baltimore, Maryland, to J. M. Frost, Nashville, Tennessee, 26 January 1897, in *Rescue the Perishing*, 341–2.

[39] Annie Walker Armstrong, Report of the Corresponding Secretary, Woman's Missionary Union, *Annual*, 1897, 16.

[40] Woman's Missionary Union, *Annual*, 1897, 37.

[41] Ibid., 52.

[42] Annie Walker Armstrong, Baltimore, Maryland, to J. M. Frost, Nashville, Tennessee, 2 July 1897, in *Rescue the Perishing*, 345; idem, Report of the

or she may have come alone, but Burroughs later wrote in a eulogy for Armstrong that "Often, in the early years of my service, I came to Baltimore to confer with 'my inspiration'. My reaction after each conference was 'she understands! 'She cares!'"[43] During the time Burroughs spent with Armstrong, Burroughs decided that she wanted to try to become the corresponding secretary of the organization they were planning to form in the NBC. "I was not dedicated to any great cause," Burroughs wrote, but "to me, Miss Armstrong was a symbol—a marvel of what a woman could do. She fired my soul. I decided to try to be a Corresponding Secretary for Negro Baptist women, similar to the fine woman to whom I had listened. I have not succeeded, but I have tried."[44] Of course, Burroughs would likely not criticize Armstrong when eulogizing her, but the two do seem to have had a good working relationship, and Burroughs seems to have followed most (although not all) of Armstrong's advice.

The 1898 meeting of the WMU indicated that Armstrong had managed to garner more interest among its members in aiding the African American population. Armstrong read a series of recommendations from the WMU Executive Committee to the group, all of which the women adopted. Among these was that the women should display "an attitude of Christian helpfulness" with regard to "organized Christian work" among "the colored people around our homes."[45] They also adopted the recommendation of Tichenor, the corresponding secretary of the SBC's Home Mission Board with whom Armstrong had been in frequent correspondence, regarding aiding African American women: "The colored women in and about our homes should not look to us in vain for spiritual help."[46] At last, a state other

Corresponding Secretary, Woman's Missionary Union, *Annual*, 1898, 22 and 1899, 13.

[43] Nannie Helen Burroughs, Washington, DC, to W. Clyde Atkins, Baltimore, Maryland, 28 January 1939, Baptist Center History Library, Baptist Convention of Maryland-Delaware, Baltimore, Maryland. My thanks to Shannon Baker, journalist for the Baptist Convention of Maryland-Delaware's *BaptistLIFE*, for sending me this document.

[44] Burroughs to Atkins, 28 January 1939. Shannon Baker quotes a portion of this in her article, "Following in the Footsteps of Annie Armstrong in Baltimore," (Baltimore) *BaptistLIFE*, March 2006, 2.

[45] Woman's Missionary Union, *Annual*, 1898, 29.

[46] Ibid., 34.

than Maryland reported work with African American women. Lucinda Williams reported for Texas that "New lines of work are opening, notably among the colored people."[47] Armstrong's Maryland WBHMS reported that their efforts with the industrial schools and "Mothers' Meetings" had been "the most successful" they had ever been.[48]

Armstrong was concerned that their work must not overshadow the work of Burroughs and other African American women. Whatever organizing work they accomplished, Armstrong felt, must be their own. If the WMU helped, it must be just that—help, not supervision: "Our object is to help the colored people, and certainly the best help is to train them to do their own work."[49] "I am looking and hoping for a great work to be done by the colored people themselves," she wrote. "I believe they are our best agents."[50] She began emphasizing this in her annual reports to the WMU. She then added, "Continued effort has been made towards helping the colored people help themselves," saying that Bible classes, industrial schools, and teaching in homes were the best ways the WMU could help.[51] The WMU Executive Committee answered apparent expressions of confusion about what to do with the assertion that "Sanctified, individual common sense will suggest various ways of helping the colored people."[52] In May 1900, Tichenor's recommendations for the WMU suggested that these volunteer efforts needed a financial supplement. The volunteering (however sparse it may have been) had been popular in the SBC at large because it avoided arousing controversies related to giving the convention's money to African Americans, yet "On the plea of poverty, we can no longer excuse ourselves."[53] Armstrong and her SBC allies in the Home Mission Board, with her connections in the NBC and the WC, which would form a few months after the WMU's meeting in 1900, would find a new way to help

---

[47] Woman's Missionary Union, *Annual*, 1898, 45–46.

[48] Ibid., 44.

[49] Annie Walker Armstrong, Baltimore, Maryland, to J. M Frost, Nashville, Tennessee, 2 July 1897, in *Rescue the Perishing*, 344.

[50] Annie Walker Armstrong, Baltimore, Maryland, to R. J. Willingham, Nashville, Tennessee, 2 June 1902, in *Rescue the Perishing*, 350.

[51] Annie Walker Armstrong, Report of the Corresponding Secretary, Woman's Missionary Union, *Annual*, 1899, 13.

[52] Woman's Missionary Union, *Annual*, 1899, 38.

[53] Woman's Missionary Union, *Annual*, 1900, 47.

African American women help themselves. In 1901, the WMU reported that the SBC had begun giving money to the NBC "to help them in reaching their people."[54]

In September 1900, perhaps bolstered by the determination she had developed in observing Armstrong, Burroughs did something Armstrong and the women of the WMU would never have done: she addressed her convention to advocate the establishment of a women's organization. Her "inspiration" was in Indian Territory and could not attend, although those working on organizing the women had invited her.[55] Burroughs was scheduled to follow an address on "Heathen Women: Their Condition" by another woman, named in the NBC's *Annual* as Mrs. L. A. Coles of Richmond. Burroughs was originally supposed to give an address titled, "How Their Sisters in the Land of Light May Help Them,"[56] but when she rose to speak she had a more provocative title, "How the Sisters are Hindered from Helping."[57] There were words of reassurance in her speech: "We come not to usurp thrones nor to sow discord."[58] These were not women seeking to take over the leadership of the NBC; they wanted to help the men who were already leading it. When Armstrong met with the group's new president, Sarah Layten, she encouraged her to do things as the WMU had performed, not attempting to work independently of the NBC but to allow the NBC's boards to direct them. Armstrong had firsthand experience with the sort of conflict women's organizations could cause among Baptists. Later, Armstrong would write, "This policy is entirely different from that adopted by Northern women," about her discussion with Layten, "but in the fourteen years in which it has been tried by Southern Baptists, it has proved successful, and I believe the colored women will find that their work will increase, and friction will be prevented, if they will adopt this method."[59] A group of women met at the local American Methodist Episcopal church to

---

[54] Woman's Missionary Union, *Annual*, 1901, 55. In SBC parlance, "reaching" people meant evangelizing them. They were giving money to the NBC in hopes of making more Baptists.

[55] Sorrill, *Annie Armstrong*, 180.

[56] National Baptist Convention, *Annual*, 1900, 14.

[57] Ibid., 68.

[58] Nannie Helen Burroughs, National Baptist Convention, *Annual*, 1900, 196.

[59] Annie Walker Armstrong, Baltimore, Maryland, to R. J. Willingham, Nashville, Tennessee, 2 June 1902, in *Rescue the Perishing*, 350.

discuss the possible national organization of NBC women. Like the WMU before them, most likely due to the controversial nature of their meeting, they chose not to convene in a Baptist church. Upon Jordan's motion that the WC form, the NBC's vote indicated that they agreed that the women should not be hindered, and thus, the WC was born, with Burroughs as its corresponding secretary.[60]

Burroughs wrote to Armstrong prior to the WC's 1901 meeting, saying that she hoped Armstrong would come and "speak to us on 'Why and How,'" saying she had concerns about how to proceed with the organization of the black Baptist women "and yet not antagonize the 'powers that be.' ... [O]ur women must know how to meet these things in a sisterly way, not get discouraged and yet not fight." She also had questions for Armstrong about how to exercise her own duties as corresponding secretary, wishing to follow Armstrong's model in the more minor logistical matters of compiling reports.[61]

Armstrong was, true to her typical methods for handling things, not inclined to act without first seeking the advice of a few male Southern Baptist leaders. She was particularly worried about "the practice at the North and also among the Colored People to hold mixed meetings," she wrote to M. M. Welch. She was not sure she could convince Burroughs and the WC to disallow men from attending while she spoke.[62] Welch sent a hurried telegram: Armstrong should speak, but only to women. He followed up with a letter advising, in the strictest terms, "your going, or at least your speaking should be conditioned upon being allowed to address an audience of women only."[63] Bolstered by his advice, Armstrong wrote back to Burroughs, explaining, as she later told J. M. Frost, that she could only come if "the audience was to consist only of feminines." Burroughs sent a telegram

[60] Higginbotham, *Righteous Discontent*, 155–56. See also National Baptist Convention, *Annual*, 195.

[61] Annie Armstrong's transcription of a letter from Nannie Helen Burroughs, Louisville, Kentucky, to Annie Walker Armstrong, Baltimore, Maryland, 11 July 1901, James Marion Frost Papers.

[62] Annie Walker Armstrong, Baltimore, Maryland, to M. M. Welch, Atlanta, Georgia, 12 July 1901, James Marion Frost Papers. See also idem, to J. M. Frost, Nashville, Tennessee, 12 July 1901, James Marion Frost Papers.

[63] M. M. Welch, Atlanta, Georgia, to Annie Walker Armstrong, Baltimore, Maryland, 12 July 1901, James Marion Frost Papers.

add euphemism

agreeing that the audience would be "Women only." Armstrong was pleased that Burroughs had asked for her to come. She wrote to Frost, happy that "even in the northern territory the brunettes are willing to adopt Southern ideas ... The Northern people have made such tremendous efforts to control the colored people ... and yet, now that the colored people have organized, they turn of their own accord to the Southern white people and ask for our assistance and advice..." She hoped this would result in "a much better state of feeling among the white and colored people than has existed since the war."[64]

The WC's minutes from 1901 show a clear connection to the WMU. The constitution and bylaws they adopted followed those of the WMU word for word with only a few sentences being added or removed (most of the changes had to do with criteria for membership and voting; the WC also added explicit reference to education as one of their goals).[65] Armstrong spoke at the meeting, with women alone in her audience. WMU women never spoke to mixed audiences to avoid accusations that they were trying to be preachers. The NBC Baptists, she wrote to Frost later, found her insistence on a female-only audience "very funny," although she did believe her talk had been well received.[66] The minutes note, "Her address was full of wise suggestions and helpful directions, referring to the successful Baptist white women of the South had achieved in the past thirteen years, indicating how we might advance and do likewise." Armstrong "expressed the desire to assist us in carrying forward our work as she might be able. We mark Miss Armstrong's visit as a new and important step in our onward march in the development of Christian womanhood."[67] In her eulogy, Burroughs later

---

[64] Annie Walker Armstrong, Baltimore, Maryland, to J. M. Frost, Nashville, Tennessee, 17 July 1901, James Marion Frost Papers. It is not clear where Armstrong came up with the term "brunettes" for black women, but she used it relatively frequently.

[65] See Constitution and By-Laws of the Woman's Missionary Union, *Annual*, 1900 and Constitution and By-Laws of the Woman's Convention, in National Baptist Convention, "Journal of the Woman's Convention," *Annual*, 1901. See also Allen, *A Century to Celebrate*, 243.

[66] Annie Walker Armstrong, Cincinnati, Ohio, to J. M. Frost, Nashville, Tennessee, 13 September 1901, James Marion Frost Papers.

[67] National Baptist Convention, "Journal of the Woman's Convention," *Annual*, 1901, 29. The statement that they marked her visit as something "new" may

wrote of Armstrong's visit, "Her presence was a benediction. She stayed with us, and took part. In the afternoon, she delivered one of the most inspiring addresses of the entire Convention."[68]

Yet despite Burroughs's remembrance of Armstrong as a staunch supporter of the women of the NBC, it also seems there were limits to what Armstrong was willing to do for them. Burroughs made an "appeal to the Christian white women of the Southland" to help end the unfair treatment that African Americans received due to a recent law segregating travel on streetcars, which Armstrong must have heard.[69] However, when she reported on her activities in 1901 at the 1902 meeting of the WMU, she did not mention the "separate coach law." As stated earlier, Armstrong's interests were mainly religious, not political, and she does not seem to have connected the two in the way Burroughs did. Armstrong understood the category of "help" as evangelistic, not social justice, and her report on her trip indicates that the work Burroughs and others had done pleased her and that she felt the WMU should help the WC in its work (although apparently not in its political work to combat Jim Crow). There were many opportunities if the WMU would step up, she said. Armstrong had become known among African American Baptists, and "unexpectedly ... addressed meetings of Colored people" upon receiving several invitations in Louisiana and Florida in her usual travels throughout the South. "[T]he Colored people are most appreciative of the interest we are taking in them and are looking to us for help." This time, the help Armstrong suggested was financial support of evangelistic missions, following the precedent of the Home Mission Board in 1901. The NBC was beginning to appoint female missionaries and asked the SBC for $250. Armstrong found "a lady in Maryland" who was willing to make the donation.[70] Layten's report to the

---

be what led Higginbotham to mistakenly characterize Armstrong's visit as part of a "new spirit of cooperation that emanated from southern white church women." See Higginbotham, *Righteous Discontent*, 197.

[68] Nannie Helen Burroughs, Washington, DC, to W. Clyde Atkins, Baltimore, Maryland, 28 January 1939.

[69] See Nannie Helen Burroughs, Report of the Corresponding Secretary, in National Baptist Convention, "Journal of the Woman's Convention," *Annual*, 1901, 23–24.

[70] Annie Walker Armstrong, Report of the Corresponding Secretary, Woman's Missionary Union, *Annual*, 1902, 17.

WC in 1902 states that she, Burroughs, and R. H. Boyd of the NBC's Home Mission Board had called upon Armstrong to ask for her help in raising the funds for the missionary.[71]

Burroughs's report that same year seemed to echo Armstrong's sentiments about "Helping Those who Help Themselves," saying, "The Southern white women, among whom most of us live and labor, have convinced us, once for all, that they have hearts that can be touched with our needs, if we only demonstrate a desire to help [our]selves."[72] In the following years, mention of volunteer work among African Americans would fade from Armstrong's reports, replaced by reports of the financial contributions of the WMU toward the work of the WC.[73] Armstrong continued to act as a liaison between the WMU and the WC.[74] Burroughs had become the crusader for work with industrial schools, Bible studies, and "Mothers' Meetings," and Armstrong and the WMU gradually gave up those projects as Burroughs and the WC took them on,[75] although she did meet with the WC to give her advice on how to carry out educational work among African American women.[76] Armstrong was very optimistic about the state of affairs under the leadership of the WC. In 1904, she predicted that if the women of the WMU would continue its efforts with the WC, it would be "a mighty

---

[71] Sarah Layten, Report of the President, in National Baptist Convention, "Journal of the Woman's Convention," *Annual*, 1902, 16–18.

[72] Nannie Helen Burroughs, Report of the Corresponding Secretary, in National Baptist Convention, "Journal of the Woman's Convention," *Annual*, 1902, 29.

[73] See Annie Walker Armstrong, Report of the Corresponding Secretary, Woman's Missionary Union, *Annual*, 1903, 12–13; 1904, 20; and 1905, 20. See also Nannie Helen Burroughs, Report of the Corresponding Secretary, in National Baptist Convention, "Journal of the Woman's Convention," *Annual*, 1903, 306.

[74] See Annie Walker Armstrong, Report of the Corresponding Secretary, Woman's Missionary Union, *Annual*, 1904, 22; and Sarah Layten, Report of the President, in National Baptist Convention, "Journal of the Woman's Convention," *Annual*, 1903, 295–96.

[75] Burroughs began pushing for the WC to educate black women in 1901. A large section of her reports to the WC included information about this work.

[76] Sarah Layten, Report of the President, in National Baptist Convention, "Journal of the Woman's Convention," *Annual*, 1905, 244.

power in obliterating feelings of friction ... Faithfulness on our part will, we believe, bring about a complete revolution."[77]

Armstrong introduced Layten to the WMU that year.[78] Layten was enthusiastic about the progress the groups were making, reporting to the WC that "the greatest movement in women's work THIS YEAR ... [is] the meeting of the Woman's Missionary Union ... held in Nashville ... and the Woman's Convention ... held in Austin."[79] Layten felt that "The white women of the South are the power behind the throne and dictate conditions; they are more powerful than the law makers in our Congressional Halls. Therefore, let us take fresh courage."[80] Layten believed Armstrong was the key to any progress made, remarking when Armstrong came to visit the WC meeting in 1905 on "the sweet womanly modesty of that woman, wielding an unlimited power in the Southland.[81]

Layten's words were more perceptive than she could have known at the time, for Armstrong's report of her 1905 activities at the WMU's annual meeting in 1906 would be her last and that would severely hinder the cooperation between the two groups. Due to a disagreement over the decision to begin allowing women to attend the SBC's Southern Baptist Theological Seminary in Louisville, Kentucky, Armstrong offered an ultimatum: either the women would have their own school elsewhere, or she would leave all SBC mission activities for the rest of her life. Armstrong felt that women should have theological training but that attending seminary classes was not the way to do it. She thought that being in close proximity to the men would hinder the education of both the men and the women and that seminaries should train preachers, not female religious workers. The WMU and the SBC called her bluff, and Armstrong kept her word.[82] Armstrong said that

---

[77] Annie Walker Armstrong, Report of the Corresponding Secretary, Woman's Missionary Union, *Annual*, 1904, 22.

[78] Woman's Missionary Union, *Annual*, 1904, 42.

[79] Sarah Layten, Report of the President, in National Baptist Convention, "Journal of the Woman's Convention," *Annual*, 1904, 326.

[80] Ibid., 328.

[81] Sarah Layten, Report of the President, in National Baptist Convention, "Journal of the Woman's Convention," *Annual*, 1905, 241.

[82] See Armstrong's correspondence on this subject in *Rescue the Perishing*, 261–307.

there was a need for continued cooperation with the WC,[83] but without her, the WMU's partnership with the WC would stagnate. Her successors did not have the relationships and history with the women of the WC that Armstrong had, and after Armstrong was no longer there to plead for the cause of African Americans, the WC would find the white Baptist women of the North in more readiness to help them than the WMU.[84] Meanwhile, Armstrong cut ties with her local mission society as well, and although she continued to attend Eutaw Place Baptist Church in Baltimore, she did not associate with other women in the church who were prominent in the WMU. Instead, Armstrong turned her attention to work the SBC was not doing, evangelistic efforts among the Jews of Baltimore and charity work with immigrants in the city. She taught Sunday school for children in her church, and she also began conducting "Mothers' Meetings" of her own again.[85]

Armstrong died on 20 December 1938, and Burroughs wrote a eulogy for her, although she heard of the memorial service that Eutaw Place held the following January too late to attend it. Burroughs believed that "no purer soul ever entered the heavenly portals."[86] She remembered her as a "trail blazer ... No woman in America has ever done more to encourage Negro Baptist women in their work than our recently departed friend, Annie W. Armstrong." To Burroughs, Armstrong had been a "Devoted friend, wise counsellor [sic], the *real pioneer* in Christian, interracial understanding and cooperation between white and Negro Baptist women of the South."[87]

---

[83] Annie Walker Armstrong, Report of the Corresponding Secretary, Woman's Missionary Union, *Annual*, 1906, 20.

[84] Allen, *A Century to Celebrate*, 245. See also Higginbotham's account of Burroughs's relationships with white Baptist women of the North in *Righteous Discontent*.

[85] Sorrill, *Annie Armstrong*, 275–80.

[86] Nannie Helen Burroughs, Miami Beach, Florida, to [W. Clyde] Atkins, [Baltimore, Maryland], 9 February 1939, Baptist Center History Library, Baptist Convention of Maryland-Delaware, Baltimore, Maryland. My thanks to Shannon Baker for sending me this document.

[87] Nannie Helen Burroughs, Washington, DC, to W. Clyde Atkins, Baltimore, Maryland, 28 January 1939, Baptist Center History Library, Baptist Convention of Maryland-Delaware, Baltimore, Maryland.

Many years following Armstrong's departure from the WMU, some of its leaders would begin the work of "interracial understanding and cooperation" again in earnest. Researchers sifting through Burroughs's large collection of papers at the Library of Congress will note extensive correspondence between Burroughs and WMU leaders beginning in the 1930s, including Kathleen Mallory, Alma Hunt, and Una Roberts Lawrence. In this collection, a lingering conflict is prevalent over whether or not the right strategy to encourage cooperation would explicitly mention racial issues, or whether the focus would be entirely on religious matters. True to Armstrong's legacy, Lawrence insisted that the best thing to do would be to never mention "a *single race problem*," warning Burroughs, "I truly believe the race prejudice and supersensitiveness of our Negro leaders is the greatest stumbling block now in the elimination of all these wrongs."[88]

For Burroughs, although continually concerned with addressing these types of problems head on and not inclined to agree that African Americans were primarily at fault for them, the relationships she had with women in the WMU were nonetheless valuable in improving the lives of black Baptists. In response to Lawrence, she lamented, "I love your race a great deal more than they love mine..."[89] Despite their conflicts, it ultimately appears that they did agree that the best focus would be spiritual, rather than immediately pragmatic or political. While they published a magazine collaboratively, Lawrence reminded Burroughs of the power of their friendship as an example to others: "Why not pour your heart out in these editorials along that line [of love] and even as you and I have forgotten race and color of skin in a very real friendship, let us bring that same forgetfulness of race and color to every Baptist woman who reads its pages."[90] Burroughs assented to the plan. "Instead of talking about the rightness and wrongness of things racial, we can talk about the goodness and the beauty of things spiritual."[91]

---

[88] Una Roberts Lawrence, Kansas City, Missouri, to Nannie Helen Burroughs, Washington, DC, 19 June 1935, Nannie Helen Burroughs Papers, Manuscript Room, Library of Congress, Washington, DC.

[89] Nannie Helen Burroughs, Washington, DC, to Una Roberts Lawrence, Kansas City, Missouri, 29 June 1935, Nannie Helen Burroughs Papers, Manuscript Room, Library of Congress, Washington, DC.

[90] Lawrence to Burroughs, 19 June 1935, Nannie Helen Burroughs Papers.

[91] Burroughs to Lawrence, 29 June 1935, Nannie Helen Burroughs Papers.

Regardless of what they chose to focus on, it is clear that for some Baptist women in the South, denominational segregation did not mean a lack of cooperation or even of friendship across racial lines. The story of the relationship between white and black Baptist women in the South is a complicated one, and still not yet completely told, but if there is anything to learn from Armstrong and Burroughs, it is that further research will likely uncover other surprising turns in this narrative. As Burroughs herself wrote, "We are not performing miracles, but we are making headway and someday somebody, somewhere will understand some things which they do not understand now."[92]

---

[92] Nannie Helen Burroughs, Washington, DC, to Una Roberts Lawrence, Kansas City, Missouri, 5 April 1935,

Nannie Helen Burroughs Papers, Manuscript Room, Library of Congress, Washington, DC.

5

"The Holy Spirit Come to Us": Black Baptist Organizations and Cultural Practices from Reconstruction to the Rise of Gospel Music

Paul Harvey

For much of the twentieth century, scholars interested in African American religion were beholden to the term "the black church." The very popularity and singularity of the term "the black church" suggests a unified force formed out of the Christianization of black Americans during the Great Awakenings, the creation of black denominations and other religious structures, as well as the effective political movements that arose, in part, out of those institutions during the civil rights era. However, black church organizations have often not been able to realize their potential as central institutions powerfully speaking for a people. More often, they have been, in the words of the late black Baptist scholar James Melvin Washington, a "frustrated fellowship." The fact that there is such a thing called "the black church" in the first place, moreover, has been the subject of a recent historicizing of the topic, with scholars examining how the term actually came to be in the first place. It was, they have shown, largely a construct of twentieth-century religious sociologists and arose, in fact, at much the same time as northward migration and a major diversification of the religious institutions that black seekers could choose, from the Holiness-Pentecostal movements to quasi-Orientalist groups such as the Moorish Science Temple. [1]

The term "the black church," moreover, historically has papered over deep divisions within diverse, scattered religious institutions, from small countryside shacks meeting once a month to mammoth, urban mega-congregations servicing the needs of urban migrants in both southern and northern cities. For black Baptist churches, the paradox of independence and

---

[1] See, for example, Curtis Evans, *The Burden of Black Religion* (New York City: Oxford University Press, 2008).

internal division appeared immediately upon emancipation and deeply impacted black Baptist life for decades to come.

Black Baptist organizations came together in the late nineteenth century, resulting ultimately in the formation of the National Baptist Convention and the nation's largest black-owned publishing house, the National Baptist Publishing Board. But black Baptists remained divided over philosophies of black nationalism versus integration and over practices arising from the black folk tradition versus the "intelligent worship" advocated by denominational leaders. It would fall to twentieth-century church leaders to make black Baptists into a powerful force, in part by marrying these diverse strands within their tradition. Ultimately, it took the renewed impetus for religious organizing spurred by twentieth-century migration, together with the genius of cultural entrepreneurs and civil rights organizers who knew how to call on tradition to support change. Ministers, cultural innovators, and denominational organizers were all part of this story, all critical to the development of black Baptist cultural, political educational, and social life in the years from emancipation to World War II.

Even before the Civil War ended, black Baptist leaders in the newly emancipated regions of the South were articulating ideas that would later come to be associated with black economic independence and nationalism. The consultations during Reconstruction between government officials, including the Freedmen's Bureau, and the black clergy suggested that the "invisible institution" would make a strong case for very visible changes in the political, social, and economic structure of the South. In January 1865, African American ministers from Savannah and the Georgia low country advised Union war officers on how to assist the refugees who were set free by Sherman's march. Garrison Frazier, a black Baptist pastor in Georgia, met with Union war officers in Savannah following Sherman's capture of the city. He informed them that the best way for freedpeople to "take care of ourselves is to have land and turn it and till it by our own labor ... and we can soon maintain ourselves and have something to spare." Shortly after the meeting, General William Tecumseh Sherman set aside a strip of land from near Charleston and stretching down to Jacksonville, Florida, land that could at least be temporarily occupied by freedpeople who had become war refugees. Many of them hoped this would create a government policy to extend land and farming implements to former slaves.[2]

Throughout the South, black religious leaders followed this lead, actively shaping African American life under freedom. James Simms serves as one example among many. Born a slave in Savannah, he purchased his freedom in 1857 with money raised from working as a master-builder. During Reconstruction, he worked with the Freedmen's Bureau and the American Baptist Home Mission Society, served as a Union League organizer, and later won election to the Georgia House of Representatives. During this time, he became the only black district judge in the state, which left him vulnerable to Klan attacks that eventually chased him from the low country region into Atlanta. As Simms later explained, socially conscious black clergymen at that time "had to leave their flock and legitimate field of labor to enter the arena of politics to secure right and justice for their people ... notwithstanding the white citizens among whom they lived and served, and the late owners, [who] constantly spoke disparagingly of the ministers who served in these positions." Simms also testified before Congress on behalf of the freedpeople and edited the Savannah-based *Freedmen's Standard*. His ministerial colleague Thomas Allen, a politician in Jasper County, reminded his congregants that the Yankees had freed them and that "they ought to vote with them; to go with the party always. They voted just as I voted."[3] Historians of Reconstruction have detailed both the importance

---

[2] Clipping from *New-York Daily Tribune*, 13 February 1865, "Negroes of Savannah," Consolidated Correspondence File, ser. 225, Central Records, Quartermaster General, Record Group 92, National Archives, http://www. history.umd.edu/Freedmen/savmtg.htm (accessed 27 March 2014). This meeting is also recounted in Andrew Billingsley, *Mighty Like a River: The Black Church and Social Reform* (New York City: Oxford University Press, 1999) 30–34.

[3] William Montgomery, *Under Their Own Vine and Fig Tree: The African American Church in the South, 1865– 1900* (Baton Rouge: Louisiana State University Press, 1993) 157, 179; James M. Simms, *The First Colored Baptist Church in North America Constituted at Savannah, Georgia, January 20, A.D. 1788*, with biographical sketches of the pastors (Philadelphia: J. B. Lippincott, 1888) 151–52,

http://docsouth.unc.edu/church/simms/simms.html (accessed 23 September 2013); For an example from Alabama, see Howard Rabinowitz, "Holland Thompson and Black Political Participation in Montgomery, Alabama," in *Black Leaders of the Reconstruction Era*, ed. Howard Rabinowitz (Urbana: University of Illinois Press, 1982) 249–79.

and the limitations of black churches as avenues of political organizing. Just as significantly, churches were as moral and spiritual guides during dangerous and difficult times for the freedpeople. As a British observer in the late nineteenth century wrote, "visit them in their churches, and observe them in praying, and singing, and preaching, and the reason why they themselves do not ask or desire to be admitted to the communion of the white churches will be readily understood." Church gatherings reunited families scattered under slavery, provided avenues for courtship and sociability, and sustained a social life important to impoverished freedpeople scattered through the countryside and congregated in towns and cities. The freedpeople "made their churches their rallying places, and poured out their souls in praise and thanksgiving," a later black Baptist historian wrote. The pastors of large congregations spent much pulpit time "advertising and reading letters from all parts of the South making inquiries for members of scattered families ... who were sold like cattle in the market," a visitor to Richmond observed.[4]

As much as political power, it was the affective feeling of sociability—of the need to be together—that sustained black congregations and ministers through harsh times. In forming one of the first state conventions in 1868, black Baptists in Virginia evoked the trials they faced with so many freedpeople scattered, searching for work, or spiritually demoralized by the physical struggle for existence in this promising but economically difficult period: "The great struggle between contending political parties in this country has scattered, and virtually exiled, many of the children of God, and caused them to be as sheep without a shepherd and a flock, and are hungering and thirsting after righteousness, as presented in the gospel and its melodious sound, and panting, not only for spiritual food, but also for spiritual protection." Black people congregated in churches "to worship, to hear the choir sing, to listen to the preacher, and to hear and see the people

---

[4] Elizabeth Banks, "The American Negro and His Place," *Nineteenth Century* 46 (September 1899): 463; N. H.

Pius, *An Outline of Baptist History: A Splendid Reference Work for Busy Workers* (Nashville: National Baptist

Publishing Board 1910) 62; *Christian Watchman and Reflector*, 23 November 1865 (B.); Charles Dudley Warner, *On Horseback: A Tour in Virginia, North Carolina, and Tennessee* (Boston: Houghton, Mifflin, and Co., 1899) 7– 10; H. S. Bennett, "The Religion of the Negro," *Independent* (New York), 15 July 1875, 12– 13.

shout," Benjamin Mays, future president of Morehouse College and a preeminent black Baptist educator of the twentieth century, remembered of his boyhood in South Carolina; and further, "The young people went to Mount Zion to socialize, or simply to stand around and talk. It was a place of worship and a social center as well. There was no other place to go." Mays was "motivated by people in the church who made me believe that I could become something worthwhile in the world." When his buggy accidentally threw dust on some whites passing by, Mays's father apologized profusely to the offended white. "Did this mean that my father mentally accepted or emotionally approved this cringing behavior?" Mays asked, "I doubt it. It was a technique of survival. But I have always wondered how long one can do a thing without eventually accepting it."[5]

Benjamin Mays went on to graduate training at the University of Chicago and later to become a professor and president of Morehouse College during the years of Martin Luther King's attendance. What Mays did was to take the black evangelical tradition of the later nineteenth century, add to it Social Gospel and liberal Protestant developments from seminary training, and combine those in ways that would be hugely influential for figures such as King. Thus, Mays is not so much forgotten as relegated to the role of schoolmaster, important largely because of his association with others, notably Martin Luther King.[6]

There is a good reason that figures like Mays tend to be left to the side—they were so busy in everyday organizational work, especially fundraising for struggling black institutions and ministering to ordinary black folk in churches, that they often did not leave behind a sizable body of published or easily accessible writings. Thus, they do not pop up on the short list of major thinkers/writers. Moreover, they were generally older by the time of the outstanding events of the civil rights years, somewhat on the sidelines as compared to the drama experienced by younger people in groups such as SCLC and SNCC. In other words, people like Mays did not become "known" as great (even if aloof, *á la* W. E. B. Du Bois) thinkers, nor

---

[5] Minutes, *Virginia Baptist State Convention*, 1868, 14; Benjamin Mays, *Born to Rebel* (New York: Scribner's, 1971) 13–17. All Baptist association and state and national convention minutes were consulted on microfilm at the Southern Baptist Historical Library and Archives, Nashville, Tennessee.

[6] Randal Jelks, *Benjamin Elijah Mays, Schoolmaster of the Movement* (Chapel Hill: University of North Carolina Press, 2012).

as full-time activists in the Ella Baker mode, nor as civil rights heroes—even though, in May's case, he had his foot in all three at the same time.

To northern missionaries of both races during Mays's childhood, however, the worship of the freedpeople smacked of barbarism. Denominational leaders imbued with a drive for black advancement and a politics of respectability feared that black religious customs would prevent newly freed African Americans from gaining full freedom and citizenship. Conflicts between black Baptist organizers (many of them free before the war) and the local ministers (most of whom were freedmen themselves) were widespread, as a national evangelical culture of denominationalism encountered African American folk traditions that had been preserved through slavery. A Savannah missionary recounted to Northern Baptists of preachers who professed support for "intelligent" and "progressive" practices yet preached in an unrestrained style to their congregants. The different masks they wore and different roles they placed according to the situation would, by his estimation, undermine the work of progressive-minded church leaders. He warned: "Believe me when I tell you that I have found much of this amongst our people."[7]

As part of this effort towards organizing, educating, and uplifting African American freedpeople, black Baptists during Reconstruction organized associations and state conventions throughout the South. Black Baptist associations, local groups of churches banded together to pursue projects of mutual interest, figured centrally in aiding educational institutions (academies, high schools, and colleges). Although churches were members of associations by voluntary consent, and the associations held no formal powers, they exerted considerable local influence.

For ministers, leadership in local groups offered an early stepping stone to career advancement. "There is as much scheming to get churches to join some associations," a Texas Baptist association acknowledged, "as there is practiced in political circles."[8]

---

[7] See William Troy, *American Baptist (AB)*, 4 May 1869. Similar accounts pervade the pages of papers such as the *American Baptist* and other white northern Baptist papers of this era.

[8] See Daniel Stowell, *Rebuilding Zion: The Religious Reconstruction of the South, 1863–1877* (New York City: Oxford University Press, 1998) passim; Quotation from Minutes, *Missionary Baptist State Convention of Texas*, 1885, 5.

Whites refused to meet in the same associations with churches that would send black delegates. Relationships with black Baptists in churches before the Civil War was one thing, for it operated under an entirely different regime. Under freedom, interaction with blacks at a local level, such as at the association or local body level, seemed an unacceptable, even impure, mixture of religion and "social intercourse." Black Virginians responded to this lack of cooperation with the following: "The Convention will not mourn at the non-interchange, nor slacken her progress but will move on trusting in that God who has no respect of persons, [who] has proven ... to be void of prejudice, of colorphobia, of caste, or lines of demarkation." They recognized that it would be their lot to "work in the Gospel vineyard by ourselves." Black Virginians lifted themselves up as "God's freemen," unwilling to be "mere hewers of wood and drawers of water, above back seats and figure heads." They were determined to pursue the same kinds of evangelization, education, and organization that had been the glory of Baptist denominationalism through the nineteenth century."[9]

In a number of states, freed Christians followed suit, and by the 1890s, they had formed an impressive black Baptist infrastructure at state and local levels. After the war, state conventions sprang up throughout the South, replicating at a state level what associations accomplished at a local level. North Carolina Baptists led the way, organizing a state convention as early as 1866. By the late 1880s, they numbered more than 132,000 and were spreading from their original areas of concentration in the eastern part of the state into the central Piedmont and western hills and mountains. In Virginia, churches in and around Richmond organized a state convention with over fourteen thousand members after the Civil War. Black Baptists in Montgomery, Alabama, as well as black Mississippians in Jackson, followed suit in 1869. In fact, Mississippi hosted two rival black Baptist conventions until a merger in 1890 brought together nearly eighty thousand black Baptists in the State. Texas Baptists convened their state convention in 1874, numbering one hundred thousand members by the late nineteenth

---

[9] Joseph B. Earnest, "The Religious Development of the Negro in Virginia" (PhD diss., University of Virginia, 1913) quoted in Montgomery, *Under Their Own Vine and Fig Tree*, 110–12; Virginia Baptist State Convention quoted in *CABMC Report*, 1871, 13.

century. In South Carolina, the prominent minister E. M. Brawley, brought Baptists together into a state convention listing nearly one hundred twenty-four thousand members in 1895.[10]

Black Baptists understood that a strong national organization would bolster a budding African American voice in religious affairs. Forming such an organization posed particular challenges given the Baptist polity of congregational control, and the nature of the vast bulk of the black Baptist constituency that worshipped in small, desperately poor, rural churches scattered through the countryside. The attempt to form one strong, unified national organization would consume much of the post-Civil War era until the formation of the National Baptist Convention in 1895. Even then, the work was far from done, as disputes between early leaders of the NBC eventuated in the first of what would be multiple splits and schisms in the organization through the twentieth century.

Soon after the war, representatives from a number of smaller black Baptist organizations formed the Consolidated American Baptist Missionary Convention (CABMC). During its life from 1866 to 1879, the CABMC was the first attempt to bring together black Baptists in the country and to use a denominational organization to represent African American ideas of freedom, education, and respectability. By the end of the 1860s, the CABMC listed some thirteen affiliated associations, mostly in and around Richmond and central/southside Virginia. The convention's spokesmen warned of the importance of the success of their work:

> Brethren, we are watched. We are not accepted as a body or denomination qualified to manage our own missionary and educational work, and many of those who most discredit our capacity...have set themselves up as our benefactors, and call upon our friends to aid us through them. But our very

---

[10] Montgomery, *Under Their Own Vine and Fig Tree*, 100–115; J. M. Carroll, *A History of Texas Baptists: Comprising a Detailed Account of Their Activities, Their Progress and Their Achievements* (Dallas: Baptist Standard Publishing Co., 1923) 228–39, 346, 349; Frenise Logan, *The Negro in North Carolina, 1867–1894* (Chapel Hill: University of North Carolina Press, 1964) 164–65; George Tindall, *South Carolina Negroes, 1750, 1930* (Columbia: University of South Carolina Press, 1952) 186–89; Edward Freeman, "Negro Baptist History," *Baptist History and Heritage* 4 (1969) 89–100.

organization is our proclamation to the world that we are able to do this work, and that we *ought* to do it.[11]

Delegates to the CABMC advocated that white philanthropic support black missionaries and black Baptist-controlled endeavors and organizations. This was a philosophy that would guide a great deal of black Baptist work through this era, when funds were scarce or non-existent but the desire to use organizations to advance black southern interests during a perilous period was strong. Rufus Perry, a CABMC organizer, pointed out the "vast gulf" separating the races and charged that aid from the white Northern Baptist missionary societies tended to hinder the cause of black independence and freedom. He sought to encourage the principle of "helping us to help ourselves," a principle too often ignored by well-meaning but overly controlling white Baptist paternalists. The white Northern Baptists in the Home Mission Society and other groups responded negatively to Perry's request, suggesting that making such an arrangement with the CABMC would simply lead to being swamped by requests from others. To CABMC members, this episode exemplified how whites deliberately steered the development of free black institutions away from self-reliance.[12]

The dispute over who should control the expenditure of missionary funds illustrated some of the difficulties that bedeviled relations between black Baptist men and their northern white benefactors through the remainder of the century. Early black Baptist organizers, including those of the CABMC, learned that white aid came with little involvement of African Americans involved in determining use of the money. Black Baptists were already pointing out the paternalism that always seemed to accompany the distribution of philanthropic money. Some observers suggested that former abolitionists should merge with black nationalists to resist the paternalistic policies exercised by mainline white religious societies. The Home Mission Society followed its characteristic policy of funding white missionaries rather

---

[11] For more information, see James M. Washington, *Frustrated Fellowship: the Black Baptist Quest for Social Power* (Macon, GA: Mercer University Press, 1986); Montgomery, *Under Their Own Vine and Fig Tree*, 227. Quotation from *CABMC Report*, 1869, 9.

[12] *AB*, 15 September 1868; *CABMC Report*, 1869, 16; *AB*, 29 September 1868. The full story can be traced in Washington, *Frustrated Fellowship*, 95–100.

than encouraging black independence in religious endeavors. Such efforts ignored the truth that "our elevation must be emphatically the result of self-help and individual effort." Black leaders resented the lack of meaningful black participation on the committees of the Home Mission Society. The Society's "mode of operation," one black Baptist declared, "makes the colored people entirely passive and completely unmans us."[13]

During the war, the American Baptist Home Mission Society initiated work among the freedpeople, directing its money especially at the creation of academies and colleges. At its height, sixty-eight missionaries worked the southern field. By 1879, however, as the society sought to stretch its resources to projects scattered across the country, only twenty-one missionaries of the American Baptist Home Mission Society were left working among freedpeople. The contacts Home Mission Society leaders developed with officials of the white Southern Baptist Convention heightened the frustration with white paternalism. Prominent Virginians Jeremiah B. Jeter and John Broadus maintained ties with Northern Baptist officials, although they occasionally complained that Northern Baptists "interfered" and misunderstood the freedmen's needs. While preferring to maintain control over missionary work, white Southern Baptist officials recognized that laborers from the North were bound to be present and would require suitable advice from southern whites. "By thus co-operating with good men in this work," Jeremiah Jeter suggested, "we neutralize the effect of ultraists who may come from the North to preach to the colored people."[14]

Partly in reaction, black Baptists continued to develop arguments towards separate and distinct national organizations. One white Northern Baptist recounted his experiences at a conference where "nearly every speaker announced himself as a 'race man' and avowed his determination to 'stand by

---

[13] *AB*, 11 August 1870 (H. H. White, 8 June 1869). Douglass's views on black independence and black abolitionism are discussed in William McFeely, *Frederick Douglass* (New York City: Oxford University Press, 1991) 104–82; and Waldo Martin, *The Mind of Frederick Douglass* (Chapel Hill: University of North Carolina Press, 1984).

[14] Montgomery, *Under Their Own Vine and Fig Tree*, 189; Ed Crowther, "Interracial Relations Among White and Black Baptists in Alabama, 1865–1890" (paper delivered at Southern Historical Association, November 1994); Jeter quoted in *American Baptist*, 30 July 1867; See also *Baptist Record* (Mississippi) 27 May, 1880.

his race.'" He found this alarming: "Even the more sensible colored men themselves confess to its unwisdom and danger." Black Baptist officials responded that requests for greater participation in religious and educational work among their own people were not equivalent to an unthinking separatism. After all, as one black minister reminded their white brethren, "it is the whites who want to keep separate."[15]

The language of separatism, helpful in energizing black Baptist organization, often proved less useful in formulating specific policies on issues particularly regarding educational institutions and publishing endeavors. In the state conventions, which served as intermediaries between local congregations and large national organizations, no clear victor emerged from internal philosophical battles in black Baptist organizations between what historians have termed "separationists" and "cooperationists." Likewise, and in a broader sense, no clear intellectual victor came out of the "debate" between integrationism and separatism. Ultimately, these racial strategies drew from an ideology of uplift and improvement that missed the depth, extent, and depravity of the rise of new forms of anti-black racism in the late nineteenth century. Uplift implied that success led to acceptance, when in many cases, quite the opposite was the result. Moreover, black Baptists struggled with the same questions that bedeviled the leaders of numerous black organizations in the late nineteenth century. If whites donated money to black institutions on the condition of white leadership, was this a sacrifice of the principle of black autonomy? What counted as tokenism versus real participation in governing educational institutions? If blacks tried to support separate educational and publishing endeavors, would they be so weak as to embarrass rather than credit the race?

In the 1880s, black Baptists fought through such intra-racial controversies, and the results that emerged would impact much of the new leadership of what was to become the National Baptist Convention. Black Baptists in south and east Texas in 1884 founded Guadalupe College in Seguin, supported primarily by the Guadalupe Baptist Association. In 1888 the black convention in Texas voted to divide its money between two preparatory schools and two colleges, Bishop College (established by the American Baptist Home Mission Society in 1881 in Marshall, Texas) and Guadalupe. White Northern Baptists, however, devised a plan to make

---

[15] *National Baptist*, 11 January 1883 and 1 February 1883.

Guadalupe a "feeder" institution, servicing mostly primary grade needs, and then concentrate higher educational plans at Bishop. The resulting debate split those who supported the plan as a necessary division of financial resources and those who argued that Guadalupe should serve as an example of the independent black Baptist educational projects. In fact, black Baptists working for white missionary agencies in the state had to fend off attacks that they were simply working for white interests. One missionary for the Northern Baptist home mission society encountered congregants who believed that "every dollar a white man turns loose on a colored man he sees where he can make two out of it."[16]

Meanwhile, black Baptist supporters of work that would remain separate and distinct from that of white Northern Baptists included future founder of the black Baptist Sunday School Board Richard H. Boyd, and Richard Abner, son of a Reconstruction legislator and a former faculty member at Bishop. These leaders formed the General Missionary Baptist Convention of Texas, justifying their move with language that even the cooperationists could appreciate: "The Holy Spirit came to us and forbid the Negro taking a second place." Sutton Griggs argued that white money and power, funneled through the home missionary agencies, hindered the development of "black manhood": "We believe in letting all our Baptist schools live.... [Whites] simply say let your field grow up in weeds and work my land for fifty years. Let your wife and children do without the home for fifty years, and work for me; but they forget when the fifty years are out the Negro is just where he was when he started. Not one whit higher, cornered and unprotected." Several of the black separatists in Texas, such as Richard H. Boyd, later became key figures in the formation of the National Baptist Convention.[17]

In the early 1890s, the gathering currents of black separatism came to a head, resulting in the formation of the National Baptist Convention in 1895 and, soon thereafter, the National Baptist Publishing Board. Here, the controversy involved the use of printed materials from the white Northern American Baptist Publication Society, which distributed educational

---

[16] Minutes, *Baptist Missionary State Convention of Texas*, 1887.

[17] Minutes, *General Baptist State Convention of Texas*, 1894, 20–32. For more on Bishop and Guadalupe, see Michael Heintze, *Private Black Colleges in Texas, 1865–1954* (College Station: Texas A&M University Press, 1985) 40–70, 129–32; Montgomery, *Under Their Own Vine and Fig Tree*, 249–51.

materials throughout the South. It was an instrumental part of the work of the American Baptist Home Missionary Society. Black Baptists interested in cultivating their own work sought to create a separate publishing endeavor and national denomination; they were opposed by black authors who wrote for the American Baptist Publication Society.

Opponents of the new board defeated a proposal floated by some of their leading opponents, mostly employees of northern publication societies, who "felt that such steps would be construed as enmity against our white brethren and friends who had given so much, and endured so much for us." E. M. Brawley, a well-educated South Carolinian who headed up black Baptist cooperative endeavors with the northern Publication Society, warned black Baptists not to "rush poverty-stricken, comparatively, into the face of wisdom, experience, and might." African Americans should "want no organizations on the color line," especially in matters of religious benevolence.[18]

Backers of the publishing house pointed out that such an agency would serve as a vehicle for resisting the growing tide of white supremacist rhetoric and action. "All races have a literature," one advocate pointed out. A black Baptist publishing effort could help African Americans avoid "absorption" into the white mainstream. Such a publishing endeavor, moreover, could provide opportunities for black Baptist scholars and theologians who would be denied them elsewhere. Black Baptists would "never attain to the broad influence and elevated dignity worthy of so vast a body of Baptists so long as our literary productions remain unpublished," a black denominational leader explained in 1893. Elias Morris, soon to become president of the National Baptist Convention for twenty-five years, explained that a black Baptist publishing agency would provide "race employment" and spur "race development." Black Baptists should assume the responsibility "to provide better things for our children, than our fathers were allowed to prepare for us."[19] Boyd, Morris, and others represented a growing black entrepreneurial

---

[18] Lewis G. Jordan, *Negro Baptist History, U.S.A.: 1750, 1930* (Nashville: Sunday School Publishing Board, 1930) 250; E. M. Brawley, "The Duty of Negro Baptists: In View of the Past, the Present, and the Future," in Brawley, ed., *The Negro Baptist Pulpit*, 297–8.

[19] L. C. Garland, "Why We Should Use the Sunday School Literature Published at Nashville, Tennessee," *National Baptist Magazine* (*NBM*) September 1901, 352–57; *American National Baptist Convention Journal*, 1893, 36; E. C.

spirit, which saw the kind of "separate economy" forced upon blacks in the South as an opportunity to cultivate businesses, organizations, and agencies. In so doing, black independence would be fostered in a way unforeseen by whites who were busy imposing Jim Crow restrictions.

By the mid-1890s, influential black ministers such as Emmanuel K. Love, pastor of a large congregation in Savannah and president of the Missionary and Educational Baptist Convention of Georgia, supported a separate publishing agency. Love had been employed by the American Baptist Publication Society, and had become one of the most successful ministers and authors of his era, well situated in a state that boasted the first two historic congregations of black Baptists (in Savannah and Augusta). Eventually, however, he came to feel that through their dependence on white Northern Baptists, black Baptists had "grown too largely to be parasites" and too prone to assume a "begging attitude." The color line had been drawn, and blacks were going to turn this to their advantage. By 1896, Love found "as strong an argument in favor of a distinctive Negro publishing house as there is for distinctive Negro churches, schools or families." By 1897, he proclaimed that "there is not so bright or glorious a future before a Negro in a white institution as there is for him in his own ... A people who man no enterprises show that they can have no spirit of progress ... and a people without this cannot command the recognition of nations and the respect of the world."[20]

The arguments of supporters such as E. K. Love proved successful. In 1896, the National Baptist Publishing Board, headed by black religious entrepreneur Richard H. Boyd, was chartered; in 1898 it was incorporated in Tennessee. In the early twentieth century it became the largest black-owned publishing enterprise in the country. Besides denominational literature, pews, hymnbooks, and other accoutrements for church life, the National Baptist Publishing Board was one of the first enterprises (perhaps *the* first) to produce black dolls for a black children's audience, a development usually

---

Morris, "The Demand for a Baptist Publishing House," *NBM*, January 1894, 18–20.

[20] Minutes, *Missionary Baptist Convention of Georgia*, 1897, 35–45, 52–3; Montgomery, *Under Their Own Vine and Fig Tree*, 246–248; Quote from 1896 in Jordan, *Negro Baptist History*, 122–123; Emmanuel K. Love quoted in Edward Freeman, *The Epoch of Negro Baptists and the Foreign Mission Board, National Baptist Convention, U.S.A.* (Kansas City: Central Seminary Press, 1953) 87.

ascribed to the Garveyites of the 1920s. Boyd's publishing house venture eventually led him into a small business empire in Nashville, including a Savings Bank and, for a short period, a streetcar line designed to counter the rise of segregation and second-class seating on the main lines of the by then Jim-Crowed city.[21]

Unlike the white Southern Baptist Convention, the National Baptist Convention was not specifically a southern organization, but a national one. And yet it was, in effect, southern at a time when more than ninety percent of black Americans lived in the region. The great migration of African Americans starting in World War II and extending into the early 1960s would change that demographic, but also helped to spread the convention and make it the largest black organization in the country. But while the largest, it was not necessarily the most "powerful" in some social, economic, or political sense. Its real power lay in the cultural forms that it helped to nourish, cultivate, and spread. And ironically, over the course of the twentieth century, those cultural forms increasingly encompassed and incorporated the very kinds of spiritual expressiveness that black Baptist organizers after the Civil War had tried to extirpate from church life.

In the 1890s, black religious organizers knew that their battle only had begun. Baptists had been "classed as the most ignorant of the race" with a manner of worship "called a modified form of heathenism," E. C. Morris told his fellow organizers. While the "intelligent and progressive elements in our churches have composed the vanguard of God's great army among the Negro Christians of the world," he suggested that most of the nearly two million Negro Baptists remained "crude and underdeveloped." Morris's protestations of confidence in the "leading and progressive element" of black Baptists together with his despair about "crude and underdeveloped" congregants captured the hopes and fears of the black religious leadership. During the progressive era, both white and black Baptists found in "intelligent worship" a strategy for bringing their denominations into a new

---

[21] Paul Harvey, "Richard Henry Boyd: Black Business and Religion in the Jim Crow South," in Nina Mjagkij, ed., *Portraits of African American Life Since 1865* (Lanham, Md.: Roman & Littlefield, 2003) 51-67.

era of separate racial development, and they hoped, "all things working together for mutual progress."[22]

The expressive styles cultivated and preserved during this era resulted in decidedly divergent political consequences for whites and blacks. The politics of respectability, however, united white and black denominational leaders of this era. Recent historical works have emphasized the tensions, contradictions, and ambiguities within white and black Baptist groups, finding that the struggle between traditionalists and progressives characterized the history of white and black Baptists, seen especially in the struggle over what constituted "intelligent worship."

Organizers of black Baptist associations and state and national conventions focused on a rhetoric drawn from the notion that cultural respectability would result in greater access to civil, political, and economic rights. They used the progressive-era language of control, regulation, and scientific management. Elias Camp Morris, president of the National Baptist Convention from its origins in 1895 until his death in 1920, explained how improved worship practices would better reflect on the rising race. "We make no effort to eliminate the worship from our worship or our service," he said, "but we think the right to regulate it, so that it may be more profitable than injurious, should be reserved by the leaders and disseminators of thought who are laboring faithfully to advance the Christian system."[23] As another worship reformer put it, "God demands of us a regular, systematic, steady, and forceful course of procedure."[24]

The reformation of southern religious ritual was a central aim of the white Baptists from the north who educated black ministers of the late nineteenth century in denominational schools and colleges. However, even some of those educated in the black Baptist colleges found themselves still

---

[22] E. C. Morris, *Sermons, Addresses, Reminiscences*, original (Nashville: National Baptist Publishing Board, 1901) 17, 102; The reference to "all things leading to mutual progress" comes from Booker T. Washington's famous address at the Atlanta Exposition of 1895, in Booker T. Washington, *Up From Slavery* (New York: Airmont Books, 1967) 150.

[23] *NBC Journal*, 1909, 34; *NBC Journal*, 1907, 86.

[24] L. C. Simon, "The Real Value of Christian Organization," (address before Louisiana Baptist Convention reprinted in *National Baptist Union*, 21 November 1908, 1).

attracted to black worship styles, unwilling to relinquish them to meet norms of respectability.

The struggle for respectability especially focused on music, which always had been central to black Baptist life. Black religious music in the late nineteenth century grew more diverse as congregations absorbed musical influences from missionaries, popular secular tunes, and the writings of black and white gospel hymnists. Observers of services commented on the range of styles on which congregants drew, as well as on how African American expressive culture influenced the singing of any style of song. At services on Alabama sharecropper plantations in 1894, Henry Morehouse, director of missions efforts for the American Baptist Home Mission Society, heard plantation songs, standard hymns, and Gospel songs, all of which were lined out, or "deaconed out." Morehouse approved of musical modernization in black services but realized that "nothing so alters their souls like the plaintive, weird, old plantation songs born of their bitter experiences, old slave songs of supplication to God for deliverance from their woes." The only antidote to this primitive slave music, he wrote, was to "teach good music in our schools."[25]

By producing and promoting hymnals, African American Baptists sought to teach their parishioners in norms of "intelligent worship." The first National Baptist hymnal, which was close to a reprint of a previous compilation of the American Baptist Publication Society, began to incorporate a few songs authored by African Americans. Richard Boyd, who ran the National Baptist Publishing Board, advised black Baptists to adopt the "old-established hymns" and then "hold to them. Do not be carried away by 'catchy' tunes adapted to words that may be either destitute of all sentiment or full of that which would be positively injurious. Many an error is sugar-coated by music popularizers."

Boyd's thriving Nashville-based National Baptist Publishing Board soon jumped headlong into the hymnal-producing business. His denominationally-based company put out hymns for all types of use, from the most formal to the most "camp meeting" like settings. "Doctrine can be more easily taught in poetry set to music than it can be by dry prose," he said. In 1916, the Board published a collection of African American Spirituals,

---

[25] H. L. Morehouse, "Plantation Life of the Colored People," *Baptist Home Mission Monthly*, March 1894, 95.

marking a major advance in incorporating black-authored material into songbooks used in black churches. "These melodies express the emotion of the soul of the Negro race as no other collection of music—classically or grammatically constructed could possibly do," Boyd wrote. He hoped that the hymnal would "build a monument to the memory of our Negro ancestry and show the rising generation who may yet become a great and educated people that they sprang from a deep and prayerful religious race."[26]

Just a few years later came the landmark publication *Gospel Pearls*, which proved to be a milestone in the move towards "blackening" the officially approved music of the National Baptist Convention and, thus, of music enjoyed by congregants even in the most upstanding northern urban churches. In the years to come, prominent black hymnists, performers, and musicians incorporated the "gospel blues" into their work. They overcame resistance from black congregations proud of their heritage of "classical" music, and imparted an African American sensibility even to hymns that were standard in the American Protestant oeuvre of songs.

In the 1920s, black denominationalists sponsored contests to encourage new hymns, reintroduced congregations to the spirituals, and fostered the growth of a new sensibility about African American religious music. The notation of the spirituals was a key turning point in this process, because it allowed print to communicate and pass down a folk tradition that once had been wholly oral. Thomas Dorsey's composing and Lucie Campbell's writing and performing, A. M. Nix's promotion, and increasingly enthusiastic crowds for gospel music performances and churches and black Baptist conventions grew during the 1920s and 1930s; during and after World War II, the new genre had its first superstar, the great black Baptist singer Mahalia Jackson, who was first supported by a funeral home director but soon teamed with Dorsey and others to spread the gospel music message nationwide and on the radio airwaves. Gospel might be said, in fact, to have grown up first in northern cities and then traveling back South (in a reverse pattern from the migration itself). Gospel grew into a widely appreciated

---

[26] Boyd quotes from John Spencer, *Black Hymnody: A Hymnological History of the African American Church* (Knoxville: University of Tennessee Press, 1992) 80, 84.

(and, very early on, highly commercialized) form that profoundly influenced the later course of twentieth-century American popular music.[27]

Beginning in the late nineteenth century but advancing with astonishing rapidity during World War One and into the 1920s, the great migration of African Americans from South to North reshaped black life in America, including religious life. The center of gravity shifted from the rural South to the urban North. Black religious leaders seeking upward mobility followed denominations northward, where more opportunities, higher pay, and noted status as community brokers between the white political structure and the African American community beckoned. Black northern churches also helped to birth a variety of new musical styles, most notably gospel music. That cultural transformation emerged slowly and over much resistance, but took black churches by storm by the World War Two era.

The great black gospel singer, Mahalia Jackson, and "father of gospel music" Thomas Andrew Dorsey, helped to revolutionize black Protestant cultural life in the middle years of the twentieth century. They also helped black Baptists determine how best to integrate African American musical currents into black Christian practice – how to weld the power of secular sound on behalf of sacred ends. Both grew up in the South – Dorsey in rural Georgia and Atlanta, Jackson in New Orleans. They both came from black Baptist families, but had their ears attuned to a variety of influences, including the blues and the powerful beat emerging in Holiness and Pentecostal churches. In the 1920s, both made their way to the black Midwestern mecca of Chicago, and from there developed innovative musical sounds, established important entrepreneurial ties, and discovered the power of mass media in spreading their influence. In particular, Jackson's early recordings and radio performances and Dorsey's organization of black choirs and choruses into a national force reshaped black religious music nationally. Perhaps most importantly, they learned to tap into the power of direct contact with the spirit, African rhythms and movements, and the kinds of "holy dancing" that religious reformers had long tried to discourage. Growing up in New Orleans, Jackson remembered black Holiness and Pentecostal folk who "stomped their feet and sang with their whole bodies."

---

[27] Lawrence Levine, *Black Culture and Black Consciousness: Afro-American Folk Thought from Slavery to Freedom* (New York City: Oxford University Press, 1977); Harris, *The Rise of Gospel Blues.*

Their "powerful beat" was something "we held on to from slavery days, and their music was so strong and expressive it used to bring the tears to my eyes."[28]

In 1927, Jackson moved to Chicago, where she met "Professor" Thomas A. Dorsey. Thomas Dorsey's father and mother were respectable sorts but were also very poor. In Villa Rica, Georgia, Dorsey's father held a prominent position as a minister while toiling the other six days a week as a tenant farmer. After graduating from Atlanta Baptist in 1894, however, Thomas Madison Dorsey did not become "race leader" but an itinerant preacher. "This abrupt change of course," Dorsey's biographer writes, "reflected a deep ambivalence toward assuming his duties in the acculturative church over which the Society had trained him to preside."[29] Dorsey's own family suggests the same ambivalences that many black Baptist congregants felt toward moving to respectability even while sensing the power of their own expressive styles.

Dorsey's years as a musician took him to juke joints, blues haunts, and holiness storefront churches as well as some of Chicago's largest and most respectable Baptist congregations. Gradually, he married blues feeling to gospel message. Unlike many other evangelicals, he did not reject blues as inherently ungodly, for as a musical form blues was a cry of the soul that could be cleansing and healing: "When you cry out, that is something down there that should have come out a long time ago."[30]

Dorsey's blues-influenced innovations in gospel music perfectly suited Jackson's powerfully emotive, expressive voice. At first, they met rejection from the established black churches in Chicago. "They were cold to it," Jackson later remembered of those congregations. "They didn't like the hand-clapping and the stomping and they said we were bringing jazz into the church and it wasn't dignified."[31] A sympathetic black minister and funeral home director began sponsoring Jackson's musical singing tours. He introduced her also to the radio, which proved an ideal medium for her

---

[28] Mahalia Jackson, *Movin' On Up* (New York City: Hawthorn Books, 1966) 32–3.

[29] Harris, *The Rise of Gospel Blues*, 19.

[30] Quoted in Nick Salvatore, *Singing in a Strange Land: C. L. Franklin, the Black Church, and the Transformation of America* (New York City: Little Brown and Co., 2005) 32.

[31] Jackson, *Movin' On Up*, 63.

talent. In her early musical career, Jackson sang everywhere, and began to pick up a fan base that propelled her and the new music of black gospel into national prominence.

One of her most influential earlier recordings came from the black Baptist minister and gospel song writer William Herbert Brewster. This Memphis-based pastor thrived in any number of musical styles, including the religious "pageant," a kind of sacred opera set for church audiences. As pastor of East Trigg Baptist Church in Memphis, he composed in ways that set black history in a sacred context, including in multi-part compositions such as "From Auction Block to Glory."[32]

Mahalia Jackson took Brewster's song of encouragement and hope, "Move On Up a Little Higher," and turned it into an early gospel mega-hit. Jackson's recording of that tune, whose lyrics seemed to reflect the African American experience from slavery to the Great Migration, sold over eight million copies, sealing black gospel's place in the history of American popular religious music. The organizational, musical, and entreprenrial talents of Dorsey, Jackson, and a rising generation of black gospel songwriters and performers propelled gospel into the American mainstream.

In addition to blues and gospel music, black churchgoers also flocked to buy recorded sermons of black ministerial superstars. In the 1920s and subsequent decades, talented ministers in both the South and North discovered the art of recording their sermons and then selling them to the black community. The earliest master of the form was the Reverend J. M. Gates. The Atlanta-based minister's three-minute recorded side "Death's Black Train is Coming" sold over 50,000 copies, so many that Columbia Records found it difficult to press enough copies to keep up with the demand. Gates inspired a legion of recorded sermonizers in the 1920s, but until the early 1930s he remained the king of the recorded three-minute sermonizers. Not all were as successful as he was, of course, but those who were made their names known nationally, and enjoyed the fruits of their labor with income far exceeding those of most pastors. Perhaps most

---

[32] W. Herbert Brewster, "Rememberings," in Bernice Johnson Reagon, ed., *We'll Understand it Better By and By: Pioneering African American Gospel Composers* (Washington, D. C.: Smithsonian Institution Press, 1992) 185-201.

importantly, these recorded innovators of the 1920s set the stage for the radio and (much later) television superstars to come.[33]

In that sense, the successor to the Reverend J. M. Gates was Clarence LaVaughan (C. L.) Franklin, father of soul singer Aretha. Franklin first developed his talents in his home state of Mississippi, but used the recordings (45s and LPs) and radio broadcasts from his congregation in Detroit to establish his presence in ways that built on but exceeded those of Gates and others from the 1920s. With his home base in a northern city, moreover, Franklin served as a key facilitator of the African American migration to industrial jobs, helping Detroit's employers by supplying names and references for migrants looking for work. Franklin preached in an exuberant "southern" style, but linked the poetry and artistry of that style to a message that derived from the contemporary African American experience. He could excite congregants with an evangelical message but also address directly issues of oppression, migration, discrimination, and African Americans' desires for the American dream. After World War Two, he drew a huge national audience to the live radio broadcasts of his sermons, which he used to promote his recordings. His church also nurtured the astonishing musical talents of his daughter Aretha. Once freed from the straitjacket of her early attempts to record jazz for Atlantic records, Aretha discovered her true voice when she brought her voice to the marriage of soul, gospel, and rhythm and blues in the 1960s.

Dorsey's music, Jackson and Franklin's performances, Brewster's "pageants," and the rise of what is now called the "Golden Age of Gospel Music" all point to the accomplishment of twentieth-century black Baptists in learning how to transcend more conventional norms dictated by the politics of respectability, employing, instead, African American cultural history to the ends both of pleasure and politics. Buying recorded sermons and gospel tunes married both successful entrepreneurship on the parts of the cultural producers with a desire of a consuming black audience to hear messages that could inspire and motivate. The Reverend C. L. Franklin's classic sermons, such as "The Eagle Stirreth Her Nest," also show how southern-derived sermonic styles translated into mid-twentieth century northern urban (and broadcast) form could touch a national audience. And

---

[33] See Lerone Martin, *Preaching on Wax: the Phonograph and the Shaping of Modern African American Religion* (New York: New York University Press) 2014.

the explosion of gospel quartets, star soloists and instrumentalists, and other performers during the golden age of gospel from about the early 1940s to the 1960s provided part of the soundtrack of black Baptists who were about to enter the civil rights era.

To put this in a more scholarly sense, what this article suggests is how scholars may marry two approaches that are often seen as being antithetical—denominational or institutional history on the one hand, and "lived religion" on the other. The first arises from traditional schools of "church history," even if applied to unconventional subjects such as African American churches. The latter draws from more recent work that assumes that church institutions and denominations, while important organizations, do not define people's lived religion, which can draw from diverse sources and has to do with how religious expression feels to the believers. Where historians have (until recently) generalized about the regional religion, scholars from other disciplines, especially folklore, musicology, and religious studies, have brought their expertise into the study of practices that exist on the margins of dominant evangelicalism. Scholars have addressed subjects such as ring shouts, conjure rituals, chanted sermonizing, and blues hollers. In such activities, students of religious culture have discovered a rich tradition of expressive culture underneath the smothering rhetoric of "uplift" pervading church organizations. Those studies have been particularly fruitful in looking at Baptist congregations, which have been the fount of folk religious life and expression precisely because of their tradition of congregational autonomy.

As this essay has argued, even mainstream and established denominations such as the Baptists contain a great deal of diversity. These assertions would certainly not have been news to White and black denominational leaders, who understood that their constituency cherished emotional exuberance over what they would have perceived as a stilted respectability in their worship. Twentieth century black Baptist leaders, moreover, were constantly tormented by institutional divisions and ugly episodes of denominational power politics. Nevertheless, black Baptist church folk managed to find ways to marry uplift and respectability, ecstatic and musical forms of worship, and civil rights protest and ways that fundamentally reshaped America both politically and culturally.

6

Racial Destiny and Christian Ideals:

M. C. Allen and the National Baptist Convention of America

Alan Scot Willis

Madison Crencha (M. C.) Allen saw race as the greatest threat to America in the years following World War II. For Allen, African Americans presented the nation with a paradox: the "Negro Problem" was the one problem capable of sundering the nation; simultaneously, African American spiritual superiority was the answer to a white civilization crippled by materialism and militarism.

Throughout the 1950s, Allen reached a broad audience of black Christians with his race-conscious assessment of America's problems and promise. As president of the Virginia Theological Seminary and College, he influenced the lives and perspectives of future ministers. As editor of the *National Baptist Union Review*, the official organ of the National Baptist Convention of America (NBCA), he addressed the nation's second-largest African American Baptist denomination, with churches in northern urban centers and throughout the South.

Allen's race-conscious editorials appeared a mere three or four pages before the virtually race-neutral articles of the "Every Woman's Page" published weekly in the *Union Review*. There, readers encountered stories, primarily intended for women, offering advice about parenting and living a Christian life, and stories for children in the "Starlight and Sunshine Band Corner." The stories on the "Every Woman's Page" not only lacked the race-consciousness of Allen's editorials, but many were actually written by whites and were often reprints from other publications. Unlike Allen's editorials, stories running on the "Every Woman's Page" assumed a normative whiteness, not blackness,[1] and while many stories cited materialism as

---

[1] Although the basic storyline in "Peter, a True Witness," a children's story appearing in the "Starlight and Sunshine Band Corner" of the *Union Review*, could

rotting the nation's soul, the solution typically had nothing to do with race but, rather, was to be found in the spread of Christian ideals and Christian homes—views shared by leaders of the overwhelmingly white Southern Baptist Convention.

On their own, Allen's race-conscious, Afrocentric editorials and the race-neutral stories on the "Every Woman's Page" make sense, but together, however, they present an intriguing paradox of African American Baptist thought in the 1950s. Indeed, historian David Chappell has argued that the civil rights movement might better be understood as a religious revival, in which religious culture spilled out from African American churches to shape broad regions of political and social life in America. The religious vision required broad appeal to create a "movement culture" that, as Larry Isaac has pointed out, would both "change and augment mainstream cultural stock." In the 1950s, much of "mainstream" America accepted that black preachers would challenge the long-standing traditions of racism and segregation, along with the indictments of rampant materialism which emanated from both black and white pulpits; far fewer were prepared to accept Allen's declarations of black superiority, spiritual or otherwise. Indeed, as Carolyn Renée Dupont noted in *Mississippi Praying*, many white evangelicals in the South attributed the economic and social disabilities faced by African Americans to their "natural spiritual inferiority." In the face of such prejudice, and undeterred by the fact that his views failed to dominate even the NBCA, Allen never wavered from his central philosophy of black spiritual superiority. As a result, black Baptists reading the *Union Review* found stories with broad appeal on the "Every Woman's Page" while being simultaneously challenged by Allen's race-conscious Jeremiads.[2]

---

have been embraced by nearly any Christian, it revealed an underlying assumption of witness when the protagonist, Peter, offered to tell a wayward newsboy whom he had invited to Sunday School all the things his grandmother had taught him about the Bible back in Scotland. "Peter, a True Witness," *Union Review*, 7 February 1959, 9. The author wishes to thank A. J. Fletcher for her assistance in preparing the manuscript.

[2] David Chappell, "Religious Revivalism in the Civil Rights Movement," *African American Review* 36.4 (Winter 2002), http://www.jstor.org/stable/1512419; Larry Isaac, "Movement of Movements: Culture Moves in the Long Civil Rights Movement," *Social Forces* 87.1 (September 2008): 36, http://www.jstor.org/stable/20430849; Carolyn Renée Dupont, *Mississippi Praying: Southern*

Born in 1880 to former slaves Cary and Cornelia Allen of Buckingham County, Virginia, M. C. Allen obtained his bachelor's degree from Virginia Seminary in 1918 and his Doctorate of Divinity in 1938. Allen became president of the seminary in 1946 after having served as an army chaplain in World War I, a pastor, a high-school principal, and a superintendent of education at the seminary. Upon becoming president, Allen expanded the curriculum by creating a Department of Black History.[3]

Allen led a seminary dedicated to "self-help" that explicitly rejected financial aid from whites. Indeed, Allen condemned African American educational leaders who sought white donors for their "begging."[4] By the time he entered Virginia Seminary as a student, the division among Virginia's black Baptists over the role of northern whites, particularly those associated with the American Baptist Home Missionary Society, had been settled. The fallout left the state with two African American Baptist conventions, one rejecting the aid of the northern whites and sponsoring Virginia Seminary in Lynchburg, and the other accepting their aid and sponsoring a school in Richmond, which eventually became Virginia Union University. The Lynchburg school suffered severe financial setbacks through the early years of the twentieth century, but its dedication to "self-help" and independent black education never wavered. Throughout its early years, the seminary sent forth ministers who, like Allen, considered themselves "Race Men" and believed in "the God of Black Christianity: benevolent and loving, but also an avenging God, a deliverer with a special concern for the oppressed."[5]

Throughout the 1950s, Allen stayed in Virginia as head of the seminary, while the *Union Review* was published in Nashville, Tennessee, by

---

White Evangelicals and the Civil Rights Movement, 1945–1975 (New York City: New York University Press, 2013) 32.

[3] E. Renée Ingram and Charles W. White, *Buckingham County*, Black America Series (Chicago: Arcadia Publishing, 2005) 20.

[4] M. C. Allen, "Editorial: Negro Private Education," *Union Review*, 5 August 1950, 4.

[5] Adolph H. Grundman, "Northern Baptists and the Founding of Virginia Union University: The Perils of Paternalism," *The Journal of Negro History* 63.1 (January 1978): 36–37; Andrew Rosa, "The Roots and Routes of 'Imperium in Imperio': St. Clair Drake, the Formative Years," *American Studies* 52.1 (2012): 55–57, http://muse.jhu.edu/journals/american_studies/v052/52.1.rosa.html.

the R. H. Boyd Publishing Company. The distance no doubt contributed the seeming disjointed views presented in the paper. R. H. Boyd, who had been born a slave in Texas, founded the publishing company. Boyd had sought to free the Sunday schools for African American Baptists from the influence of northern whites in the American Baptist Home Mission Society by establishing an independent publishing company to supply the needs of black Sunday schools. While Boyd faced numerous challenges, none was more serious than the efforts by the National Baptist Convention to take control of the publishing board of which he was the head. The confrontation led to a split in the convention, and Boyd's supporters formed the NBCA. Boyd succeeded in maintaining his independence, and the National Baptist Publishing Board continued to publish Sunday school literature through the publishing company. With its own presses, and even its own bank to aid in its financing, Boyd's publishing business was very nearly self-contained.[6] When the Convention appointed Allen as editor of the *Union Review* (the convention's official organ published by the board and printed by Boyd), their separate backgrounds had long pointed in the direction of independent black Christianity.

However, Boyd and his publishing business were less independent of white influence than was Virginia Seminary. When he began his publishing company, Boyd had to face the simple reality that he did not yet have a printing press. Boyd turned to an unlikely ally with its own reasons for wanting to limit the influence of northern whites on southern Blacks: the Southern Baptist Convention.[7] While Boyd eventually obtained his own presses, becoming a major publisher of religious literature, that early alliance with the Southern Baptists on issues common to evangelical Christians

---

[6] Bobby L. Lovett, *A Black Man's Dream: The First One Hundred Years* (Nashville: Mega Corporation, 1993) passim, especially 1, 13–30, 48–49. See also Bobby L. Lovett, *How it Came to Be: The Boyd Family's Contribution to African American Religious Publishing from the 19th to the 21st Century* (Nashville: Mega Corporation, 2007). In 1988 the National Baptist Convention of America split with about 25 percent of its membership following the Boyd faction in creating the National Missionary Baptist Convention of America. No one in the 1950s, however, could have foreseen this later schism. C. Eric Lincoln, *The Black Church in the African American Experience* (Durham, NC: Duke University Press, 2003) 36.

[7] Lovett, *A Black Man's Dream*, 1–2, 27–30.

continued well into the twentieth century, most obviously in the articles appearing on the "Every Woman's Page."

The apparent paradox, then, of having Afrocentric editorials and white normative articles within just a few pages from each other in the *Union Review* grew out of differing strategies for limiting northern white influence among southern black Christians in the years following Reconstruction. That juxtaposition, however, could not have continued throughout the 1950s, a decade when black ministers—including Vernon Johns, a former president of Virginia Seminary—rose to the national civil rights scene, unless it met the needs of the diverse membership of the nation's second largest black Baptist organizations.

M. C. Allen rooted his race-conscious interpretation of history in his fundamental belief that God had created racial distinctions for a particular purpose. While some scholars have argued that the "Afrocentric paradigm" developed fully with the establishment of the Africana Studies doctoral program at Temple University in the late 1980s, Allen's views, publically disseminated through the *Union Review*, clearly anticipated the main currents of Afrocentrism; hence, his ideas often faced the same barriers to broader acceptance and those of later Afrocentric scholars.[8]

To fully understand the African world view, Allen argued, African Americans needed to learn at the hands of members of their own race and not from whites. Indeed, Allen criticized black Baptists who did not read black-written Sunday school materials. He argued that reading black-written materials for the Sunday schools taught readers "to appreciate the writings, ideas, and the literary works of members of their own race." For Allen, this was indeed "Racialism" but, he said, "It is the type [of racialism] that aims to discover and explore **God's purpose in racial distinction**. It is the type of **racialism** that Jesus made plain to the woman at Jacob's well. When she flung race prejudice in his teeth, he relieved the tension by presenting a philosophy of **racial understanding** [emphasis in original]."[9] It was God-ordained racialism to train a divinely chosen people in the nature of their God-given destiny.

---

[8] Adisa A. Alkebulan, "Defending the Paradigm," *Journal of Black Studies* 37.3 (January 2007): 410–27, http://www.jstor.org/stable/40034783.

[9] Allen, "Editorial: The 'As Others' Leadership," *Union Review*, 24 January 1953; Allen, "Editorial: Race Problem: Ignorance—Fear—Conscience" *Union Review*, 23 June 1951.

According to Allen, time was running short, and African Americans had to fulfill their destiny post-haste. He explained the crisis using a sports analogy: "Speaking in terms of baseball, racially, civilization is at the 'bottom of the ninth.'" The white race, he said, "had a chance to score with social justice or the quality of race" but had, instead, "batted the fouls of economic exploitation and political domination all over Africa, India, and China and then 'struck out' in Western Europe." The African, whose spiritual interpretation of life gave people hope, offered the last chance for civilization. Allen proposed, "Since innately the Negro is a deeply spiritual and apparently without a major urge for political and economic world domination—in things spiritual he has a good chance to score."[10]

Allen believed, "it is up to the Negro to save civilization and to advance democracy," and he consistently interpreted this in terms of "the unusual opportunity of the American Negro to save civilization." For Allen, the black man's history in America would not be what it was "without some fundamental meaning in relation to world history." Undoubtedly, Allen would have rejected the criticism that he constructed a particular vision of the American past, and of the role of African Americans in it, which fit his pre-ordained meta-narrative of world redemption at the gentle spiritual hands of African Americans. Instead, history revealed to Allen that "no people of the world are better situated than the American Negro to preserve and use the best in human nature for the good of man." Blacks appreciated the blessings of democracy and freedom in ways that whites could not because whites had not been denied the privileges democracy was supposed to bestow on citizens. To transform the rich resources America held "into a blessing for America and the world instead of a curse" the "Negro needs Christianity, or has no hope now or hereafter."[11]

A divinely and historically ordained racial destiny necessitated an insurmountable racial difference. Allen thoroughly rejected emerging

---

[10] Allen, "Editorial: Thank God," *Union Review*, 5 October 1957, 4.

[11] Allen, "Editorial: The Negro's Challenge" *Union Review*, 31 January 1959, 4; Hayden V. White, *The Content of the Form: Narrative Discourse and Historical Representation*, ACLS Humanities Ebook (Baltimore: Johns Hopkins University Press, 1987), http://hdl.handle.net/2027/heb.04929.0001.001. The idea that those individual denied freedom are most appreciative of freedom is both logical and firmly established by Orlando Patterson, *Slavery and Social Death: Comparative Study* (Cambridge: President and Fellows of Harvard College, 1982).

scientific evidence that supposedly demonstrated that there were no real differences among the races.[12] Allen told readers to, "never mind about what the authorities say about climate being responsible for your racial distinction, never mind what the scientists say about the myth of racial distinctions, never mind about what the theologians say about racial distinction" and then he expounded upon the falsity of their ideas. Calling those authorities, scientists, and theologians who doubted God-created, innate racial distinctions "little smarties," he said that they had had "a field day on this subject for thousands of years, and when it comes to peace and good-will among the different people of the earth, they are nearer hell today than ever before." If Allen exaggerated by suggesting that the "little smarties" had been denying innate racial distinctions for "thousands of years," he insisted that, "The true African leader is interested in being what 'the others' have never been. He wants to become conscious of God's purpose in his racial distinction." The problem, for Allen, was simply this: The long history of racism had led blacks to develop an inferiority complex because "the average Negro leader has never seen or understood that his racial distinction is of divine origin."[13] The divine racial distinction was as ancient as Africa.

Even if the Black races' destiny was to be played out in the Americas, that destiny was as ancient as the race itself. Allen sought to locate great historical achievements in Africa, typically Egypt, in an effort to lay claim to a glorious racial past. To lay claim to black spiritual superiority, he tied Africa's heroic heritage directly to Christianity. Blacks' spirituality would redeem the world the materialist, militarist white civilization had run roughshod over for the past several centuries.[14] Here, again, Allen presaged later Afrocentric scholars who would argue: "Afrocentric methods, as well as Afrocentrically generated knowledge, must reflect the primacy of the spiritual."[15] According to Allen, "nature is God's first and most accurate revelation of himself," giving Africans primal spiritual advantage over all

---

[12] Mia Bay, "The Historical Origins of Afrocentrism," *Amerikastudien* 45.4 (2000): 509, http://www.jstor.org/stable/41157604.

[13] Allen, "Editorial: The 'As Others' Leadership,"; Alkebulan, "Defending the Paradigm," 414.

[14] Allen, "Editorial: Ancient Negro History," *Union Review*, 21 March 1959; Allen, "Editorial: Imhotep: A Negro Father of Medicine," *Union Review*, 14 September 1957, 4; Mia Bay, "Origins of Afrocentrism," 505–6.

[15] Alkebulan, "Defending the Paradigm," 414.

other races because they were "the only major race on earth who has learned the art of living with and from nature."[16]

Allen moved beyond natural spirituality by locating the origins of monotheism in ancient Egypt. For Allen, African spiritual leadership had proceeded in an unbroken line from the Pharaoh Ikhnaton to African Americans. In an editorial lionizing J. C. Sams, Florida pastor and vice president of the NBCA, Allen called Sams a spiritual leader "who by precept and example can teach, preach, and racially practice the height, depth, and breadth of the universal doctrine of the Fatherhood of God and the brotherhood of man."[17] Allen explained that African spiritual leadership dated from the fourteenth century BC when Ikhnaton, "a Negro leader," first discovered and taught the idea of "One God" and thus "gave to man the concept of the superiority of moral force and spiritual values" over mere military might. Allen suspected that "this analysis of the Negro's religious background is sure to be foreign language to millions."[18] While Allen's analysis likely was a "foreign language" to millions of Americans, in Tunde Adeleke's analysis such a "foreign language" was a necessary part of the "reconstruction of African history and the experience of peoples of African descent abroad with a view to debunking prevailing historical fallacies and misrepresentations."[19] Indeed, Allen's analysis was a direct debunking of racist history; when he wrote, some scholars were insisting that the "superstitious Egyptians" lacked originality, and thus, Ikhnaton's genius was attributable to his Aryan and Syrian heritage.

---

[16] Allen, "Editorial: Spiritual Emphasis Education," *Union Review*, 3 June 1950, 4.

[17] Allen, "American Negro Leadership," *Nashville Globe and Independent*, 2 July 1954, 12. During 1954, the *National Baptist Union Review* was not published as a separate paper, but rather its content was published by *The Nashville Globe and Independent*. The situation had little impact on the content, except that the "Every Woman's Page" was not included every week as it was in the *Union Review*, and M. C. Allen's columns were not labeled "Editorials," perhaps to avoid confusion with the *Globe and Independent's* own editorials.

[18] Allen, "Editorial: Dr. Sams and Christian Statesmanship," *Union Review*, 3 August 1957, 4; Bay, "Origins of Afrocentrism," 505.

[19] Tunde Adeleke, "Black Americans and Africa: A Critique of the Pan-African and Identity Paradigms," *International Journal of African Historical Studies* 31.3 (1998): 508, http://jstor.org/stable/221474.

For Allen, Ikhnaton was a part of the Negro's heritage, a spiritual bloodline inherited by men like Sams. Africans had "for several centuries successfully taught, preached and believed in the superiority of Moral Force and Spiritual Values over military force and economic values." Clearly, also, Allen's drawing a direct connection between Ikhnaton, the Egyptian pharaoh, and J. C. Sams, the Baptist minister, showed that he embraced "the idea of a transhistorical racial personality" that scholar Mia Bay claims is a cornerstone of Afrocentric thinking.[20]

The story of Iknhaton was likely to be a quite foreign—perhaps too foreign—limiting its resonance even among African American Baptists in America. Where Allen used the Bible to demonstrate Africa's spiritual heritage, his message was undoubtedly more familiar. Allen cited the story of Abraham and Hagar, the bondswoman who bore Abraham a son. Allen transformed the story through his Afrocentrism, writing, "When Abraham was living in Hebron, he became the father of Ishmael, by the **Negro maid, Hagar—an Egyptian** [emphasis in original]." The Bible, however, merely indicates that Hagar was an Egyptian, Allen determined for himself that that meant she was a negro. From Hagar's son, a mighty nation had sprung; Allen referred here only to Arabs, but not at all to Muslims.[21]

Further explaining Africa's importance, he noted that the ancient world had been subject to periodic droughts leading to famines, and argued: "Egypt, or Africa, throughout the history of the world has been a land of plenty. No matter who they were, Hebrew travelers, Hittite soldiers, Phoenician traders and others, Egypt was the only refuge and hope when these dry spells prevailed."[22] Allen saw Africa as a land of refuge and security, citing the commonly known story of Joseph and Mary's flight into

---

[20] Allen, "Editorial: Dr. Sams and Christian Statesmanship"; Bay, "Origins of Afrocentrism," 505. The influence on Ikhnaton on monotheistic thought was certainly debated by Allen's contemporaries and the pharaoh was widely credited with a religious and political revolution that gripped Egypt in the fourteenth century, but it seems unlikely, as Allen suggested, that such debates were widely known outside of academic circles. Leslie A. White, "Ikhnaton: The Great Man vs. The Culture Process" *Journal of the American Oriental Society* 68.2 (April–June 1948): 94, http://www.jstor.org/stable/596342.

[21] Allen, "Editorial: Hagar's Child—A Mighty Nation," *Union Review*, 19 October 1957, 4. See also the Book of Genesis 16:1 (KJV).

[22] Allen, "Editorial: Hagar's Child—A Mighty Nation."

Egypt after Jesus' birth to avoid the wrath of King Herod, a story widely known among American Christians.[23] Finally, while admitting that both sacred and secular histories were unfortunately incomplete about early Christian history in Africa, Allen pointed to the conversion of Ethiopia under the guidance of Philip as clear evidence of the ancientness of African Christianity, noting that "a few of the ancient traditions are still prevalent among Ethiopians."[24] Hence, Allen was able to wed his Christian and his Afrocentric beliefs in a narrative in which Egypt took the prized place in religious history, rather than one focusing on the enslavement of the Hebrews and the exodus across the Red Sea.

Intriguingly, M. C. Allen said very little about Moses in his editorials. He did refer to Moses in a column lionizing President G. L. Prince of the National Baptist Convention of America, whose work at Mary Allen College in Texas had distinguished him as a "national symbol of fundamental principles in race initiative—'self-help.'" Allen wrote that the "idea of 'self-help' and spiritual independence in Negro education like Moses' burning bush in the back side of the desert will burst forth into a flame of hope and security for the world."[25] Nevertheless, the story of Moses leading the Hebrews out of Egypt is ever popular with children because of its drama and its miraculous resolution; hence, it appeared in the "Starlight and Sunshine Band Corner" where children could read, or have read to them, "Into the Sea."[26]

Allen worked to create a particular Biblical memory for his readers, one in which Africa was a land of refuge, not of enslavement. As historian Ralph Luker has noted, Moses can serve many purposes: foundling, liberator, or law-giver. For Martin Luther King, Jr., Moses often served as the liberator-leader who would never make it to the Promised Land. For Vernon Johns, who preceded Allen as president of Virginia Seminary and King as pastor of Dexter Avenue Baptist in Montgomery, Alabama, Moses was the avenger for the oppressed. Both of those interpretations of Moses, which resonated strongly with mainstream American Christians, cast Africa, especially

---

[23] Allen, "Editorial: The 'As Others' Leadership."

[24] Allen, "Editorial: The Conversion of the Man from Ethiopia," *Union Review*, 19 July 1958.

[25] Allen, "Editorial: President Prince: Symbol of Progress," *Union Review*, 27 January 1951, 4.

[26] Allen, "Into the Sea," *Union Review*, 4 October 1958, 7.

Egypt, in a negative light that Allen could not accept. For Allen, if biblical memory and biblical narratives, like historical narratives, could be used "to give meaning to experiences that would otherwise be disabling," then biblical and historical narratives could also be used to create an unambiguously meaningful past pointing toward a glorious future. Of course, neither history nor the Bible are so clear as to unambiguously support those unambiguous narratives. For Allen, no part of the Moses story truly fit Africa's meaning in the world as a land of refuge and security, and his approach, apparently, was to simply avoid Mosaic entanglements.[27]

If Allen avoided Moses, a favorite of other black preachers, he embraced the Pilgrims, undeniable favorites of Baptists and Americans in general. Whether black or white, Baptists prized religious freedom as the root of all other freedoms, and they located its origins in America in seventeenth-century Plymouth. Later Baptist heroes such as Roger Williams and John Leland expanded and defended religious freedom until it was finally enshrined in the Bill of Rights. M. C. Allen lauded the Pilgrims' courage, as they not only came in search of religious freedom, but also "triumphed with the Christian Spirit over Europe's materialistic interpretation of the whole meaning of life." Hence, while African Americans embodied spiritual anti-materialism in modern America, the Pilgrims demonstrated that even whites could obtain such a state. Nevertheless, Allen had reached back more than three hundred years to highlight a group of whites who had managed to overcome the endemic materialism of mercantilist Europe.[28]

Children encountered stories of the Pilgrims on The "Every Woman's Page," particularly—predictably—in the November issues, which offered stories of the "First Thanksgiving." Seeing Thanksgiving as an opportunity to remind young people to be thankful to God, George T. B. Davis, well-known evangelist and author of *When the Fire Fell*, wrote, "The Pilgrim Fathers were God-fearing and Bible loving people. They wanted to set apart a day for thanks to God for all His great goodness to them." Davis noted, too, that the Pilgrims "wanted others to rejoice with them in praising God

---

[27] Ralph E. Luker, "Murder and Biblical Memory: The Legend of Vernon Johns," *Virginia Magazine of History and Biography* 112.4 (2004): 404–6.

[28] Allen, "Editorial: The Genuine Thanksgiving Spirit of the Christian Faith," *Union Review*, 23 November 1957, 4.

for His goodness" and invited friendly Indians to join them.[29] The most famous Indian to join them was, of course, Squanto. In a story for children offered in the "Starlight and Sunshine Band Corner" of the "Every Woman's Page," Esther O. Smitle offered a story, clearly fictionalized, about the children of Elder Brewster, who realized "God must have sent Squanto to help our people." Considering the first thanksgiving itself, Brewster wrote, "Such a wonderful day the Pilgrims and the Indians had. There was a time of worship and then they gathered around the wood-hewn tables for their feast. Elder Brewster thanked the Lord for his many blessings and mercies. There were games in the afternoon and a military drill under Captain Miles Standish."[30] Such stories offered virtually the same vision of the Pilgrims that Southern Baptists regularly presented to their young people in November Training Union programs.[31]

Allen did not extend such praise to other colonists. Diverging considerably from the patriotic narrative of a chosen nation offered on the "Every Woman's Page" or to Southern Baptist youth, Allen identified another group of colonists, settling further south, as made up of "crackers" and criminals. The United States Constitution, a powerful document for freedom, descended directly from the Pilgrim Fathers; the "crackers" and criminals of the South had bequeathed the country a very different document, the Constitution of the Confederate States of America, which enshrined racial slavery. The problem had not ended with the demise of Confederacy. Allen offered a direct analysis of the problems facing the United States in the 1950s, saying that the fights over segregation "may be traced to the early white immigrants to this continent."[32]

For Allen, then, the pious heritage of the Pilgrims had been overrun by the materialist and racist heritage of the "crackers." America had clearly fallen, despite the South's defeat. For some Black religious leaders, the narrative of the Civil War involved the "fortunate fall" in which the sin of slavery was redeemed and the nation was purified in the fires of war, but

---

[29] George T. B. Davis, "Praising God on Thanksgiving Day—And Always," *Union Review*, 30 November 1957, 7.

[30] Esther O. Smitle, "Squanto, Good Friend of the Pilgrims," *Union Review*, 13 December 1958, 7.

[31] Willis, "Symbolic History in the Cold War," 276.

[32] Allen, "Editorial: Legal Forced Integration vs. Illegal Forced Segregation," *Union Review*, 13 September 1958, 4.

Allen rejected the idea that the nation had been redeemed.[33] He believed, instead, that the same problem was at the root of both the Civil War and the racial problems of the mid-twentieth century: blackness was simply too powerful a moral force within a corrupt white society dominated by the twin evils of materialism and militarism. Slavery and the racism that continued long after Appomattox offered Allen an opportunity to expose the corruptions of white civilization.[34] Wedding these ideas to the power of blackness, Allen offered an interpretation of the Civil War and the emerging civil rights movement that revealed that blackness was more powerful than Americanism, a particularly dangerous position to take in the midst of the Cold War.

The power of blackness rooted in black spiritual superiority, streamed in black blood. It mattered not whether blacks were in Africa, or the Americas, their spiritual superiority was in their blackness. In America, blacks regularly demonstrated their spiritual superiority over whites. For Allen, the very fact—and he took it as fact—that blacks were not embittered toward whites after centuries of slavery and decades of segregation was proof positive of black spiritual superiority.[35] While Baptists, both white and black, saw Communism as a tyrannical system that denied the most essential freedom—liberty of conscience—as serious threats to America, Allen believed it was not capable of destroying America: only blackness was.[36] In his analysis, the United States had met, and survived, every internal and external threat posed to it, save one: blackness. Only blackness had nearly sundered the union. Only blackness would bring the union to the brink again. Perhaps paradoxically, only blackness could—and would—save the nation from materialism and militarism.[37]

---

[33] Patrick Rael, "Black Theodicy: African Americans and Nationalism in the Antebellum North," *The North Star: A Journal of African American Religious History* 3.2 (Spring 2000), https://www.princeton.edu/~jweisenf/northstar/volume3/rael.html.

[34] Bay, "Origins of Afrocentrism," 509.

[35] Allen, "Editorial: Negro Labels," *Union Review*, 14 January 1950, 4.

[36] Andrew M. Manis, *Southern Civil Religions in Conflict: Civil Rights and the Culture Wars* (Macon, GA: Mercer University Press, 2002) 73–5.

[37] Allen, "Editorial: America's Skin Color Cancer," *Union Review*, 26 July 1958, 4.

Allen, who had initiated a black history program at Virginia Seminary, saw a dangerous trend in histories of the Civil War. He argued that "in an effort to minimize the significance of the Negro's 'racial' color distinction as being one of the basic reasons for the Civil War in the U. S. A., some writers have tried to make it purely an economic problem based on 'states' rights'. The truth is this Republic has been able to solve all of its domestic and foreign problems... [that have threatened] its independence—with one exception, which is the Negro's racial color distinction."[38] Allen examined a variety of other threats to the union, including the controversies over the Bank of the United States, President Andrew Jackson's "Pet Banks," and the tariff law and resulting Nullification Crises. The Union, he concluded, had withstood the strain of each event, but "the only thing that has been great enough to snap the strength of the Union was the Negro's racial distinction." That evidenced the great power of blackness: "Historically, the strength of the Negro's color is the weakness of the republic."[39]

Little had changed from the Civil War to the early days of the civil rights movement. Writing in March 1954, in anticipation of the Supreme Court's decision in *Brown vs. the Board of Education*, Allen likened the strain on the Republic to the days of the Missouri Compromise and the outbreak of the Civil War, but he remained sure of the power of blackness to save the nation. Allen believed that "If his black face and curly hair can close the class room doors to all of the white children in any state or states, or community," then:

> his brain, his intellect, his ability of spiritual insight, his moral courage or creative genius, if submitted to the influence of stimulation of the infinite power of the love of God and the truth of Jesus Christ would be able to give this country and the world a concept of education and a spiritual interpretation of life that would make it possible for any race, every race, any and every individual who has the ability and character to live in a school, a college, or university community, an opportunity to learn.

Allen, however intentionally or unintentionally, exposed the tension between the rights of the groups and of the individual, a tension which had long created difficulties in the struggle for civil rights. Whites could point to

---

[38] Ibid.

[39] Allen, "The Negro's Racial Distinction—A Test of American Democracy," *Nashville Globe and Independent*, 5 March 1954, 12.

individual African Americans who had succeeded despite the system and claim those individual who, as Allen indicated, had the "character and ability" did indeed have the opportunities. Nevertheless, Allen thought in racial terms, not individual terms. However much individuals within a race varied, Allen was sure that racial prejudice represented the "weak link" in the Republic and that it had to be "replaced with a sympathetic understanding between all peoples." When that happened, "each racial group will find pleasure in following GOD'S PURPOSE OF ITS RACIAL DISTINCTION [emphasis in original]."[40] Hence, in 1954 as the nation began its tumultuous move away from legal racial distinctions, Allen maintained the idea of an unchanging, divinely ordained, natural racial distinction that privileged Black spirituality. For Allen, the racial collective would always outweigh individual members of the race.

After *Brown*, the state government in Virginia moved to close the public schools rather than allowing them to be desegregated. When the Supreme Court forbade such solutions, Allen announced that the decision had "definitely proven that the Negro's legal mind is supreme or superior to the best legal minds of Arkansas, Virginia, and several other states." For Allen, the winning arguments transcended case-by-case considerations and the talents of individual lawyers; it reflected, instead, the racial heritage of the lawyers. He boasted, "it must be awfully embarrassing or humiliating to the governors and state attorney generals as well as to the mothers and fathers of white children, who have claimed 'WHITE RACIAL SUPERI-ORITY' to their children and the world or who have taught and preached that the Negro is inferior, and now, before their children and the world are forced, by the supreme law of the land to bow to their Negro masters of the law [emphasis in original]."[41]

Allen was not, of course, oblivious to the fact that some people departed, in opinion and character, from the norms of their racial group and recognized that some whites agreed with the Supreme Court. He also noted the indisputable fact that the justices themselves were all whites. He concluded his editorial saying, "Let us thank God for the federal judges and the white lawyers, the white men and women in all walks of life ... who have

---

[40] Ibid.

[41] Allen, "Editorial: Supreme Court vs. Supreme Negro Lawyer," *Union Review*, 27 September 1958, 4.

lent their influence at the expense of prestige in this fight to save the prestige of the greatest nation on earth."[42] He never, however, fully clarified those people's departure from the white racial norm. Indeed, while Allen clearly identified the Africans' racial destiny, he never identified precisely what he believed was God's purpose in the *white* racial distinction, but only that the white race had, generally, succumbed to racism, militarism, and materialism.

The legal wrangling over segregation provided Allen with evidence for an updated version of the "fortunate fall" ideology. One central theme of the "fortunate fall" and its concomitant vision of African Americans as a "chosen people" who would redeem America was that slavery, for all of its evils, had Christianized the slaves. In the 1950s, Allen believed that segregation had had a not-too-dissimilar effect.[43] He wrote, "Racial segregation forced upon the Negro has made him conscious of his potential mental, moral, and spiritual resources of power. Racial segregation has made the Negro conscious of the fact that the race possesses the fundamental requisites for a distinct culture."[44] Segregation had allowed, indeed forced, African Americans to develop a spiritual, rather than materialist, culture by denying them access to the material progress of the nation; thus, it had prepared them to be a saving force.

Racial distinctions, however, were notably absent from most discussions of America's history appearing on the "Every Woman's Page." There, in child-friendly language, readers encountered a much more common, 1950s-style narrative of American history filled with white heroes. Stories about George Washington and Abraham Lincoln were particularly common in February editions, while nothing was said of "crackers" or even of slavery. Washington's reputation for telling the truth grew out of the oft-told myth of the cherry tree. Writing for the "Starlight and Sunshine Band Corner," Virginia Fisher admitted, "Historians say that the young George probably did not cut down the tree and so did not need to tell his father the truth about it." Nevertheless, the story's moral teaching remained and she

---

[42] Ibid.; "Virginia's 'Massive Resistance' Laws Declared Unconstitutional," *The Journal of Negro Education* 28.2 (Spring 1959): 163–72, http://www.jstor.org/stable/2293723. See also Bob Smith, *They Closed Their Schools: Prince Edward County, Virginia, 1951–1964* (Chapel Hill: University of North Carolina Press, 1967).

[43] Rael, "Black Theodicy."

[44] Allen, "Editorial," *Union Review*, 14 January 1950, 4.

concluded, "We still like the story. We admire young George Washington's truthfulness, and we still use hatchets as decorations on his birthday."[45] Fisher added another story, selecting a perhaps more peculiar hero, Henry Clay. She wrote, "We remember, too, that other great American statesman Henry Clay for his famous declaration 'I would rather be right than be President' of the United States." Clay, she reminded her young readers, never became president despite the fact that many of his friends believed he would be a good president. She concluded, "We remember him for the high value he put on doing right."[46] Like Southern Baptist writers on early American heroes, Fisher overlooked both Washington's and Clay's slaveholdings. Indeed, the article "George Washington's Regard for Mother" referred directly to Washington's "servants" rather than his slaves.[47]

The *Union Review* rarely published materials submitted by readers, much less by children, but one eleven-year-old girl from Pecos, Texas, Margaret Ramage, had her poem lauding Washington as the "Hero of Our Nation" published on 18 February 1950 in the "Starlight and Sunshine Band Corner." Washington, she wrote, had "fought in a battle/for me and for you." In February 1957, Tara Teagan had her poem published in the "Starlight and Sunshine Band Corner," saying about Washington "He and many others/Made our Country strong/Tried to have it stand for/Right instead of Wrong." She finished by noting that "If I love my country/I will do the same—Cherish truth and honor/More than gold or fame."[48]

Along with Washington, Abraham Lincoln ranked high among American leaders. Everett E. Jackman, who had authored the centennial history of Methodists in Nebraska, argued, "Probably every American will agree that George Washington and Abraham Lincoln are the two outstanding Americans of our nation's history." According to Jackman, "We might say that Washington founded our union of states and Lincoln saved it

---

[45] Virginia S. Fisher, "About Telling the Truth," *Union Review*, 24 January 1953, 5.

[46] Ibid.

[47] "George Washington's Regard for Mother," *Union Review*, 18 February 1950, 8.

[48] Margaret Ramage, "The Hero of Our Nation," *Union Review*, 18 February 1950, 8; Tara Teagan, "Washington," *Union Review*, 25 February 1957, 8.

from ruin," and Lincoln "hated slavery as he hated hell and devoted most of his mature life to fighting it."[49]

Jackman noted that both Washington and Lincoln were Christians, a point commonly made by Southern Baptists as well. Christian leaders often saw how stressing the piety of the nation's heroes served as a counter-point to flawed secular histories. In 1950, the *Union Review* posthumously published "What Lincoln Said" by British-born, American-educated evangelist G. Campbell Morgan, who had died in 1945. In it, Morgan specifically amended the common understanding of the Gettysburg Address. Morgan argued that most people who quoted the address stopped short of grasping Lincoln's full meaning. Lincoln had said, Morgan reminded readers, "We highly resolve that the dead shall not have died in vain, that this nation **under God** shall have a new birth of freedom ... [emphasis in original]." Morgan suggested that when people thought of the address, they add "under God" to each of the well know phrases, so it would read "of the people under God, by the people under God, for the people under God."[50]

The heroes of American history presented on the "Every Woman's Page" and in stories for children in the "Starlight and Sunshine Band Corner" offered an American history that could easily have been transferred to Southern Baptist Training Union and Sunday school sessions. Just as official Southern Baptist literature in the Cold War either downplayed or rejected outright the white supremacy endemic in the South, the "Every Woman's Page" was devoid of "crackers," criminals, and African American superiority. On the other hand, the "Every Woman's Pages" was also devoid of any claims about the God-given racial purpose of African Americans, while Southern Baptist literature was peppered with a clearly national chauvinism. And such are the problems with divine choseness. Southern Baptists consistently presented the United States as God's chosen nation, chosen to deliver the word from the grips of Communist materialism and

---

[49] Everett E. Jackman, "Washington and Lincoln," *Union Review*, 7 February 1959, 7.

[50] G. Campbell Morgan, "What Lincoln Said" *Union Review*, 6 May 1950, 8; "George Campbell Morgan," *Pleasant Places Press*, http://www.pleasantplaces.biz/authors/morgan_gc.php. The *Union Review* also carried a story about a study done by Robert S. Barton in which he examined the various copies of the Bible Lincoln used and notated. "Abraham Lincoln's Bible," *Union Review*, 16 February 1952, 8.

militarism. M. C. Allen consistently presented African Americans as God's chosen people, chosen to deliver America from the grips of white materialism and militarism. Given its peculiar existence at the crossroads of the Southern Baptists and M. C. Allen, the "Every Woman's Page" was devoid of claims of divine choseness, for the United States or for African Americans.

Not everyone, not even all African American leaders, had discerned the divine meaning of the negro's history in the Americas. Allen worried that too many black leaders suffered from an inferiority complex despite the spiritual and moral superiority of their race.[51] They had allowed whites, "the opposite race," to define cultural creation and assign negros an inferior status. Allen sought to change that. He argued that, "if the American Negro were to cease thinking of what the opposite race thinks about him and begin to think in terms of his rapidly developing culture and of his cultural heritage, he would instantly be cured of his inferiority complex."[52] Allen admitted, "Some Negro leaders want to be 'as other' races, they ignore the creations of their own race and seek 'crumbs' from other races." This, he said, was the "seedbed" of the inferiority complex affecting African Americans.[53] The ultimate danger lay in the possibility of African Americans forfeiting the divine inheritance and pursuing the worldly materialism that had been the undoing of white civilization.

Allen warned, "The god of mammon is riding high in the saddle" leading to "selfish greed, race hate, and intolerance among people." Materialism had undermined white education and white spirituality, and had led to wars causing untold destruction. Materialism had even won the battle for the white man's churches. Allen declared white churches "scarcely more than good business institutions" concerned more with "budgets, dependable membership fees, swelling treasuries and well organized church departments than in brotherhood, social justice, every-day Christianity, and world peace." Notably, even examining their own churches some Southern

---

[51] Rael, "Black Theodicy."

[52] Allen, "Editorial: Negro Cultural Heritage," *Union Review*, 2 September 1950, 4. See also, Herbert Apatheker, "Afro-American Superiority: A Neglected theme in Literature," *Phylon* 31.4 (Winter 1970): 330–40.

[53] Allen, "Editorial: the 'As Others' Leadership."

Baptist leaders shared his concerns, and evangelist Billy Graham worried that too many churches had really become socials clubs.[54]

Materialism won the day in the United States; specifically, it had won Independence Day. Allen lamented that when President Eisenhower had called for the Fourth of July to be a day of prayer instead of a day of commercialism and play, materialism had won out. Such calls for prayerful days went unheeded, Allen believed, because "the public generally has learned how to respect and obey those who control material wealth and political power. The only time men take God and religion seriously is when they are either threatened or are in the grasp of danger, disaster, or hopelessness."[55] Materialist education had promised to make the world safe for democracy, but at the hands of whites, it had led to totalitarianism and war; it had promised freedom from fear but created a more fearful world than had ever existed before.[56]

Herein lay the key to African American destiny in saving America from itself: "Generally speaking Negro people are more susceptible to things religious or spiritual than they are to things material or political." For Allen, this was an inherent racial trait, not a function of prevailing political and economic conditions. Hence, it was fitting for African Americans to lead a great spiritual awakening because "a spiritual awakening can only be made by those who are spiritually awakened."[57]

However, as the evangelist Billy Graham and other Southern Baptists routinely demonstrated, white Christians were well aware of the dangers posed by materialism. The nation's dire need for Christian homes and Christian education to counter rampant materialism, shorn of relationship to any particular race's divine destiny, provided a common link between the "Every Woman's Page" of the *Union Review* and a multitude of Southern Baptist publications.

---

[54] Allen, "Editorial: The Negro's Challenge"; Alan Scot Willis, *All According to God's Plan: Southern Baptist Missions and Race, 1945–1970* (Lexington: University Press of Kentucky, 2005) 96–101.

[55] Allen, "Editorial: Day of Prayer or Day of Play," *Union Review*, 11 July 1953, 4.

[56] Allen, "Editorial: Higher Education," *Union Review*, 6 July 1957, 4.

[57] Allen, "Editorial: S. S. C., World's Greatest Need," *Union Review*, 7 April 1951, 4.

Materialism could affect the even the youngest members of a household. In one "Why, Mommy?" an advice column regularly published in *Royal Service*, the magazine of the Woman's Missionary Union of the Southern Baptist Convention. The *Union Review* reprinted Mrs. Douglas Harris's column concerning the problem of "things" on the "Every Woman's Page." She wrote about a young boy whose ambition it was to get rich and own many things, and she surmised, "The parents of this boy may talk too much about making more money so they can do the things and get the things people think they must get and do in our 1950 world." She warned, "We all have to guard against allowing things to own us instead of our owning things. There is no more destructive evil than this. It is one that will affect the entire spirit and direction of the family."[58]

Even when parents were careful, materialism invaded the home through mass media. While magazines carried advertisements, nothing threatened the home quite like television. After noting the violence involved in a Western, one writer lamented, "The next 'show' was an advertisement of beer, with a woman speaking of it as being recognized as necessary to real hospitality in every home." The children, aged seven to twelve, were watching this in a supposedly Christian home. The author worried that "our old ideas of home are being assaulted, and assaulted right in our homes."[59] Another author informed readers that advertisers had poured more than twenty billion dollars into radio and television in the thirty years prior to 1959 but added, "We wonder whether television sponsors know what they are doing to American youth" concluding that "what might be called an education in evil is now obtainable at the twirl of a knob."[60]

Parents had the primary responsibility of making sure that their children did not watch inappropriate shows or read salacious literature. However, Marceline Cutler of St. Stephen Missionary Baptist Church in Pueblo, Colorado, told readers of the *Union Review* "everyone has the responsibility of being an example for some child, whether they want it or not." She believed church leaders and members had a great responsibility to youth but worried that "we stand aloof so our youth turn elsewhere to find

---

[58] Mrs. Douglas Harris, "Why, Mommy?: Things," *Royal Service* (June 1950): 20; "Why, Mommy?" *Union Review*, 23 September 1950, 8.

[59] "The Christian Home and Television," *Union Review*, 3 October 1953, 8.

[60] "Crime in Your Parlor," *Union Review*, 14 March 1959, 7.

the love, leadership and compassion that they should receive from us. Some turn to television and radio and there adopt for themselves great leading unscrupulous characters with no true morals." Reflecting the widespread fear of skyrocketing juvenile delinquency, she concluded, "Making delinquents is easy! It's done every day in our homes."[61] For Baptists like Cutler, truly Christian homes were the answer to the nation's delinquency problem, and delinquent parents were far more to blame than their children.

Teenagers presented a particular problem. Many of them had money of their own, demanded space and privacy in their own rooms, encountered broad-based advertising, and purchased things their parents might not approve of, or even know of. The *Union Review* offered a report from a Youth for Christ International convention where Robert A. Cook called the teenage generation "moral morons" who were "sapped by materialism and humanism." Cook, a graduate of Eastern Baptist Seminary and widely known author and radio minister, had co-founded Youth for Christ with Billy Graham in 1948. In 1957, he was in his last year as the organization's president. He placed the problem of materialism squarely in the context of the Cold War, claiming, "Our young people grab milkshakes, pizzas, and hamburgers and develop into Fourth of July Christians while [the] Communists are playing for keeps." While the symptom was teenage behavior, the root of the problem was the parents: "A failure to practice Christian stewardship on the part of parents and a failure to teach Christian stewardship to children has ushered in a materialistic way of life."[62] Proper stewardship could best be taught in Christian homes.

Birthdays had become materialist celebrations centered in the home itself. Birthday parties had become, in the words of Elizabeth Ward, "A method of keeping ahead of the Joneses." Ward recognized that parents wanted their children to have "every advantage" but doubted that an "Orgy

---

[61] Marceline Cutler, "How to Make Delinquents," *Union Review*, 23 August 1958, 7.

[62] Jason Reid, "'My Room! Private! Keep Out! This Means You!': A Brief Overview of the Emergence of the Autonomous Teen Bedroom in Post-World War II America," *Journal of the History of Childhood and Youth* 5.3 (Fall 2012): 419–43; "The Teen-Age Generation," *Union Review*, 21 September 1957, 7; Alfonso A. Naraez, "Rev. Robert Cook, Author, Dies at 78; Led King's College," *New York Times*, 16 March 1991, http://www.nytimes.com/1991/03/16/obituaries/rev-robert-cook-author-dies-at-78-led-king-s-college.html?pagewanted=1.

of rivalry, ambitious entertaining, and ostentatious dressing for youngsters" actually counted as an advantage. Over time, she worried, "children learn to expect presents which is not necessarily a wholesome ambition, and one that may grow worse as the child grows older. It fosters a selfish attitude that stresses the gift rather than spirit of giving." Children learned to value superficial pleasures, just as Cooke had warned.[63] Ward's concerns also echoed M. C. Allen's analysis of the world, but without the racial overtones. For Allen, the selfishness and desire to stay ahead of the "Joneses" translated, on a world and racial scale, into a quest for the material and political domination of the world, exactly what he saw as the great sins of white civilization.

If birthdays were problematic, Christmas was worse because the fundamentally Christian message of the day was lost. In a "playlet" designed for the Juniors in the National Baptist Young People's Union, one character—Sue—summed up the materialist temptations of Christmas, saying "I don't get nearly as many presents as I give. Next year I'm not going to spend all of my money on my friends. I'm going to keep some to buy something I want." Her sister, Joan, added "I got so many things that I already have. It seems silly to me to exchange presents and give someone something that you want yourself." The children's mother reminded them that Jesus had said it is more blessed to give than to receive and Sue admitted, "I guess I am ashamed, but I was disappointed too." Still, the mother's reminder was too weak of a response to the materialism-infected Christmas celebration her family was having. Luckily, the brother—John— had learned about the true meaning of Christmas from his Sunday school teacher and reminded them about keeping Christmas the right way. While the family talked about the ways they would keep Christmas the next year, John reminded them it was not too late to salvage the current Christmas: "While everyone is deciding how you are going to keep Christmas right next year, why can't we go to the special Christmas service in Training Union tonight." The family agreed. The story ends there, but the reader is led to believe that the family attended the service.[64]

---

[63] Elizabeth Ward, "Better Than Birthday Parties," *Union Review*, 21 January 1950, 8.

[64] "Bethlehem, U. S. A.," *The Junior B. Y. P. U. Magazine Quarterly* 34.4 (1955): 27–29.

The common ground provided by National Baptist and Southern Baptist concerns about materialism laid bare a fundamental paradox in Cold War America: The material comforts afforded by a booming economy demonstrated capitalisms economic superiority over communism while it created the abundance of material comforts which eroded America's spiritual superiority over communism. For M. C. Allen, African Americans held the key to solving the paradox. Naturally spiritual rather than materialistic, African Americans could save America from itself and, hence, from the Communists as well: African Americans could—indeed, would—return America to its spiritual moorings. The National Baptists certainly believed it was important to start with the youth, and Christmas offered a splendid opportunity to capitalize on the spiritual inclinations of African American Baptist youth.

Several examples were at hand. In one case, the young woman in the missionary society at Mount Olive Baptist Church in Nashville sent Christmas boxes to missions in the Bahamas and Panama.[65] Another Junior Department began a tradition of visiting the sick and shut-ins at Christmas time, but then extended the event to Easter and finally to regular visitations throughout the year. The importance of such a program, begun for Christmas, could hardly be overestimated because "as they [the members] move into the Intermediate Department they do not forget the rich experience that was theirs during the few years in the Junior Department. Even though attitudes may now undergo a severe change, they will never quite escape from the memory of the respect and thoughtfulness they had for the aged and infirm."[66] Just as the materialist lessons of poorly spent birthdays and Christmases would haunt youth into their adulthood, so to would the benefits of well-spent time follow them into their later years.

As important as their experiences in church organizations might be, the battle against materialism would have to be won in Christian homes. Alma Robinson Higbee offered her suggestions for the NBCA's "Mother's Unions," noting that "the child who is privileged to grow up in a Christian home where a family altar is maintained will learn early in life the true value

---

[65] "Ruthite Missionary Society Sends Christmas Boxes," *Union Review*, 2 December 1950, 8.

[66] "Teaching Juniors to Love and Help Old Folks and Shut-Ins," *Union Review*, 6 June 1959, 7.

of prayer. He will know the meaning of consecration. He will not only depend upon his Heavenly Father in all things but will learn early to give of his own time and talents in the Master's service." The family altar, a time set aside for the family to worship as a unit, formed the cornerstone of a Christian home. Higbee wrote, "The smallest child in the family will understand the close unity of this family gathering, the memory of that hour in which he is closer to his Lord and Saviour through prayer will go with him into the mature years of life, lifting and sustaining him in every trial."[67]

The family altar and the Christian home, however, influenced far more than individual youth. In a semi-anonymous article, A. D. R. offered Baptists a New Year's Resolution in 1952, stressing the importance of the family altar, saying "this is not only a source of strength for the family and individual, but the keynote to Christian civilization and our country's strength."[68] While some scholars, notably Audrey Lawson Brown, have suggested that African American family patterns were more matrifocal and involved having children live with grandparents to be "raised up" in the Baptist churches, virtually every discussion of the Christian home in the *Union Review* during the 1950s reflected exactly the ideals of the Christian home presented in Southern Baptist materials of the decade.[69]

Reflecting a broad Christian concern with the decline of Christian homes, R. W. Powe of the Sweet Pilgrim Sunday School, told a gathering of NBCA young people in Hattiesburg, Mississippi, that "the revival society most needs today is the revival of the Christian home," virtually the exact words of Southern Baptist missionary leader H. Cornell Goerner. Tying the home to materialism, Powe said, "The interest of the home is more important than the interest of trade. We have sold out to the lowest bidder.

---

[67] Alma Robinson Higbee, "Suggestions For Mother's Unions: For the Citizens of Tomorrow A Family Altar in Every Home," *Union Review*, 1 April 1950, 8; Sandra Burr and Alan Scot Willis, "Policing Parents: Children's Moral Vigilance in Southern Baptist Instructional Literature, 1945–1963," *Interjuli: Internationale Kinder-und-Jugend-literaturforschung* 2 (2012): 59–73; See also, Joe W. Burton, "When Do Christian Homes Begin," *Union Review*, 30 September 1950, 8.

[68] A. D. R., "Resolved: The Family Altar," *Union Review*, 5 January 1952, 8.

[69] Audrey Lawson Brown, "Afro-Baptist Women's Church and Family Roles: Transmitting Afrocentric Cultural Values," *Anthropology Quarterly* 67.4 (October 1994): 173–86; Burr and Willis, "Policing Parents," in Willis, ed., *All According to God's Plan*, 107–9.

When we sacrifice home joy and sanctities for the many goods, this is what the many are doing. They are money mad." Powe, then, seemed to reject the relationship between a materially comfortable home and the joys of home life, a staple of Cold War idealization of American homes.[70]

For Powe, the issue impinged on the question of race. He noted, "The sanctity of the home is more important than all of the questions which center in the latest schemes of racial integrity." Powe believed

> we are fighting some great battles for human rights here in America. We must have leaders who possess courage and strength to stand against the evil of life, and citizens whose ideals are high and clean, and who place the moral welfare of society above party, schemes, or private gain. For the making of such leaders and citizens we must have Christian homes. No nation is better than the homes of its people.

For Powe and Higbee, then, redemption from materialism would rise from the Christian home, and institution that transcended race, significantly differentiating their views from M. C. Allen's race-conscious assessment of African American spiritual superiority.[71]

If the Christian home stood as a Christian, but not racial, bulwark against the materialism corrupting civilization, then Christian spiritual education, as M. C. Allen described it, was a specifically race-conscious antidote to the same poison. Allen believed that the world had tried political, scholastic, materialist, and militarist education but that no nation had ever had a genuinely spiritual education. Indeed, the dominant "secular education with a materialistic interpretation of the whole meaning of life is **miseducation** [emphasis in original]." While the idea of Christian spiritual education could have transcended race, Allen's vision drew on his belief in the natural spirituality of African peoples. He announced that "the African by nature is qualified to give to the world a new brand of philosophy of education—spiritual emphasis education." For Allen, the necessity of a spiritual emphasis in education was clear. Jesus of Nazareth had emphasized a spiritual, not material, Kingdom; as a result, a spiritual emphasis in education "enables men to commit acts of God." Somewhat circularly, those

---

[70] "Reverend Powe Delivers Message," *Union Review*, 19 September 1953, 1, 4; Willis, *All According to God's Plan*, 107–9.

[71] "Reverend Powe Delivers Message," *Union Review*, 19 September 1953, 1, 4.

acts of God enabled by a spiritual emphasis in education were "required to maintain spiritual emphasis education in this age of militarism and materialism."[72]

Allen attended, taught at, and eventually led a seminary and college that had been born of a declaration of independence from outside influences. As Virginia and the entire South struggled with the implications of *Brown vs. the Board of Education,* Allen declared, "Education by the state or the rich is undemocratic and both economically and morally unsound." Indeed, Allen had long argued that private education was a key to independent education for African Americans. Although Allen cast the problem in economic rather than racial terms, the long trajectory of his analysis made clear the racial implications of his claim. The racial implications were clear, too, as the editorial appeared at the end of the 1957 school year, a year marked by massive resistance to the *Brown* decision throughout the South and, most conspicuously, in Virginia.[73]

Allen fervently believed that Black spiritual superiority was the key to a spiritual emphasis in education. Both his racial ideology and as his understanding of economic power underpinned his claim that "An education system with a spiritual emphasis in the development of the student's potential mental and moral resources, would disqualify the rich from setting themselves up as idol gods for those who are economically poor to bow down and worship their capitalistic charity in education." Allen believed that a spiritual emphasis in education, coupled with the ideas of "self-help" and "spiritual independence"—ideals he believed institutions like Virginia Seminary embodied—"are ideas that grab the creative energies of the student with the GRIP OF GOD. It is as mental serum of inspiration that makes students hate ease, gifts—charity. It makes men choose to die for WHAT IS NOT or the things that OUGHT TO BE, rather than to have

---

[72] Allen, "Education: An Evolution," *Union Review*, 14 October 1950, 4; Allen, "Editorial: Spiritual Emphasis Education."

[73] "Virginia's 'Massive Resistance' Laws Declared Unconstitutional"; Allen, "Editorial: President Prince: Symbol of Progress"; Douglas Smith, "'When Reason Collides with Prejudice': Armistead Lloyd Boothe and the Politics of Desegregation in Virginia, 1948–1963," *The Virginia Magazine of History and Biography* 102.1 (January 1994): 5–46, http://www.jstor.org/stable/4249409.

all that is, as acts of charity from those who BOSS WITH MAMMON [emphasis in original]."[74]

Black education, Allen contended, was spiritually superior. It was also free of racial prejudice. Indeed, after centuries of slavery and segregation, "The Negro has to his credit the clearest record of non-prejudiced leadership of any racial group in America." Whites, with their supposed superiority, had succumbed to the stupidity of prejudice. Blacks had not, and therefore could claim leadership in the democracy. Allen explained, "The fundamentals of a culture or a democracy are the home, church, education, and business. Negro leadership is without race prejudice in either, or all, of these fundamentals." Blacks had not kept whites out of their schools, their churches, or their businesses. Hence, "Any honest student of American history must admit that American Negro Leadership is genuine."[75]

Genuine and heroic Black leadership grounded in the Black religious experience rose to the fore in the 1950s, but rarely did those leaders mirror the Christian Afrocentrism espoused by M. C. Allen in the *Union Review,* the official organ of the NBCA. Allen's editorials, and the stories and columns of the "Every Woman's Page" both provided a mechanism for making sense of the problems faced by black Christians in the 1950s. Ultimately, they offered fundamentally Christian solutions—education with a spiritual emphasis, Christian homes centered on a family altar, and a broad refocusing on spiritual life in place of the materialism and militarism that had so corrupted civilization and led to war after war. Both stressed the urgency of the social problems facing the nation and demanded a Christian solution.

M. C. Allen's interpretation was thoroughly race-conscious, whereas the message for women and children was virtually race-neutral. These apparently contradictory voices appeared but a few pages from each other in the *Union Review.* Both engaged, as Sandra L. Barnes suggests of the black church more broadly, the religious symbols and vocabulary that helped congregants by providing "meaning and clarity for historical events such as slavery and present day discrimination and poverty as well as possible

---

[74] Allen, "Editorial: Higher Education."

[75] Allen, "American Negro Leadership," *Nashville Globe and Independent,* 2 July 1954.

avenues for collective redress."[76] While the message found on the "Every Woman's Page" appears to have had a broader, mainstream audience, M. C. Allen found in history and religion a message of uplift based on black racial superiority; African Americans, however downtrodden they might feel in the world, were superior in the spiritual realm, and their spiritual superiority would be the salvation of the nation. Allen's view, imbued with the symbolism and language of evangelical Christianity, anticipated the academic Afrocentrism that followed two decades later. African Americans might be downtrodden and poor, Allen argued, but: "We must get a new perspective on life and historical forces. The virile forces come not from the mansion but from the hut. The Saviour of Mankind was not born in a castle but a stable!"[77]

---

[76] Sandra L. Barnes, "Black Church Culture and Community Action," *Social Forces* 84.2 (December 2005): 969, http://muse.jhu.edu/journals/social_forces/v084/84.2barnes.html.

[77] Allen, "Editorial: The Negro's Challenge."

7

"Living in the Face of Death":
Prathia Hall in Southwest Georgia

Courtney Pace Lyons

Rev. Dr. Prathia Laura Ann Hall was an important figure in the civil rights movement with the Student Nonviolent Coordinating Committee (SNCC) and became a highly significant Baptist minister. Although scholarship has tried to address the relative silence on women in the Civil Rights Movement, most narratives of the Movement revolve around its male leaders. Literature on religious leaders in the Movement is no different. Prathia Hall was a considerable religious leader of the movement in her own right, and her story sheds light on the important role that female religious and community leaders played.[1]

Raised in North Philadelphia, Hall assisted her father, Rev. Berkeley Hall, in his social gospel-oriented church ministry. Her father was her primary spiritual and intellectual mentor. Having attended predominantly white schools, Hall first experienced Jim Crow segregation at age five when traveling south to visit her grandmother, and it galvanized her commitment to racial justice. She was involved with Fellowship House, a Philadelphia social justice organization for youth and college students, where she studied the philosophy of non-violence. After her father's death in 1960, Hall became a leader in the SNCC's work in Southwest Georgia (SWGA), Selma, and Mississippi Freedom Summer. When King visited Albany in

---

[1] Even as civil rights historians have transitioned their focus beyond Martin Luther King, Jr., to include groups like SNCC, only in the past two decades have scholars published widely on women in the Civil Rights Movement. For a list of the most relevant titles, refer to *Further Reading* at the end of this chapter. Even with the depth of current scholarship on the Civil Rights Movement, SNCC, and women in the movement, most of which mention Hall's name, however, the most significant/extensive scholarship of Prathia Hall is Courtney Pace Lyons, "'Freedom Faith': The Civil Rights Journey of Rev. Dr. Prathia Hall" (PhD diss., Baylor University, 2014).

1962 after several church burnings, Hall reportedly used the phrase "I have a dream" in a prayer service; he so admired her preaching that he described her as "the one platform speaker I would prefer not to follow."[2]

This chapter will focus on Hall's work in SWGA, describing her as a religious leader and highlighting the importance of women in the success of local movements. When asked about the complexity of the civil rights

---

[2] Beverly Jackson, series producer, "Prathia Hall," *This Far by Faith*, http://www.pbs.org/thisfarbyfaith/people/prathia_hall.html (accessed 23 January 2014). For more on Hall as the originator of "I have a dream," see Pace Lyons, "Freedom Faith." Hall resigned from SNCC in 1966 because of rising militancy in the organization. Hall's experiences in the movement helped her discern and confirm her call to womanist preaching and religious education. Hall became one of the first African American Baptist women to be ordained by the American Baptist Churches USA (1977) and was the first woman accepted into the Baptist Minister Conference of Philadelphia and Vicinity (1982). She completed her MDiv (1982), ThM (1984), and PhD (1997) degrees at Princeton Theological Seminary, and she taught womanist theology, Christian ethics, and African American church history. She served as Associate Dean of Spiritual and Community Life, Director of the Harriett L. Miller Women's Center, and Dean of African American Ministries at United Theological Seminary in Dayton, Ohio (1989-1998) and held the Martin Luther King, Jr., Chair in Social Ethics at Boston University School of Theology (2000-2002). In 1997, *Ebony* magazine named her first in its list of "15 Greatest Black Women Preachers," and she was the only woman considered for its list of "10 Greatest Black Preachers," ultimately placing eleventh. In 1999, the International Theological Center in Atlanta awarded her its annual Womanist Scholar Award. She pastored Mt. Sharon Baptist Church in Philadelphia, her father's church, for nearly a quarter century. She mentored more than two hundred African American clergy women, and there is a prominent blog for African American clergywomen named "Prathia's Daughters." See "Episode Four: Freedom Faith," *This Far By Faith*, PBS, 2002; Roger Fritts, "The Most Famous American Sermon of the 20th Century" (sermon given at Cedar Lane Unitarian Universalist Church, Bethesda, MD, 13 January 2002), http://www.cedarlane.org/02serms/s020113.html (accessed 29 September 2008); Jim Haskins and Kathleen Benson, *Black Stars: African American Religious Leaders* (San Francisco: John Wiley & Sons, 2008); "WPS Scholars—Dr. Prathia Hall," Interdenominational Theological Center, http://www.itc.edu/pages/wsp/WSPDrHall.htm (accessed 29 September 2008); "15 Greatest Black Women Preachers: Experts and Leading Blacks Name Select Group of Ministers." *Ebony* (November 1997), http://www.prathiasdaughtersvoices.ning.com (accessed 23 January 2014).

movement, Hall replied: "The movement was so much more than Dr. King ... It was largely women."[3]

SNCC, SCLC, and the Albany Movement

SNCC, created in 1960 at Shaw University in Raleigh, North Carolina, organized voter registration and non-violent direct action in conjunction with local activists and organizations. Whereas Martin Luther King, Jr.'s Southern Christian Leadership Conference (SCLC) typically led short-term campaigns, SNCC students moved into communities for long-term voter registration drives in the "Black Belt": former plantation rural counties in which African Americans outnumbered whites and where most (white) congressmen had had great power from long tenures in office. The organization recognized that if African Americans could vote senior congressmen out of office, they could very quickly change the dynamic of Congress and its committees.[4]

On 17 November 1961, the Albany Movement in SWGA officially formed the cooperative effort between the local Baptist Ministers' Alliance, Federated Women's Clubs, Lincoln Heights Improvement Association, NAACP Youth Council, SNCC, Albany State University students, and other local supporters, including several Albany gang members.[5] Albany

---

[3] Rhiannon Varmette, *(Boston) Daily Free Press*, 16 January 2001.

[4] Charles McDew, interview by Courtney Pace Lyons, 3 June 2011, in Albany, GA, compact disc, Institute for Oral History, Baylor University, Waco, TX. See also "Southwest Georgia Voter-Registration Project," undated, Student Nonviolent Coordinating Committee (v.s.) Papers, 1959–1972, Sanford, N.O.: Microfilming Corp. of America, 1982 (hereafter SNCC Papers), reel 8, Martin Luther King Jr. Center for Nonviolent Social Change, Atlanta, microfilm.

[5] Faith Holsaert, and others, *Hands on the Freedom Plow: Personal Accounts by Women in SNCC* (Chicago: University of Illinois, 2010) 85; "Method of Revolution," undated, SNCC Papers, reel 8; Annette Jones White, "Expression of My Discontent," in *Hands on the Freedom Plow*, 116; Peter DeLissovoy, interviewed by Courtney Pace Lyons, 16 April 2010, in Raleigh, NC, compact disc, Institute for Oral History, Baylor University, Waco, TX. Sherrod compared the Albany project to Ezekiel's wheel within a wheel. Albany was the center, organizing work in surrounding counties: "Together, hub and spokes drove the wheel." Faith Holsaert, "Resistance U," in *Hands on the Freedom Plow*, 186; Howard Zinn, "Albany," 8 January 1962, SNCC Papers, reel 19. According to a SNCC survey of African Americans in Terrell County, the average African American family earned less than

became the first massive African American "uprising" since Montgomery in 1955. Most importantly, Albany confirmed the reluctance of the federal government "to protect constitutional rights in the Deep South," demonstrated through the mass arrests and the repeated failure of the government to intervene to protect civil rights workers.[6] SCLC left Albany by late August 1962 after white city leaders refused to negotiate with civil rights workers and persisted in their segregation arrests using only the language of maintaining peace and public order.[7]

Prathia Hall Joins SNCC

In 1962, Prathia Hall told her mother, Ruby, that she wanted to join SNCC's work in the South. In Hall's second week in Atlanta, she was recruited to work with Charles Sherrod, the leader of SNCC's project in SWGA, based in Albany.[8] For Hall and others, the Albany Movement prioritized voter registration over direct action, as "We soon discovered that [lunch counter desegregation] was not where it was at. Then we went into the Black Belt with voter registration. The people there couldn't eat at lunch counters because they were only making twenty-three cents an hour. That was where it was at."[9]

---

one fourth of the average white household income, and less than one-fifth of the national household income. Twenty-five percent of African Americans had no more than a sixth-grade education. In 1960, African Americans composed 64.4 percent of the population of Terrell County yet represented only 0.04% of voters. See "In 'Terrible' Terrell: Night Riders Shoot Worker," *The Student Voice* 4.7 (December 1963), quoted in Clayborne Carson (Ed). *The Student Voice, 1960–1965: Periodicals of the Student Nonviolent Coordinating Committee* (Westport, CT; London: Meckler, 1990) 87, 89.

[6] Howard Zinn, *SNCC: The New Abolitionists* (Cambridge: South End Press, 2002) 123.

[7] Claude Sitton, "Albany, Ga., Police Break Up Protest by 2,000 Negroes," *New York Times*, 25 July 1962.

[8] The 1960s civil rights project of SNCC in Albany is most commonly called "The Albany Movement." The SWGA Project is a larger name to the multi-decade initiative in Albany and surrounding areas to promote racial and economic equality. To this day, Charles Sherrod continues to direct the SWGA Project in Albany.

[9] Guy and Candie Carawan, *Sing for Freedom: The Story of the Civil Rights Movement through its Songs* (Montgomery, AL: New South Books, 2007) 176.

To head this effort, SNCC field secretaries canvassed door-to-door to talk with locals about registering to vote, building trust, and acknowledging the physical, social, and economic consequences for attempting to register. With time, Hall noted that "After several visits, the fearful and the skeptical usually allowed us to come in or to sit on their porches and visit. The topic of the imminent danger soon made its way into the conversation. They told us of people who had 'just come up missing' or had been found floating in the river after some minor assertion of personhood or an infraction such as trying to register to vote."[10] In addition, Hall appreciated the "two-way educational exchange" of voter registration canvassing:

> We spent long hours on those porches. It took a long time. You didn't just walk up to somebody and convince them to register to vote and take their life in their hands. And so you talk to a person sometimes two weeks before you had permission, the time was right even to broach the subject. But during that time, we had the information about political empowerment, voter registration, literacy ... They had the wisdom of the ages. And that's what we received. And this was especially true in my experience in Southwest Georgia.[11]

Those who feared voter registration, or even association with SNCC workers, understood the "entrenched white supremacy backed up by violence" that ruled SWGA.[12] Since whites controlled most African Americans' employment, housing, and utility infrastructure, registering to vote could mean losing one's job, personal property, or home.[13] SNCC

---

[10] Prathia Hall, "Freedom-Faith," in *Hands on the Freedom Plow: Personal Accounts by Women in SNCC* (Chicago: University of Illinois, 2010) 175.

[11] Prathia Hall, interview by Sheila Michaels, 25 February 1999, Title no. 12458, Film and Media Archive, Washington University, St. Louis, MO.

[12] Stephen Tuck, *Beyond Atlanta: The Struggle for Racial Equality in Georgia, 1940–1980* (Athens: University of Georgia Press, 2001) 163.

[13] Those who mustered the courage to register to vote typically found excessive constraints arbitrarily imposed by voting clerks. Since the law permitted African Americans to vote, cities and counties created their own barriers. Voting officials often charged exorbitant poll taxes or required voters to pass difficult exams in American history. Many elongated the process by requiring a two-week waiting period between registration and eligibility to vote, during which time the names of all who registered to vote were printed in the newspaper. To circumvent these intimidation tactics, SNCC implemented freedom schools to help people pass voter registration exams. Since

workers, too, were taking their lives in their hands to live interracially and promote civil rights.[14]

When Hall arrived in Albany in late summer 1962, she and Sherrod became kindred spirits almost instantly.[15] Their shared commitments to social justice, education, and Christian leadership helped them form a strong bond, which Sherrod described as "closer than boy and girl friend."[16] Carolyn Daniels remembered their special connection: "Sherrod was a minister. And the two of them could communicate, you know. So they would always be, you know, doing their little thing."[17] "She was a beautiful person, in more than one way," Sherrod explained of Hall's leadership: "She was smart. She could write. She was tactical."[18]

Although Sherrod was the primary leader of the SWGA project, Hall played a vital role. When Sherrod was out of town, which was somewhat often by 1963, Hall was in charge. Sherrod trusted her implicitly and later reflected, "I can think of nobody who didn't respect Prathia Hall."[19] Although some of the SWGA staff had tension at times with Sherrod, Hall was widely respected.[20] True to her nature, however, when SNCC veteran Sheila Michaels mentioned Hall's reputation of being a co-leader with Sherrod, Hall modestly responded: "Really? I didn't think that. I didn't

---

sharecroppers had to meet daily quotas, many SNCC workers helped sharecroppers in the field to meet their quotas so that they could attend evening meetings.

[14] Fred Powledge, *Free At Last?: The Civil Rights Movement and the People Who Made It* (Boston: Little, Brown and Co., 1991) 343-4.

[15] Faith Holsaert, interview by Courtney Pace Lyons, 19 May 2010, compact disc, Institute for Oral History, Baylor University, Waco, TX.

[16] Charles Sherrod, interview by Courtney Pace Lyons, 16 April 2010, in Raleigh, NC, compact disc, Institute for Oral History, Baylor University, Waco, TX.

[17] Carolyn Daniels, interview by Courtney Pace Lyons, 24 May 2010, in Atlanta, GA, compact disc, Institute for Oral History, Baylor University, Waco, TX.

[18] Sherrod, interview by Lyons.

[19] Sherrod, interview by Lyons.

[20] Faith Holsaert, "Staff Relationships or Personnel Politics," undated, SNCC Papers, reel 6; particularly as the SWGA project expanded into Lee, Terrell, Sumter, and other counties, SNCC workers in those counties had strong disagreements with Sherrod's strategy and leadership style.

know that."[21] Similarly, at Ella Baker's funeral, a male SNCC colleague told Hall, "We would have followed you anywhere you told us to go. That's how we respected you." Hall laughed and said, "Had I only known!"[22] These testimonies reflect her significance, as her name often appeared before or adjacent to Sherrod's in SNCC correspondence.[23]

Hall spoke often in mass meetings, and Sherrod frequently selected Hall to speak on behalf of the SWGA project and for fundraising. "She spoke well," Sherrod noted, "She went to talk with people well. She recruited other students to work with us very well. She did everything well. She was a great speaker. Little known to the world, she would awe Martin Luther King, Jr. down there in Southwest Georgia she spoke so well."[24]

In interviews with Hall's SNCC colleagues, more often than not, the first thing interviewees mentioned was amazement at her preaching, that she had a captivating "presence" about her and was a "powerful" speaker, even at twenty-two. Even those who were not religious relayed feeling spiritual stirrings around her, that something about her oration and demeanor invited them into God's presence. Faith Holsaert, from a nominally Jewish family, was "blown away" by Hall's preaching, "of a caliber and intensity and seriousness comparable" to prominent speakers like King. SNCC secretary Judy Richardson recalled transcribing one of Hall's sermons: "She was so powerful, even from this little tape recorder, that I started crying ... The tears started just dripping down my face ... It's an image that I will always have ... And I am not churched, so for Prathia to get to me meant a whole

---

[21] Hall, interview by Michaels.

[22] Prathia Hall, interview by Barbara Ransby, 25 June 1997, in Denver, CO, Prathia Hall Papers (Prathia Hall's papers are privately held; hereafter cited as "Hall's Papers"); Vincent Harding listed Prathia Hall with Bob Moses, Charles Sherrod, and Bob Zellner as leaders of the modern civil rights movement who were inspiring and empowering thousands to realize their capability to change the world. Vincent Harding, *Hope and History: Why We Must Share the Story of the Movement* (Maryknoll, NY: Orbis,1999) 74.

[23] Mary King to Burrelle's Press Clipping Bureau, 6 November 1963, SNCC Papers, reel 5; Barbara Ransby, *Ella Baker and the Black Freedom Movement: A Radical Democratic Vision* (Chapel Hill: University of North Carolina Press, 2002) 345–6.

[24] Sherrod, interview by Lyons.

lot." She described Hall as "a woman who could absolutely magnetize a mass meeting ... such a command of the language."[25]

Peggy Dammond Preacely saw Hall as a pastor even before Hall realized her calling; Preacely immediately recognized Hall's spiritual leadership and felt that the SNCC team "were a part of her early ministry."[26] Sherrod heartily agreed that Hall was "already a minister. She knew more Scripture than I did."[27] Additionally, SNCC historian Wesley Hogan described Hall as "one of the Movement's most powerful young preachers" and listed her with Lawson, King, and Sherrod as leaders of the African American church in the 1960s.[28]

Holsaert wrote the following anecdote: "[Sherrod] selected a female staff member, Prathia Hall, the daughter of a minister, to preach at the Albany Movement's first anniversary program, a night when Dr. King spoke from the same pulpit. I was bowled over by Prathia—I had not imaged a young woman my age could possess such oratorical power."[29]

Mary King was particularly taken by Hall's preaching, the pacing of her words, her imagery, and her "grasp of words and their emotive power." King recalled SNCC's respect for Hall's preaching: "In SNCC, we were not interested in hierarchies, but in authenticity. So Prathia was completely accepted. And whenever she would rise to speak, everybody gave her rapt attention. She was a riveting speaker. And nobody ever would talk, whisper, or cough while she was talking. She had such a strong, powerful presence."[30]

Bob Zellner recognized Hall's commitment to Christian non-violence and her spiritual maturity gave her rapport with King and other ministers: "[King] was actually captivated in some ways by Prathia, because she was a

---

[25] Judy Richardson, interview by Courtney Pace Lyons, 30 April 2010, compact disc, Institute for Oral History, Baylor University, Waco, TX.

[26] Peggy Dammond Preacely, interview by Courtney Pace Lyons, 16 April 2010, in Raleigh, NC, compact disc, Institute for Oral History, Baylor University, Waco, TX.

[27] Sherrod, interview by Lyons.

[28] Wesley Hogan, *Many Minds, One Heart: SNCC's Dream for a New America* (Chapel Hill: University of North Carolina Press, 2007) 73, 229.

[29] Faith Holsaert, "Resistance U," in *Hands on the Freedom Plow: Personal Accounts by Women in SNCC* (Chicago: University of Illinois, 2010) 187.

[30] Mary King, interview by Courtney Pace Lyons, 15 April 2010, in Raleigh, NC, compact disc, Institute for Oral History, Baylor University, Waco, TX.

woman with a voice, a woman with great power and presence. And he couldn't help but be admiring of her ability as a communicator, even as a preacher." Zellner believed that King "learned a great deal from Prathia" about preaching.[31] Wyatt Tee Walker believed King connected with Hall because of her maturity and wisdom.[32] Hall "was like a female Dr. King, because she had such a prayerful and statuesque way of standing and being," commented Preacely. "She had a calmness about her, but she also had a fire. And when she spoke, you listened, because she had a wonderful speaking voice."[33]

Holsaert found Hall "extremely generous" and noted that although Hall was raised by a "race man," she never felt any barriers in friendship with Hall. Holsaert also appreciated Hall's leadership in taking them to church every Sunday and guiding them in the mores of Southern culture: "We should wear [stockings] … and iron your clothes for Sunday church, et cetera."[34]

Julian Bond, later a twenty-year Georgia congressman and chairman of the NAACP, found Hall's wisdom remarkable and characterized her as "a young Ella Baker."[35] Mary King also compared Hall to Baker because of Hall's "paying close attention to what community people felt, attuned to unarticulated yearning."[36] Larry Rubin, who previously met Hall through Fellowship House in Philadelphia, appreciated that "she was able to communicate with local people very, very well" and that she carried a principled commitment to non-violence for life.[37]

---

[31] Bob Zellner, interview by Courtney Pace Lyons, 15 April 2011, in Raleigh, NC, compact disc, Institute for Oral History, Baylor University, Waco, TX.

[32] Wyatt Tee Walker, interview by Courtney Pace Lyons, 1 May 2012, in Waco, TX, compact disc, Institute for Oral History, Baylor University, Waco, TX.

[33] Preacely, interview by Pace Lyons.

[34] Holsaert, interview by Pace Lyons.

[35] Julian Bond, interview by Courtney Pace Lyons, 3 May 2010, compact disc, Institute for Oral History, Baylor University, Waco, TX; Hall saw herself in Ella Baker as well, though she was extremely modest in making this comparison. She admired Baker's leadership and courage: "I was a wandering pilgrim trying to find my identity … I would find myself in her." See Ransby, *Ella Baker & the Black Freedom Movement*, 258.

[36] King, interview by Lyons.

[37] Larry Rubin, interview by Courtney Pace Lyons, 18 November 2010, compact disc, Institute for Oral History, Baylor University, Waco, TX.

Chuck McDew noted Hall's hospitality: "She didn't make people feel that they were talking to a minister. She was not at all prudish." He was impressed by her ability to overcome social barriers: "These people here, and people in Georgia, would not see Prathia as being other than another good sister who was a hard worker ... that we're all sitting at the same table."[38]

Similar to her hospitality, many of her colleagues noted her maternal nature, even though she was their same age.[39] Richardson agreed that Hall "seemed much more adult than some of us were."[40] Rubin echoed: "She was rather formal in the way she conducted herself ... old-fashioned, polite."[41] Barrett agreed: "She had a dignity that most people don't have. I think she was born with dignity."[42] Her strength and power made them feel safe: "Prathia had that kind of prayerful way about her that you could just kind of get under her wing."[43]

Georgia State Representative John Lewis made similar observations about Hall. "Sometimes you would see her in a meeting, during a discussion. It seemed like she would just sit in there, not saying anything, but taking it all in, just absorbing; and sometimes in a prayerful mood." He remembered her dramatic flair for captivating storytelling: "She was known for her commitment, her dedication, her stick-to-it-ness; for hanging in there, for never giving up or giving in." He noted more than once that Hall "did not speak ill will or have bad feeling toward a fellow human being." Struck by her example, Lewis noted: "She was known for not just trying to be on the scene—be there for when the cameras were around—but going into places where you didn't see a camera." Lewis saw her "without a doubt, as a leader; that she was a leader in her own right." On Hall in the SNCC executive meetings, Lewis shared: "She didn't speak a great deal, like some people ...

---

[38] McDew, interview by Lyons.

[39] Some in SNCC used to call Hall "the mother of the church" because of her deep religious convictions. Hall, interview by Ransby.

[40] Judy Richardson, interview by Courtney Pace Lyons, 30 April 2010, compact disc, Institute for Oral History, Baylor University, Waco, TX.

[41] Rubin, interview by Pace Lyons.

[42] Barrett, interview by Pace Lyons.

[43] Preacely, interview by Pace Lyons.

She didn't just run her mouth. When she spoke out or spoke up, she had something to say. And people would listen to her."[44]

Sherrod echoed: "She could sing. And she could use the King's English, and get her way. She's a great speaker … She wasn't just a great speaker in a mass meeting. She was a great speaker in our meetings as well. When she was getting her point—wanted to make her point, if what we needed to do or what we needed not to do, she was also great at doing that."[45]

Her friends and those she organized with expressed something exceptional about Hall, something difficult to articulate, that set her apart from her SNCC peers. Betty Garman Robinson said, "I was always … inspired by her presence … She had a presence that was beyond the ordinary … I don't know what the best word would be, but a very steady, strong, passionate, inspiring presence."[46] Don Harris agreed that Hall had an "extraordinary presence" of "dignity" and that she had a "sense of elegance and grace" that was "very, very clear."[47] Preacely described her as "so in charge of herself, and more assured than the rest of us."[48]

Hall was also very responsible with money. Those staying with Daniels received $30 monthly for host home expenses, which Hall stretched to feed the entire group. Daniels compared Hall to Jesus feeding the multitude with the five fish and two loaves: "That's just the way Prathia was … Whatever needed to be done, she would try to do it … She was just a leader. She was just a spiritual person. You could just feel it." Daniels also noted that Hall insisted the group say grace every time they ate and that Hall had an extremely proper, respectable mannerism; she even carried white gloves in her purse.[49]

One of the most influential aspects of Hall's leadership was her guidance in training new SNCC volunteers. Her unique background

---

[44] John Lewis, interview by Courtney Pace Lyons, 11 August 2009, in Albany, GA, compact disc, Institute for Oral History, Baylor University, Waco, TX.

[45] Sherrod, interview by Pace Lyons.

[46] Betty Garman Robinson, interview by Courtney Pace Lyons, 4 May 2010, compact disc, Institute for Oral History, Baylor University, Waco, TX.

[47] Don Harris, interview by Courtney Pace Lyons, 16 April 2010, in Raleigh, NC, compact disc, Institute for Oral History, Baylor University, Waco, TX.

[48] Preacely, interview by Pace Lyons.

[49] Daniels, interview by Pace Lyons; Preacely, interview by Lyons.

prepared her for the challenges SNCC workers faced in the rural South; she was raised in the North by parents from the South, an African American educated in predominantly white schools and familiar with the African American Baptist tradition. Hall could educate Northern white college students about the idiosyncrasies of Southern African American culture, etiquette, and propriety to help them better connect with local people. Hall set an example for how activists should conduct themselves: "Tall, gentle, and fearless, Hall effortlessly reconciled a Northern élan with Southern roots and folkways."[50] Hall had a firm grasp of the different cultures involved—North, South, African American, white, religious, non-religious—and could easily foster communication between them. She stressed the importance of behaving according to Southern social mores, and finding a healthy balance between embodying the integration of the beloved community without needlessly causing a revolution against Southern sensibilities.

Because modeling this new community involved interracial living, Sherrod and Hall demanded moral excellence from their team: "They live by a strict personal discipline ... No behavior that could even give the appearance of anything but strict morality."[51] Even the non-religious were expected to "keep the Sabbath" and attend church services.[52] Interracial teams were particularly careful about avoiding black males and white females sleeping under the same roof because of the danger this posed for the black males.[53] This was especially difficult, however, as according to Hall, "There was no way not to because the very color of your skin and living with these black people and the whole gender thing and the whole white Southern fixation on white womanhood and living with black men and all of those kinds of things placed on you restrictions of the movement."[54]

Hall realized that many of the students she trained "had never had to 'take low,' to use the idiom, for anything." Once they came South, "Now ... whatever they did they were doing with Black people, which immediately put everybody's lives at risk ... You had younger students who had to be

---

[50] Hogan, *Many Minds, One Heart*, 73.

[51] Anne Braden, "The Images are Broken: Students Challenge Rural Georgia," *The Southern Patriot* 20.10 (December 1962).

[52] Barbara Schwartzbaum, Press Release of the Student Nonviolent Coordinating Committee, Albany, Georgia, 17 July 1962, SNCC Papers, reel 19.

[53] Holsaert, "Resistance U," in *Hands on the Freedom Plow*, 186.

[54] Hall, interview by Michaels.

oriented in a hurry. And there is no way that you could give the same kind of responsibility to those people in that situation."[55] Hall's tremendous insight trained new student workers in how to survive in the rural South:

Northern people who were never told that they couldn't go anywhere, couldn't do anything, go to the bathroom they wanted to or the drinking fountain or the restaurant, were not used to any restrictions. And we were in an extraordinarily dangerous world. We were in a brutally dangerous world where especially the fact that we were racially mixed was dynamite. And I did not find those kinds of restrictions irritating.[56]

When asked about sexism within SNCC, Hall did acknowledge "tremendous sexism, chauvinism and even some misogyny among SNCC men," but said, "Even as a religious woman, I would never have had the freedom in SCLC that I had in SNCC. The difference in SNCC was that we could talk about it." She continued: "I don't believe that any men in SNCC ever disrespected me because of my gender. I never had the sense that I was not taken seriously."[57] By and large, "women felt themselves to be an important and integral part of SNCC."[58]

Reflecting later in her life, Hall described the "complicitous ... partnership" that African American women had with men. On the one hand, the dominance of male leaders and interactions with the press were examples of sexism. On the other hand, "women often went along with that,

---

[55] Prathia Hall, quoted in Belinda Robnett, *How Long? How Long? African American Women in the Struggle for Civil Rights* (New York City: Oxford University Press, 1997) 126.

[56] Hall, interview by Michaels.

[57] Ransby, interview by Hall.

[58] Hall, quoted in Robnett, *How Long? How Long?*, 111. For multiple perspectives of women in SNCC regarding gender discrimination, see *Deep in our Hearts: Nine White Women in the Freedom Movement* (Athens: University of Georgia Press, 2000) and *Hands on the Freedom Plow* (Chicago: University of Illinois Press, 2010); Prathia Hall believed that African American women had an easier time asserting themselves for leadership than white women did: "There is a sense in which our social incubator in the Black community trained and nurtured Black women to do whatever was necessary," whereas white women "came out of that whole pedestalization and trivialization of women that the southern power establishment imposed on them." Prathia Hall, quoted in Robnett, *How Long? How Long?*, 123.

feeling that it was important to our community that Black males be seen as competent, standing up and giving strong leadership. I don't think, at the same time, that women felt that taking that posture was depriving them or taking anything away from them ... At that time, there was an attitude of partnership."[59] Lewis lamented that the movement did not recognize its own discrimination against women's leadership and noted, "Prathia, if she had been a man and not a woman, people would know much more about her ... She would have been much more visible—not just within SNCC, but in the whole movement and in America."[60]

Hall was key in preparing SNCC volunteers to adapt to the psychological realities of working in the "overlay of terror and violence" in the rural South, living with the reality that "at any moment and at any time, someone could come and kill you ... If a car was heard too late at night, everybody just froze because we didn't know whether that was friend or foe."[61] Hall taught SNCC workers to manage their fear:

> We lived with the fear, we came to understand it and then our job was to work with it and to help people not to be afraid, to learn how to keep fear from paralyzing you and to take necessary action in spite of fear and that was a slow process. We worked in the fields sometimes, we sat on porches, listening and talking before the subject of voter registration was mentioned. In that process, we were learning together how to allow the yearning for

---

[59] Hall, quoted in Robnett, *How Long? How Long?*, 42–43.

[60] Lewis, interview by Lyons. In a collection of narratives from women in SNCC, *Hands on the Freedom Plow* (2010) eight women from the SWGA Project relay their experiences in the Movement, demonstrating the critical roles of support, organization, and courage. Holsaert, an editor of *Hands on the Freedom Plow*, noted that almost everyone who addressed gender treatment within SNCC reported being "treated more democratically and in a more egalitarian fashion than anywhere else in culture at that time." Martha Prescod Norman Noonan, another editor of *Hands on the Freedom Plow*, remembered a general understanding among SNCC "that there would be women in front of the press, women giving talks, women deciding strategy, philosophy.... We grew up in the era of Daisy Bates, Rosa Parks ... so it's sort of like you could be all that you could be." Annette Jones White, "Expression of My Discontent," in *Hands on the Freedom Plow*, 114; Martha Prescod Norman Noonan, interview by Courtney Pace Lyons, 3 June 2011, in Raleigh, NC, compact disc, Institute for Oral History, Baylor University, Waco, TX.

[61] Preacely, interview by Pace Lyons.

freedom which was lived so deeply, so profoundly within the being of the people to not only surface but to surround and transform the fear.[62]

During those hours, days, and weeks locked in infested jail cells, SNCC workers sang freedom songs as a practical tool for survival. Hall explained: "When fear was so real and so powerful we could taste it, we would sing those songs ... That was where the community was."[63] When jailers demanded silence, civil rights workers knew their message was getting across: "We knew we were being heard, and we could just sing louder and longer."[64]

Hall often spoke of the power of the music of the movement:

Music was a lifeline, a source, a well from which we could draw, a source of courage and strength in the face of eminent danger. With these forces of death with their guns loaded and sometimes drawn, surrounding you and taking down your name or license plate number, to be able then to sing and the relationship between the songs of the movement and the songs of the church is of one fabric, that's a continuous thread.... In the movement rallies there would be some slight variation from the old prayer meetings that ... has a different phrasing of the melody, those pregnant pauses, those are underlying, underscoring, it's almost like you're gulping for breath in the face of fear.[65]

One incident in particular struck Peter DeLissovoy about Hall's leadership respect in the SWGA community. On his second day in SWGA, the new recruits returned to the house where they were staying to find that all of their belongings had been stolen. The group immediately asked Hall and Sherrod about what to do. Hall walked up to James Daniel, an Albany gang leader who had become a major supporter of SNCC's work in SWGA, and demanded, "James, get those things back." "Within three hours James Daniel had located the bunch of thieves in the Ritz movie theater with all

---

[62] Prathia Hall, interview by Meredith Woods, 4 October 1999, Title 53 Film and Media Archive, Washington University, St. Louis, MO; Prathia Hall, quoted by Charles Wheeler, "Revealing Voices for Civil Rights," Greensboro News & Record (20 March 2011).

[63] Prathia Hall, interview by Vincent Harding, 25 June 1997, "Interview by Prathia Hall," Ghandi-Hamer-King Center, Washington, DC.

[64] Bernice Johnson Reagon, "Laid My Burden Down," in Hands on the Freedom Plow, 150.

[65] Hall, interview by Woods.

these goods, watches, sleeping bags, everything. And they were right back. Everything: typewriters, every possession was returned the same day."[66]

As Hall trained student volunteers to operate within Southern culture, she was also teaching them how to relate compassionately to the local people and to each other, to understand the multi-layered, systemic oppression of Southern African Americans, and to build relationships across these divides:

> The new community was really strange because we were black and white. We were Northern and Southern.... We had come from different places, different spaces. Some of us were very religious in our motivations. Others were very political.... But, we had a common goal, and we had a common commitment. And I think that's what kept us together. And we had a common task, which was to stay alive today.... Your differences begin to pale in the face of a need to stay alive...And we could not stay alive without depending on each other.... Just the nuances of being black and white and living together in the same houses, or walking down the street together would so enrage the local whites that we could be shot down just like that.... So we were living together and working together because of what we believed. And that took precedence over our differences.[67]

Freedom Faith in Action

Very soon after Hall arrived in Albany, she experienced police scare tactics first hand. Police raided a July mass meeting at Mount Olive Baptist Church, the second police raid on a mass meeting in two weeks. After recording plate numbers of parked cars, thirteen "hat-wearing, cigarette-smoking, tobacco-chewing" police officers burst through the door.[68] Deputy R. M. Dunaway beat his flashlight against his palm in the back of the room, and Terrell County sheriff Z.T. Mathews told a reporter: "You know, Cap, there's nothing like fear to keep niggers in line."[69]

---

[66] DeLissovoy, interview by Pace Lyons.

[67] Hall, interview by Harding.

[68] Hall, "Freedom-Faith," in *Hands on the Freedom Plow*, 178–9; Claude Sitton, "Sheriff Harasses Negroes at Voting Rally in Georgia," *New York Times*, 27 July 1962.

[69] Sitton, "Sheriff Harasses Negroes at Voting Rally in Georgia"; SNCC News Release, Sasser, Georgia, 26 July, 1962, SNCC Papers, reel 14; Zinn, *SNCC: The New Abolitionists*, 138.

Hall described the rest of the meeting: "We sang our freedom songs with defiant and prayerful fervor."[70] As the congregation began to hum "We Shall Overcome," police withdrew from the church. *New York Times'* Claude Sitton reported: "Their voices had a strident note as though they were building up their courage to go out into the night, where the whites waited."[71] As the mass meeting dismissed, Hall and others walked into a swarm of local police officers standing outside, taunting individuals with threats of terror.[72]

Amidst police brutality, Hall showed tremendous courage and a prophetic spirit. Deputy Marshall D. E. Short of Sasser arrested Roy Daniel, Hall, Ralph Allen, and Willie Paul Berrien for speeding on August 30. Short fired two shots in the air while pulling over the vehicle. Daniel challenged the speeding charge since he was only driving 30 mph when pulled over, to which Short responded: "you think you can do anything you damn well please."[73]

Hall "answered him by looking him in the eye—which was something that was forbidden, for black people to look white people in the eye—and said to him, we're talking to people about registration and you have no right to stop us."[74] She described his reaction: "He became just enraged. Changed colors, began literally foaming at the mouth,... cursed me in, with names I had, some I had never heard before or since." She later elaborated that after Short repeatedly shouted "Shut up!" he was "trembling with rage and calling me a long-haired [yellow] bitch, he pulled a gun and began firing at the ground around our feet."[75]

After emptying his gun, Short arrested all of them and held them at "this filthy little vermin-infested hold which passed for the Sasser jail.... It

---

[70] Hall, "Freedom-Faith," in *Hands on the Freedom Plow*, 178.

[71] Sitton, "Sheriff Harasses Negroes at Voting Rally in Georgia."

[72] Ibid.; Claude Sitton, "2 Negro Churches Burned in Georgia: FBI Men Attacked: Robinson Visits Site," *New York Times*, 10 September 1962.

[73] "Two Negroes," *The Aiken Standard and Review*, 10 September 1962.

[74] "Freedom Faith," *This Far By Faith*, PBS, 2002.

[75] Ibid.; National Archives File 44-HQ-20425, Federal Bureau of Investigation. Case File 44-HQ-20425, SL: 650/73/02/05, Bx. 960, National Archives at College Park, MD NARA

Case File 173-HQ-1597, SL: 230/900/33/04, Bx. 31, National Archives at College Park. MD NARA

was about three times the size of an outhouse and smelled as bad."[76] In that moment, Hall did not fear the shooting, her arrest, or being in jail. She feared "that perhaps no friendly person had seen us, and that we might be held there, and then taken out in the middle of the night, and done away with." As Deputy Short fired at her feet, Hall felt numb, which she believed was "a gift from God":

> If I had moved one muscle, I would have given him the excuse he wanted to raise the gun point blank and fire.... I believe my numbness was a gift from God that saved my life.... And that I didn't move, I know that I was held because there were other times when we had to operate out of fear.... Fear could be a very positive thing. Because for instance, fear would make you not do, not do, not, not do something stupid, you know. But in that particular incident, I wasn't operating out of fear, I wasn't operating. I was just there. By the grace of God. I was glad to stand in that vermin infested hole because I was alive. But I came very close to not being alive.[77]

Hall and her fellow SNCC field workers survived. [78]

As the four SNCC workers left from a day of registration canvassing, they "saw a great cloud of dust, a pickup truck barreling down the road." Deputy Short pulled them over, harassed them about their vehicle registration and license plates, and demanded that the workers leave town.[79] As Allen drove away, Hall recounted that "[Short] chased three of us out of town by firing gunshots at our car and threatening to fill us full of lead and put us all in the cemetery." As they reached the edge of town, Short shouted from his car

---

[76] Ibid.

[77] "S. W. Georgia Voter Program Continues Despite Legal Losses," *The Student Voice* 4.1 (April 1963) quoted in *The Student Voice*, 66; Hall, interview by Harding.

[78] "Two Negroes," *The Aiken Standard and Review*, 10 September 1962; Hall, *Hands on the Freedom Plow*, 177; National Archives File #44-HQ-20425 (see note 75).

[79] National Archives File #44-HQ-20425 (see note 75); UPI, "Victims Pushed Voter Registration: Terrell Marshal Charged with Rights 'Violations,'" *Atlanta Daily World*, 4 January 1963, SNCC Papers, Reel 37; (AP) "U.S. Accuses Sasser Officer of Harassing in Racial Case," *The Atlanta Constitution* January 4, 1963, SNCC Papers, reel 37.

window, "Get out and stay out" and fired a warning shot into the ground.[80] Hall's discernment of Short helped her survive his brutality against them: "That was another one of those moments when you look death in the face and you also look at the enemy, which is that evil, and the victim who is the bearer of that evil, in the face, and it takes care of the fear problem."[81]

On 5 September 1962, Hall was with a group gathered in Albany to welcome new recruit Jack Chatfield. They piled into "a little teeny Nash Rambler," which they filled with loud laughter, "a kind of defiant act in the middle of a tense city that had been shaken by a mass movement." After stopping at a gas station, Hall asked the group if their plans were straight for the next day as they continued to Dawson; it was around ten or eleven at night.[82]

The SNCC crew staying with Daniels settled in for the night. Chatfield was enjoying a late night snack in the kitchen, while others were already asleep. Hall described the quiet roar of a car motor: "As it slowed in front of the house, there was a hail of gunfire."[83] Shots riddled Daniels's house.[84] "When the shooting started, they all tried to hide:" Roy behind the refrigerator, Sherrod under a piece of furniture, Chatfield under a window, and Hall and Daniels on the floor in a back bedroom. Afraid that the night riders might return, Sherrod turned the lights off and insisted that everyone stay down. Hall recalled: "We hit the floor as we had been trained to do, while a blast of shotgun pellets was sprayed into the house. After the car drove off, we waited several minutes and then called to each other to learn if anyone had been hit. We were all alive, thank God. But this had been a very

---

[80] National Archives File #44-HQ-20425; (AP) "U.S. Accuses Sasser Officer of Harassing in Racial Case," *The Atlanta Constitution*, 4 January 1963, SNCC Papers, reel 37.

[81] Cheryl Lynn Greenburg, *A Circle of Trust: Remembering SNCC* (New Brunswick: Rutgers University Press, 1998) 60.

[82] Jack Chatfield, interview by Courtney Pace Lyons, 3 June 2011, in Raleigh, NC, compact disc, Institute for Oral History, Baylor University, Waco, TX.

[83] Hall, "Freedom-Faith," in *Hands on the Freedom Plow*, 175.

[84] "They Lived in the Counties: Churches Burned, Nightriders Attack SNCC Staff in Southwest Georgia Voter Registration Drive," *The Student Voice* 3.3 (October, 1962) and "In 'Terrible' Terrell: Night Riders Shoot Workers," 4.7 (December 1963) quoted in *The Student Voice*, 57, 87.

close call."[85] Hall and Chris Allen suffered minor bullet graze injuries, but Chatfield was shot twice in the arm.[86] She said: "We were crawling around on the floor for quite a while after that not knowing if they were coming back."[87]

After nearly forty-five minutes, Sherrod moved toward the phone. Knowing he could not trust the Georgia or local police, the Georgia Bureau of Investigation, or the FBI to protect them, he called *New York Times* reporter Claude Sitton, a Southerner with a reputation for fair coverage of the movement, at midnight.[88] Hall told Sitton of her father's decision to move from Virginia to Philadelphia in the 1920s: "I feel that he left the South to somehow redeem me. And now it's my job to come back and redeem somebody else."[89] Hall knew such danger was a constant possibility, but persisted: "We had been warned in orientation sessions not to go into the field unless we were prepared to die. That night any and all romantic thoughts about our freedom adventure dissolved as we came face-to-face with the real and present possibility of death."[90]

Because of the real and present danger facing those who supported the civil rights movement, SNCC often struggled to find churches willing to host mass meetings. Daniels's church, Atoc AME Church in Dawson, would not allow Daniels or the SNCC workers to meet there: "You know these white people will burn our church down."[91] Hall reflected:

> Sometimes it was frustrating to us at the time or frustrating as when the pastors would not participate in the movement and local people would slam

---

[85] Hall, "Freedom-Faith," in *Hands on the Freedom Plow*, 175.

[86] Carolyn Daniels, "We Just Kept Going," in *Hands on the Freedom Plow*, 155; "They Lived in the Counties: Churches Burned, Nightriders Attack SNCC Staff in Southwest Georgia Voter Registration Drive," quoted in *The Student Voice*, 57, 87; Chatfield, interview by Pace Lyons; SNCC News Release, Terrell County, 14 September 1962, SNCC Papers, reel 13.

[87] Hall, interview by Michaels.

[88] Hall, "Freedom-Faith," in *Hands on the Freedom Plow*, 175; Hall, interview by Michaels; Sitton, "2 Negro Churches Burn in Georgia."

[89] Claude Sitton, "Voting Drive Met By Hope and Fear: Student Workers in Georgia Tell of Rights Campaign Hope for Negroes Seek Meaning in Lives US Inquiry Under Way," *New York Times*, 11 September 1962.

[90] Hall, "Freedom-Faith," in *Hands on the Freedom Plow*, 175.

[91] Daniels, "We Just Kept Going," in *Hands on the Freedom Plow*, 153.

their doors in our faces. But we had to translate, we had to interpret that; it was a rational fear speaking. The courage was beyond reason, beyond the level of the rational! The courage to go down to the courthouse or the courage to open the doors and say let's have the meeting here was a courage that transcended reason.[92]

Hall came to understand the profound demonstration of faith made by churches that cooperated with SNCC workers: "Churches were burned down, sometimes two or three in a night. For a congregation to open their doors and say, 'you may meet here,' was again as profound a test of the Freedom Faith as ever there could be. It's almost quite miraculous that there was always at least one church that would say, come."[93] In the summer of 1962, four African American churches in Terrell and Lee Counties, all associated with the movement in some way, were burned by white supremacists.

Two churches, Mount Olive Baptist Church (Sasser) and Mount Mary Baptist Church (Chickasawatchee), were burned the night of September 9; both were wooden, located five miles apart, and were burned within one hour of each other. Hall received word via telephone that Mount Olive was on fire: "We dressed quickly and made our way to the church. There were no firefighters. The church had already burned to the ground."[94] Hall reflected:

As we stood there, more people gathered, members and friends of the church. We held hands together and sang and prayed. As we stood there watching the remains of Mount Olive, Mr. Southwell of the Georgia Bureau of Investigation arrived. I extended by hand and said, "I'm Prathia Hall." He looked at me and said, "Don't you know better than to stick your hand out there like that to speak to me?" I said, "Don't human beings speak to each other that way?" He walked away saying, "Well it ain't the way I live."[95]

---

[92] Hall, interview by Woods.

[93] Hall, interview by Woods.

[94] Hall, "Freedom-Faith," in *Hands on the Freedom Plow*, 179.

[95] SNCC News Release, Terrell County, Georgia, 14 September 1962, SNCC Papers, reel 13. The burning did not deter SNCC, but SNCC's resilience did not deter segregationists. At an open-air voter registration meeting on September 13, Terrell County's civil rights volunteers decided to raise a tent as a temporary meeting place until the churches could be rebuilt. Between 1961 and 1963, forty-one black churches in the South were burned; five were burned in SWGA in summer 1962 alone. A UPI news article related: "Since desegregation activities were stepped up

Even though mass meetings were often held at Mount Olive Baptist Church and a minister and deacon of Mount Mary Baptist Church had been supporting the voter registration drive, Sheriff Mathews told reporters that the burnings were unrelated to voter registration.[96] Prathia Hall answered Mathews's claims with bold confidence: "We may have had visits from white girls at our headquarters… but none are staying here. The fires are the latest harassment. We've been getting the works."[97]

SNCC held a prayer vigil in September 1962 at the ruins of Mount Olive Baptist Church. Sitton was also there: "As the sun sets across the cotton fields, some fifty Negroes and two whites met at Mount Olive for a 'prayer vigil.' Joining hands, they sang softly, 'We Shall Overcome.' A wisp of smoke rose from the ashes of the church … The whites in the automobiles that shuttled slowly past looked on and said nothing."[98] After the song, Hall led the group in prayer: "'Lord, help us keep our heads up,' Miss Hall said, her voice breaking. 'Help us, Lord, as Mount Olive, Shady Grove, and Mount Mary Churches rise again out of the ashes. Lord, we're going to be free. We want to be free so our children won't have to grow up with their heads bowed."[99] According to oral tradition, throughout the prayer, Hall repeated the phrase "I have a dream," of her vision for racial equality and justice.[100] Although Sitton did not include the entire text of her prayer, he was obviously moved by the power of her words to record significant portions of what she said. Sitton did not include any text from King's remarks at the same vigil, nor did Sitton customarily quote prayers.[101]

---

here last month, three Negro churches have been burned down, four Negro homes have been fired on and a white youth working in a Negro voter registration drive has been shot and wounded." See UPI, "Urge President To Stop Terror in South Georgia," *The Daily Courier*, 10 September 1962.

[96] UPI, "Urge President To Stop Terror in South Georgia," *The Daily Courier*, 10 September 1962; UPI, "Two Negro Churches Burned; White Man Held for Attacking An FBI Agent," *Albuquerque Journal*, 10 September 10, 1962; Sitton, "2 Negro Churches Burned in Georgia."

[97] UPI, "Urge President To Stop Terror in South Georgia"; (UPI) "Two Negro Churches Burned; White Man Held for Attacking An FBI Agent."

[98] Sitton, "2 Negro Churches Burned in Georgia."

[99] Rubin, interview by Lyons.

[100] See Lyons, "Freedom Faith."

[101] Sitton, "2 Negro Churches Burned in Georgia."

Larry Rubin vividly remembered her speaking at this event: "She was really quite a powerful speaker. I remember being awestruck."[102]

"We Who Believe in Freedom Cannot Rest ..."

In the fall of 1962, Hall returned to Philadelphia for a series of speaking engagements. SNCC Executive Secretary James Forman often asked Hall to speak at Northern SNCC fundraiser events: "A lot of time when something pivotal happened in the South I was in the North speaking at a rally."[103] At the SNCC Emancipation Celebration at Tenley Temple United Methodist Church, Hall spearheaded SNCC's work in Philadelphia, organized out of Fellowship House. A spectator described her talk at the Emancipation Celebration: "Her account was very simple and deeply moving."[104] Marjorie Penney appreciatively reflected on Hall's frequent connection with Fellowship House through Northern speaking engagements:

> Some of our young people who had gone South with Dr. King to work on the whole voting registration thing came back and spoke of the bravery of the black people....The intensity of the self-giving of many of these young people...in cities like Albany, Georgia; Americus, Georgia; Cleveland, Mississippi; Jacksonville, Mississippi; Florida towns; name it, and somebody from the Fellowship House was in there for a long or short time.[105]

Hall realized how difficult her movement involvement was for her family, who received harassing phone calls frequently. She called her mother a "trooper lady, warrior lady" and claimed her mother "was [her] number one supporter. She worried all the time. Wanted me to come home." Hall was aware that "Family conspired on various occasions to try to get this one or

---

[102] Rubin, interview by Lyons. For more on Hall as originator of "I have a dream," see Lyons, "Freedom Faith."

[103] Hall, interview by Woods, 6–7.

[104] "Fellowship House, Meeting of Board of Directors, October 4, 1962," and "Fellowship House, Meeting of Board of Directors, November 15, 1962," Fellowship House Papers, Acc. 723:1, 1931–1994 Temple University Archives; Hall continued to attend meetings of the Director Board of Fellowship House during her organizing time in Philadelphia. She and Barrett were granted a one year's leave of absence from their Fellowship House staff duties to join—in Hall's case, continue—the movement in the South.

[105] Marjorie Penney, interview by Rosa King Zimmerman, 20 July 1976, West Chester State College Oral History Program, Fellowship House Papers, Acc. 723:5.

that one to try to persuade me to come home, which again, which irritated me no end at the time, but once you become a parent, you certainly understand."[106]

SNCC's work in SWGA continued in spite of some difficulties. The project now included twelve field secretaries —Prathia Hall, Jack Chatfield, Carver (Chico) Neblett, John Churchville, Joyce Barrett, Don Harris, Ralph Allen, Eddie Brown, Faith Holsaert, Alfonzo Hubbard, and Joni Rabinowitz—who rotated from Albany to surrounding counties. Four lived at the Albany office, two at Koinonia Farm in Americus, and the rest with host homes in the rural counties.[107] SNCC expanded to Sumter County in November and December 1962.[108]

In January 1963, US Attorney Floyd M. Buford of the Justice Department filed suit against Deputy Short for six counts of civil rights violations against Hall, William Berrien, and Ralph Allen from late August 1962. Short pled not guilty.[109] Short's pre-trial remarks alleged that he stopped the SNCC workers' vehicle because of its out-of-state plates and its incorrect parking position, that he asked them to leave town because "Negro citizens in Sasser" had complained about the SNCC workers making threats

---

[106] Hall, interview by Harding; Hall, interview by Michaels; Many of the SNCC workers' families received threatening phone calls and hate mail. See Penny Patch, "Sweet Tea at Shoney's," in *Deep in Our Hearts: Nine White Women in the Freedom Movement*, 131–70.

[107] "Survey: Current Field Work, Spring 1963," SNCC Papers, reel 10.

[108] Braden, "The Images are Broken." Americus, the county seat of Sumter County, was a trading and manufacturing town of just over 13,000 people. African Americans composed 52.65 percent of the population of Sumter County yet only 1.01 percent of registered voters. In 1955, Clarence Jordan and his wife established Koinonia Farm, a biracial community eight miles southwest of Americus. Many whites blamed Jordan for inciting racial unrest in the community, and the farm was often the victim of nightrider attacks. For more than four years, Americus merchants boycotted the farm. Claude Sitton, "Strict Law Enforcement Stifles Negroes' Drive in Americus, Ga: 4 Integrationists Face Death Penalty as Result of Riots and Demonstrations," *New York Times*, 29 September 1963.

[109] UPI, "Victims Pushed Voter Registration: Terrell Marshal Charged with Rights 'Violations,'" *Atlanta Daily World*, 4 January 1963, SNCC Papers, reel 37.

against African Americans who would not register and that he offered to escort them out of town "for their safety and protection."[110]

Assistant Attorney General Burke Marshall supervised the investigation leading up to Short's trial, which the FBI grouped within its larger investigation of civil rights violations in Lee and Terrell counties, including the burning of four African American churches and the unlawful arrests and violence against civil rights supporters.[111] Investigators delayed pressing charges against Short, however, until his involvement in the church burnings and other shootings could be ascertained.[112]

During the January 1963 federal grand jury trial in Americus, Justice Department lawyers insisted that African Americans be identified as "colored folk" rather than "Negro" and enforced segregated seating.[113] Justice Department lawyers requested that SNCC workers refrain from interracial gathering during the trial and "would not allow one young Negro woman field secretary, Prathia Hall, to wear a hat in the courtroom" because "her dignified dress might offend Sasser farmers" and give "the impression that she was an 'uppity nigger.'" Hall described it: "I was called as a witness for the prosecution. I dressed as I had been taught was appropriate for a court appearance. I wore a business suit, hat, and gloves. As I waited to testify, I was approached by one of the Justice Department attorneys and asked to remove my hat, because the local whites were offended by the presence of a black woman dressed in such professional attire."[114]

Hall, William Paul Berrien, and Ralph Allen testified in the trial, recounting the events in which Short fired gunshots at their vehicle and at

---

[110] SNCC News Release, Sasser, Georgia, 3 January 1963, SNCC Papers, reel 14; UPI, "Terrell Marshal Charged with Rights 'Violations,'" *Atlanta Daily World*, 4 January 1963, SNCC Papers, reel 19.

[111] Other events that the Albany Movement had reported to the FBI included the beating of pregnant Mrs. Slater King, the beating of Bill Hansen, and the beating of C. B. King. "The only federal prosecution in Albany during the attorney general ship of Robert Kennedy was *against* civil rights workers who had picketed a segregationist grocer." Howard Zinn, *On Race* (New York City: Seven Stones, 2011) 74, 177–8.

[112] National Archives File #44-HQ-20425.

[113] Ibid.

[114] Hall, "Freedom-Faith," in *Hands on the Freedom Plow*, 177; William Paul Berrier, untitled document, undated, SNCC Papers, reel 37.

them, as well as arresting them on trumped up charges. Deputy Short alleged that he ran the SNCC workers out of town for their own protection from "angry white citizens." Short's lawyer made "slanderous remarks about the morals of SNCC," and particularly concerning "the language and behavior of Miss Hall." When on the witness stand, Hall could not bring herself to repeat what Short had said to her. Judge Elliot allowed her to "state that Mr. Short had been abusive."[115] In spite of obvious errors of fact in Short's testimony, Justice Department officials did not challenge Short's testimony. Short claimed that he stopped them for speeding and brought them peaceably into his office. He claimed that the arrested workers ran into the jail cell together, implying that they wanted to have sex, a common accusation by segregationists against civil rights workers. Short's defense also emphasized the Northern students as outside agitators, further strengthening segregationist animosity toward Hall and the other students.

Larry Rubin recounted that during the trial, Hall laughed, which to him "was just an example of her courage ... the way she held up when she was arrested." He was impressed that "she didn't allow herself to be intimidated." He found her reaction particularly powerful since the sheriffs were unaccustomed to such reactions from African Americans or women.[116]

After twenty minutes of deliberation, a twelve-man all-white jury acquitted Short of all charges on 25 January 1963.[117] Rubin overheard jurors saying to each other that they would not convict "a man who stood for segregation."[118]

When Hall returned to voter registration work in SWGA on 23 February 1963, she brought her childhood friend Joyce Barrett with her. Fellowship House director Marjorie Penney, as well as Aura Yores, and Claire Maier (who went to the 1960 founding meeting of SNCC) drove

---

[115] "Statements from SNCC Workers on Trial of D. E. Short," Americus, Georgia, 25 January 1963, SNCC Papers, reel 37; William Paul Berrier, untitled document, undated; (AP) "U.S. Accuses Sasser Officer of Harassing in Racial Case," *The Atlanta Constitution*, 4 January 1963, SNCC Papers, reel 37.

[116] Rubin, interview by Pace Lyons.

[117] SNCC News Release, "Sasser Policeman Acquitted in 33 Minutes; SNCC Workers Decry Lack of Justice," Americus, Georgia, 26 January 1963, SNCC Papers, reel 19.

[118] Hall, "Freedom-Faith," in *Hands on the Freedom Plow*, 177.

Hall and Barrett to Albany.[119] Sherrod distributed area SNCC workers to different locations to make room for the visitors, who arrived around 1:30 a.m.[120] Regarding her return to SWGA, Hall wrote, "It's good to be back home."[121] The next day, the SWGA team met with the visitors from Fellowship House, and in Hall's words, "The sun spread its refreshing light and warmth on my first day back in S. W. Georgia."[122] Penney, Yores, and Maier offered moral support and suggestions for effectively working with people for social change, and gifted to SNCC some needed supplies as well as assistance with odds and ends around the SNCC office.[123]

Penney, Yores, and Maier left from Albany on February 25, after an evening mass meeting. The meeting was "run in real SNCC fashion," with each county giving a report of its progress, and Hall described the people as "almost transfixed in admiration" of the reported activism. Hall appreciated multiple testimonies because "this kind of witness increases intercounty unity and at the same time gives form and backbone to the emerging leadership in the counties."[124]

While Hall had been in the North, she wrestled with the verdict of the Short trial. Hall felt "despair," but when she returned to SWGA, she realized that "the people in the counties looked on it as a measure of hope" because Short's trial was "the first time a white in this area had even been questioned and brought to trial for an injustice to a Negro." [125] In a field report, Hall lavished praise on the progress SNCC was making in Sumter County:

> People sit in the meetings with their heads high as they sing and talk about freedom. Even a *teacher* was present and offered his services in our new night school project.... Can you imagine a real live teacher? We are on our way. Mr. Weston—fire, articulate and militant—told the people "don't you go

---

[119] "Fellowship House, Meeting of Board of Directors, March 21, 1963," Fellowship House Papers, Acc. 723:1.

[120] John O'Neal, Field Report, 23 February–6 March 1963, SNCC Papers, reel 8.

[121] Prathia Hall, Letter to SNCC, Albany, Georgia, 4 March 1963, SNCC Papers, 37.

[122] Ibid.

[123] John O'Neal, Field Report; Holsaert, interview by Lyons.

[124] Hall, Letter to SNCC, Albany, Georgia, 4 March 1963.

[125] Ibid.

down to that court house with your head down, scratching when you don't itch. Stand up! And speak up!" Already they are talking about economic security and establishing a savings and loan association. Yes, Sumter may prove to be the salt of our movement.[126]

Hall returned to Daniels's house with Faith Holsaert, who described their group as a "triumvirate of female workers;" as the only white worker living with Daniels, Holsaert was "always with Prathia or Carolyn."[127] Hall spent the remainder of February 1963 there. Terrell County mass meetings were well-attended, "a tent full," and Hall noticed "a new spirit of progressiveness" among the people. She said, "Warm arms of friendship and shared suffering welcomed me into the family."[128] Hall canvassed for voter registration with Albany's Rev. Samuel Wells, whom she greatly admired, and some high school students, as well as assisted in the SNCC office as much as she should while battling the flu:[129]

There's a throbbing all over me, a never ending ache back and forth across me. It is cold pain frozen within my soul by the suffering of the years and add to this my plight—I stand within the center of a razor blade, high walls of stainless steel around me—boxed. The ugly face of Segregation hovers over me.... but this is the beginning.[130]

Around one a.m. on March 5, Hall left with Holsaert and two other SNCC volunteers for Terrell County.[131] This particular move into Terrell County was important because of Faith Holsaert. Moving white men into Terrell had been a big step, made easier by the "affectionately open personality" of Ralph Allen. Holsaert's transfer to Terrell created "havoc for the white community" because she was a white female. Holsaert stayed several nights at Daniels's house but never officially lived there because of the certain danger such news would bring.[132] During the first week of Holsaert's residency, she and Hall canvassed close to where she was staying for safety: "You see, we are trying to gauge the climate in the community in

---

[126] Ibid.

[127] Holsaert, interview by Pace Lyons.

[128] Hall, Letter to SNCC, Albany, Georgia, 4 March 1963.

[129] Prathia Hall, Field Report, 23 February–8 March 1963, SNCC Papers, reel 6; Faith Holsaert, Field Report 19 February–7 March 1963, SNCC Papers.

[130] Hall, Letter to SNCC, Albany, Georgia, 4 March 1963.

[131] Joyce Barrett, Field Report, 2–10 March 1963, SNCC Papers, reel 5.

[132] Hall, Field Report, 23 February–8 March 1963, SNCC Papers.

an attempt to control a potentially explosive situation. If there is violence we would like to feel that we have done all we could to prevent it—everything short of dishonest compromise that is."[133]

After a full day of voter registration canvassing, Hall and Holsaert met John Churchville and Rubin, who drove them to the Sumter County meeting. When they stopped in Dawson for gas, a police car that also stopped at the station followed them to Carolyn Daniels's home, where Hall and Holseart were staying, and it continued to follow Rubin and Churchville "with their bright lights on to the edge of town."[134] The next morning, after Hall saw a white man with a raised tool approaching the window, she "let out a terrific scream and went leaping like a mountain goat into the bedroom." Holsaert flattened herself against the wall, and Neblett assured them both that the man worked for the electric company and was only inspecting the meter. When Hall saw him, "she hadn't waited around to ask questions," and did not realize that he had come to disconnect their power due to an unpaid bill.[135]

Hall and several others left on March 10 for Dorchester to attend an inter-organization workshop, organized by the Fellowship of Reconciliation on nonviolence, relationship between the organizations, and strategy. Leaders such as James Lawson, Bayard Rustin, and Martin Luther King, Jr., were in attendance. Hall spoke as the SNCC representative for SWGA and emphasized the importance of leadership from within the local community. Those at the inter-organization workshop also discussed ways to encourage community economic efforts.[136] Based on their door-to-door canvassing, Hall and Holsaert suggested that, recognizing the power of education and its appeal in the rural counties, itinerant freedom school tutors offer education to those unable to come to evening mass meetings.[137] Holseart reported: "Prathia has stated very well the present situation in Dawson as far as our opposition is concerned. That is that the frenzy there is high, but that the

---

[133] Ibid.

[134] Hall, Field Report, 23 February–8 March 1963, SNCC Papers; Holsaert, Field Report 19 February–7 March 1963, SNCC Papers.

[135] Holsaert, Field Report 19 February–7 March 1963, SNCC Papers.

[136] Faith Holsaert, Field Report 9–22 March 1963, SNCC Papers, reel 6.

[137] Ibid.

authority has subjected itself to a new discipline, and that when these two elements are brought together, we will have real trouble."[138]

In May 1963, Barrett wrote to Fellowship House to describe the SWGA project's decision to focus their efforts exclusively on Albany to make it an "open city": [139]

> We've just decided to go all *out* ourselves and raise hell … Sherrod has said I'll be one of the first ones to go to jail—which may mean today or tomorrow. If I go, I'll probably stay a while. Do whatever you can for publicity for us, especially if Prathia or I are involved (she may lead a night march).
>
> We're sitting on a powder keg down here. The Birmingham riots are being felt across the nation. Students fighting in Knoxville, Nashville, sitting-in in Raleigh. Some kids shot at the police last night here—and threw bottles. We have no choice but to *move* now. I love you all.
>
> Joyce [140]

Within a week of this aggressive new recruitment campaign in Albany, both Hall and Barrett were arrested, along with Joni Rabinowitz, W .G. Anderson, and Slater King, for distributing leaflets in front of the Dougherty County Courthouse.[141]

---

[138] Ibid.

[139] Ralph Allen, Field Report, 13–26 May 1963, SNCC Papers, reel 37. Pulling workers from rural counties into Albany had a variety of effects on the still-new projects in those rural counties. The county best equipped to self-manage was Terrell County. The rebuilding of the churches burned in summer 1962 was a symbol of hope and strength for the African American community in Terrell County. Lee County had a number of willing canvassers but struggled without transportation or strong local leadership. Sumter County boasted high registration numbers.

[140] Joyce Barrett, Letter to Fellowship House, 14 May 1963, Fellowship House Papers, Acc. 723:8. After lunch, SNCC actively recruited at area schools, seeking volunteers to be arrested, and five went to jail after a mass meeting that evening. Meetings and marches continued the next day as well. At Terrell County's mass meeting, Hall and Holsaert reported that Terrell County was "carrying on fine without them" and that the meeting was well-attended: "a full tent without the Albany kids to swell the numbers." Allen, Field Report, 13–26 May 1963.

[141] SNCC News Release, 21 May 1963, Albany, Georgia, SNCC Papers, reel 13; Allen, Field Report, 13–26 May 1963.

In June, 1963, the SWGA Project was nearly halted when twenty-two of its twenty-six staff were arrested within one week in a police attempt to deter SNCC's daily demonstrations.[142] Arrests began June 20, and by June 22, more than 140 demonstrators had been arrested: "They were picked up singly and in twos and threes, during marches, while canvassing, or as they entered a local church to attend a mass meeting."[143]

When Cathy Cade's father came to Albany in June 1963 after his daughter's arrest, he went to the SNCC headquarters, where he encountered Hall and her friend Joyce Barrett: "I was introduced to Joyce Barrett, Prathia Hall, and the rest. Joyce was a young white girl very pretty, delicate face and good figure. Prathia was a young colored girl about 20-25 with a good mind and very commanding presence—somewhat masculine in her authority, I should say." Sherrod arrived, and the four conversed about the project and the status of Cathy. Cade continued: "During the next two hours of conversation interrupted by the phone ringing every 5 minutes, Joyce and Prathia constantly said to Sherrod, Don't you think this is right and he always agreed. It was apparent that the two girls were running the show." The next day, Cade attended a mass meeting at Arcadia Church at eight p.m., led by Hall: "Prathia Hall started the meeting with a reading from the Bible about the torture and martyrdom of the Christians according to Paul. Prathia is an excellent preacher with a beautiful contralto voice."[144]

In June 1963, Chief Pritchett moved twenty-two imprisoned SNCC workers to Lee County. The remaining students, including Hall, hid in the SNCC offices. A phone call informed the students to move to the home of Aurelia Noble, with no suggestion for how to get there. The group disguised themselves in dark coats and smeared soot on their faces so they could hide under the cover of night. They escaped through a back door and walked in absolute darkness, hiding from police cars whose lights were casing the SNCC office and nearby alleys. When a dog barked at them, its owners

---

[142] Annette Jones White, "Expression of My Discontent," in *Hands on the Freedom Plow*, 117.

[143] Untitled document, SNCC Papers, reel 19.

[144] Cathy Cade, "Caught in the Middle," in *Hands on the Freedom Plow*, 202, 204.

turned on backyard lights, and the group froze in an alley for almost an hour until the lights were turned off.[145]

Arriving at the safe house, they were "offered sanctuary" at Beulah Baptist Church. Rev. Samuel Wells and schoolteacher McCree Harris drove the students to Beulah. The males slept "in a room on one side of the church with the deacons, females on the other side with the deaconesses." After one of the students from the North played "jazzy blues piano," Beulah "evicted" the students. They hid in Shiloh Church for eight days, while James Christian and Monroe Gaines, guarded the backdoor of the church, "under a spotlight, with their guns across their laps," to protect the workers from the Klan that was "circling" the church after dark.[146]

Hall and Barrett spoke to SNCC reporters: "We are afraid here. We are afraid that this community may explode."[147] Demonstrations—met with police intimidation, arrests, and brutality—were the only way to communicate with city leaders or draw national attention to racial injustice in the South. Chief Pritchett stayed "one jump ahead" of SNCC's plans, however, and with insufficient funds to post bail for everyone arrested, some remained in jail "long past their time."[148] Without masses of people to back up the core two hundred local volunteers, demonstrations did not reach the potential Sherrod hoped they would.[149]

---

[145] "Frustration, Bitterness Mount in Albany, Georgia," *The Student Voice* 4.2 (August 1963), quoted in *The Student Voice*, 72; Annette Jones White, "Expression of My Discontent"; Claude Sitton, "Albany, Ga., Faces 3d Racial Crisis in 18 Months: Brutality Charged," *New York Times*, 23 June 1963.

[146] Joann Christian Mants, "Right Side Up," in *Hands on the Freedom Plow*, 135–6.

[147] "Frustration, Bitterness Mount in Albany, Georgia," *The Student Voice*, 4.2 (August 1963).

[148] Allen, Field Report, 13–26 May 1963.

[149] As Ralph Allen described, "Factually and tangibly, nothing was accomplished except the destruction of the impact of much of Sherrod's idealism.... This is not to say that Sherrod's theories about the people are not true, but rather to say that they must be taken along with an honest assessment of their context, i.e., tyranny of Pritchett, and his rather studied policies of suppression." Ralph Allen was a young African American volunteer who worked with Don Harris in Sumter County after having worked with Sherrod in Dawson, and Allen had some significant differences of opinion with Sherrod concerning strategy. Certainly not all

Hall shared Sherrod's idealism, speaking often of the inherent good in people and with faith that justice would win the day. Ralph Allen, after returning to SWGA from Atlanta on July 12, said he found "Prathia on cloud 6 ½ telling me from up there" that their next demonstration on July 13 "was the day."[150] Mass demonstrations like the multi-site event planned for July 13 required hundreds of volunteers, which SNCC had not had in SWGA since early 1962. Hall clearly had a vision for large civil rights project leadership, which may be why Forman recognized Hall's potential for project leadership within SNCC and moved her to the burgeoning Selma, Alabama project by fall of 1963.[151]

SNCC workers in SWGA held such strong view against Sherrod's tactics. Allen, Field Report, 13–26 May 1963.

[150] SNCC had planned the following mass demonstrations for July 13: a prayer meeting at a church near the pool, followed by a series of demonstrations, pickets, and boycotts across the city according to a master plan.

[151] At a subsequent mass meeting, the SWGA SNCC team was discussing their strategy to protest segregation at the Tift Park swimming pool. On 13 July 1963, when police thwarted the planned attempt to integrate the pool, Randy Battle, Phil Davis, and Pete DeLissovoy started running toward the pool: "We hit that fence and were over that fence and in that pool in a second. And we swam on cross that pool to where the ladder came up and then we went out that back gate." They ran to Arcadia church and hid in a tree. As the water dripped from their clothes and shoes, three deacons noticed them in the tree and sheltered them inside the church building. For more on this, see Randy Battle, Dennis Roberts, Curtis L. Williams, and Pete DeLissovoy, *The Great Pool Jump & Other Stories from the Civil Rights Movement in Southwest Georgia* (Lancaster, PA: You Are Perfect Press, 2010) 11–15; SNCC News Release, "Negroes Swim in White Only Pool," 13 July 1963, Albany, Georgia, SNCC Papers, reel 13.

"Look here, though, the funny part of it, the best part of it all, when we hit that water in the pool, when they looked over there and saw "them niggers" in that pool, goddam it them white folks and kids went straight up in the air, they didn't climb out, they went straight up in the air and *flew* over to the sides – I mean that's what it seemed like to me. I bet you in half a minute there wasn't nobody in the pool but the three of us. And they started screaming and hollering, "Niggas! Niggas!" Them white folks hit the air like *dolphins*, you know, right up in the air they flew."

After the jump, the city drained the pool and spent three days scrubbing the entire pool with disinfectant. Not long after, Battles and Daniel snuck back

On July 13, Hall, Holsaert, Barrett, and Ralph Allen met with C. B. King to discuss criticisms of staff relations. At a staff meeting the following day, the SWGA SNCC team decided to move from mass demonstrations toward radical, small demonstrations with a higher probability of victory, such as the Great Pool Jump. Leaders who pushed for this change did so based on their belief that "Albany could no longer bear the burden of the movement without some kind of victory." By focusing their limited resources on "smaller, more specific goals," they believed that "a series of victories may rebuild the power of the Albany movement."[152]

The interracial nature of the SWGA project remained a sore spot even for some within SNCC and the Albany Movement. While Sherrod, Hall, and Forman, remained committed to integration as necessary, others expressed more subtle resentment at the increasing number of whites in SNCC. For example, at the end of the July 14 Albany meeting, Prathia Hall returned from Atlanta with news that two new students, both white, would, in Ralph Allen's words, "descend from the heavens above to bestow their 'creativity' upon us." Allen believed that the growing number of whites in SWGA aggravated white Albany, resulted in more frequent and more expensive arrests, and enabled "a detached melancholy" spectator-mentality in Albany's African American community.[153]

Throughout summer 1963, the SWGA Project received new workers, and with the Albany "Big Push" plan gathering workers from rural areas, the population of SNCC workers in Albany was at an all-time high. The SNCC house became overcrowded with people, causing inconvenient and dangerous situations for the workers.[154] Certainly, having an interracial team

---

into the pool and poured Army dye into the water. "In the morning Tift pool was bright yellow and they had to drain it all over again! A second time."

[152] Allen, Field Report, 13–26 May 1963.

[153] Ibid.

[154] Ralph Allen elaborated on the difficulties of the larger staff in a letter to James Forman: "Actually, you take all the problems raised above in connection with the detrimental effects which whites have had upon the people of Albany, and you add to that the number ten,—ten or so people who aren't self-sufficient and who have to be told when it's time to eat and where, have to be kicked out of the Big house at night so Prathia can get to sleep, ten people who have to be closely watched because they aren't sensitive enough to know what they are

was more difficult for Sherrod and Hall to lead than an all-black team would have been.[155]

By summer and fall 1963, the "solid movement people in Albany" were tired. Police had mastered the art of mass arrests, and the city had instituted discriminatory policies to interfere with voter registration and integration.[156] By the end of 1963, however, SNCC workers in cooperation with local civil rights workers had raised the number of registered African American voters in Terrell from the 51 in 1960 to 140 (a 270% increase). The statistics remained harrowing, however, as African Americans still comprised fewer than 5 percent of voters in Terrell County.[157] Some improvements occurred in Albany by late 1963 and early 1964, but police harassment of movement activists continued in the rural counties.[158] In spring 1964, Albany attorney C. B. King announced his candidacy for Congress for the second district, which included Dougherty, Baker, Randolph, Terrell, and Worth counties. SNCC's SWGA Project expansion covered nearly every county of the second district, which sparked exponential growth in voter registrations.[159]

Freedom Faith

Hall often described these efforts as "mutual educational exchange." SNCC workers had information about how to vote, and the local people "had learned the system and how to stay alive in the system morally, mentally, and spiritually—how to live in an oppressively crushing system without being crushed."[160] She met people who had supported their families on less-than-subsistence wages earned by back-breaking labor and had weathered

---

doing in the eyes of the community, don't know that they should be afraid of being seen alone with a black chick, or that they should be afraid and wary of certain types of social intercourse." Allen, Field Report, 13–26 May 1963.

[155] Allen, Field Report, 13–26 May 1963.

[156] Barbara Schwartzbaum, Memo to James Forman, "Long Overdue VR memo," 20 July 1963, SNCC Papers, reel 19; Peter DeLissovoy, Field Report, 18 July 1963, SNCC Papers, reel 6.

[157] "Night Riders Shoot Worker," *The Student Voice*, 89.

[158] Joyce Barrett Memo to SNCC, 4 October 1963, SNCC Papers, reel 5.

[159] Don Harris, "Southwest Georgia," undated, SNCC Papers, reel 10; "King Campaign Spurs Voters," *The Student Voice* 5.18 (July 1964), quoted in *The Student Voice*, 175.

[160] Hall, "Freedom-Faith," in *Hands on the Freedom Plow*, 176.

discrimination, threats, and violence with "strength and nobility."[161] Women like Daniels inspired Hall, "just knowing that they had endured this treacherous brutality for generations, and yet it had not killed their spirit. They were not crushed, they were not victims. They were survivors. They were overcomers."[162] Elsewhere she said:

> The primary lesson I received from those black sages was that of faith for living in life-threatening circumstances. It was a faith first made manifest by our slave fore-parents who defied the teachings of the slavocracy…. Those profoundly spiritual women and men developed their own moral critique of the slaveholders' oppressive brand of religion and expressed the slaves' absolute conviction that slavery was contrary to the will of God and that God definitely intended them to be free. These sons and daughters of those enslaved ancestors continued to hold on to that freedom-faith. The freedom-faith fired and fueled the fight.[163]

Hall's father had inculcated that the theological understanding that God meant all people to be free, that "freedom and faith were woven together in the fabric of life." In SWGA, Hall learned that freedom faith meant facing one's fears with confidence that the God who led her there would deliver her from there. Hall was by no means naïve to suffering when she arrived in Georgia, but her experiences educated her in the real meaning of freedom faith. Hall's extended incarcerations added rich hues to her theology of suffering for freedom: "You can never appreciate the peace, the solace, the quiet appalling silence … unless you've been in jail. Been in jail for a just cause. There is such a purging of the soul that you feel as though you have been relieved of all of your sins. The burdens of the world have been taken off of you."[164] The person who trusted God to assist them in their pursuit of freedom in spite of their fears was "now willing to walk face to face with the forces of death in the struggle for life."[165]

---

[161] Ibid.

[162] Ransby, interview by Hall.

[163] Hall, "Freedom-Faith," in *Hands on the Freedom Plow*, 176.

[164] Hall, "Freedom-Faith," in *Hands on the Freedom Plow*, 172. British SNCC volunteer John Papworth made a similar comment in a field report, calling jail a "morale booster" John Papworth, Field Report, Albany, Georgia, 18–19 February 1964, SNCC Papers, reel 37.

[165] Hall, interview by Woods.

Hall contextualized freedom faith during the movement: "This sense that I'm not a nigger, I'm not gal, I'm not boy. I am God's child. And as God's child, that means that I am everything that I'm supposed to be." Hall praised the courage and resilience of generations of African Americans who survived the brutality of slavery and Jim Crow because of their faith in God: "How had they done that? They had done that because each generation had passed on to the next generation this thing that I call freedom faith." This same freedom faith that sustained generations of African Americans would continue to sustain them as they opposed Jim Crow: "It may cost my job, it may cost my life, but I want to be free, and I want my children to be free. So I'm going down to the courthouse, and I'm going to sign my name. And I'm going to trust God to take me there, and I'm going to trust God to bring me back. That's courage. That's faith. That's freedom faith."[166]

Prathia Hall was a significant religious leader of the movement. Her story sheds light on the important role of women both in organizational leadership and in the success of grassroots activism. Had she been male, she would be a highly recognizable historical figure. As it stands, however, too little research has been devoted to her powerful legacy. In the movement and throughout her later ministry career, she modeled the beloved community, a life-long commitment to non-violence, and freedom faith.

Further Reading

For more information on women in the civil rights movement, see: Vicki L. Crawford, Jacqueline Anne Rouse, and Barbara Woods, *Women in the Civil Rights Movement: Trailblazers & Torchbearers, 1941–1965* (Bloomington: Indiana University Press, 1990); Belinda Robnett, *How Long? How Long? African American Women in the Struggle for Civil Rights* (New York City: Oxford University Press, 1997); Bettye Collier-Thomas and V.P. Franklin, eds., *Sisters in the Struggle: African American Women in the Civil Rights-Black Power Movement* (New York City: New York University Press, 2001); Rosetta Ross, *Witnessing and Testifying: Black Women, Religion, and Civil Rights* (Minneapolis: Fortress Press, 2003); Davis W. Houck and David E. Dixon, eds., *Women in the Civil Rights Movement, 1954–1965* (Jackson: University Press of Mississippi, 2009); Danielle L. McGuire, *At the Dark End of the Street: Black Women, Rape, and Resistance—A New History*

---

[166] "Freedom Faith," *This Far By Faith*, PBS, 2002.

of the Civil Rights Movement from Rosa Parks to the Rise of Black Power (New York City: Alfred A. Knopf, 2010); Barbara Ransby, *Ella Baker and the Black Freedom Movement: A Radical Democratic Vision* (Chapel Hill: University of North Carolina Press, 2002); Kay Mills, *This Little Light of Mine: The Life of Fannie Lou Hamer* (New York City: Plume, 1993); Chana Kai Lee, *For Freedom's Sake: The Life of Fannie Lou Hamer (Women in American History)* (Chicago: University of Illinois Press, 2000); and Cynthia Griggs Fleming, *Soon We Will Not Cry: The Liberation of Ruby Doris Smith Robinson* (New York City: Rowman & Littlefield, 1998).

[handwritten margin note: not really an argument (more a story — but certainly an important one ... one of these "we need this to be visible" essays.]

8

"That the Rules be Suspended": Denominational Political Culture and Schism within the National Baptist Convention, 1895–1962

Edward R. Crowther

The crackling fire successfully battled the bitter cold of a January 2011 evening in Colorado's San Luis Valley. Seated in an oversize rocking chair, Rev. Samuel Kyles entertained his hosts with the story of the source of his nickname "Billy," after the white evangelist Billy Sunday. He interjected his humorous memoir with notes on his busy travel itinerary, one currently filled with speaking engagements to commemorate the Martin Luther King, Jr., holiday. Pastor of Monumental Baptist Church in Memphis since 1959, Kyles had recently preached at Monumental Baptist Church in Philadelphia. "And do you know who used to be pastor of Monumental in the City of Brotherly love?" he queried. Without a pause, his irenic cadence acquired an acerbic tone as he answered his own question in a sharp staccato: "J. H. Jackson."[1] Joseph Harrison Jackson, the longtime president of the National Baptist Convention (NBC), had opposed the civil rights activities of Martin Luther King, Jr., and many NBC ministers initiated and supported efforts establishing a new Baptist denomination in 1961, soon styled the Progressive National Baptist Convention (PNBC), in defiance of Jackson's iron grip on the presidency of the NBC and for his "go slow" approach to

---

[1] Notes of Rev. Kyles visit, 19 January 2011. Typescript in possession of Edward R. Crowther. Kyles, who has recently legally changed his name to Billy, was an important figure in the civil rights movement in Memphis and had been in the process of taking Martin Luther King, Jr., to dinner at Kyles's home when King was assassinated on the balcony of the Lorraine Motel on 4 April 1968. For more on Kyles, see Rev. Samuel Billy Kyles Biography, http://www.ccsu.edu/uploaded/departments/AdministrativeDepartments/Institutional_Advancement/Keyles.pdf (accessed 31 March 2013).

civil rights. Not even the passage of fifty years since the NBC schism had stilled the roiling in Kyles's soul.

The 1961 schism came after nearly a full decade of infighting within the NBC over Jackson's tenure as president. The NBC had been founded in 1895 out of three smaller "forerunner" groups. From its inception, writes Leon McBeth, the NBC was and "remains to this day as the major structure for the affiliation of black Baptist churches in America."[2] For most of its existence in the twentieth century, the NBC has beaten back the forces of disunity within, especially during the heyday of Jim Crow, and through the early years of the civil rights movement, it provided an organizational haven for African American uplift, education, and spiritual expression. In its early years, the NBC provided platforms for both Booker T. Washington and W. E. B. DuBois and directly and indirectly supported their different approaches to civil rights, while continuing the core mission of African American Baptists, missionary endeavors at home and abroad to convert lost souls. Within twenty years of its establishment, the NBC boasted 20,000 congregations and almost three million individual members. In conjunction with the white Southern Baptist Convention, the NBC operated American Baptist Seminary in Nashville, Tennessee, a major vehicle for the religious and educational edification of African Americans. By 1960, the NBC boasted five million members. Its internal politics affected the lives of scores of African Americans, and the schism within the denomination, amid the movement for African American civil rights, gave shape both to the movement and to the manner in which African American Baptists participated in it.[3]

---

[2] H. Leon McBeth, *The Baptist Heritage: Four Centuries of Baptist Witness* (Nashville: Broadman Press, 1987) 782.

[3] C. Eric Lincoln and Lawrence H. Mamiya, *The Black Church in the African American Experience* (Durham, NC: Duke University Press, 1990) 30. From its beginning, the NBC faced internal dissension. The Lott Cary Missionary Convention, centered around Washington, DC, spun off in 1897 as a separate missionary society, although many Lott Cary Baptists remained dually affiliated with the NBC. A dispute over control of the Publication Board led to the formation of the National Baptist Convention, USA, or Boyd Convention in 1915. McBeth, *The Baptist Heritage*, 782–83. For these reasons, William E. Montgomery writes, "Dissension within the National Baptist Convention tore at the organization's seams and let to expressions of disgust from outside the church over the petty jealousies and

During the 1950s, NBC leaders and laity debated the number of years in which the annually elected president might succeed himself without interruption, "tenure" as the NBC used the term. Jackson's apparent manipulation of the tenure issue garnered him ongoing support from many African American Baptists, while enraging others. By the end of the decade, dissension had seemingly spiraled into chaos. During its annual convention in Kansas City, Missouri, in September 1961, Rev. Arthur Garfield Wright, a pro-Jackson pastor from Detroit, was accidentally killed in a "march in" by NBC members seeking to remove Jackson from the presidency. Given such drama, the NBC schism garnered a great deal of press at the time and has continued to do so from historians since. Because Martin Luther King, Jr., was among those supporting Jackson's removal and given Jackson's public expressions of disdain for King's civil disobedience tactics during the civil rights movement, historians have often reduced the schism in the NBC to a debate in the African American community over means and ends of the quest for civil inclusion in the United States.[4]

---

senseless squabbling that kept it in a state of turmoil and were an embarrassment to the race." William E. Montgomery, *Under Their Own Vine and Fig Tree: The African American Church in the South, 1865–1900* (Baton Rouge: Louisiana State University Press, 1993) 335. Membership figure from William D. Booth, *A Call to Greatness: The Story of the Founding of the Progressive National Baptist Convention*, (Lawrenceville GA: Brunswick Publishing, 2001) 52. Note: The NBC is officially the National Baptist Convention, Inc.

[4] Taylor Branch, *Parting the Waters: America in the King Years 1954–63* (New York City: Simon & Schuster, 1988) 502–3; David J. Garrow, *Bearing the Cross: Martin Luther King Jr., and the Southern Christian Leadership Conference* (New York City: William Morrow and Co., 1986) 166. Wallace Best, "The Right Achieved and the Wrong Way Conquered": J. H. Jackson, Martin Luther King, Jr., and the Conflict over Civil Rights," *Religion and American Culture: A Journal of Interpretation* 16 (Summer 2006): 195–226, offers a trenchant analysis of the division between Jackson and King, noting that they shared many similarities, especially regarding social Christianity, but differed primarily "over the nature and role of black religion in the public realm" (197). Sam Hitchmough, "Mission of Patriotism: Joseph H. Jackson and Martin Luther King," *European Journal of American Studies* 1.1 (2011): 2–15, http://ejas.revues.org/9155 (accessed 30 March 2013). Hitchmough notes in his insightful article that "Histories rarely venture beyond this rift," between King and Jackson (4). Classical studies for King and Jackson include Peter J. Paris, *Black Leaders in Conflict: Martin Luther King, Jr., Malcolm X, Joseph H. Jackson, and Adam*

Such an understandable focus driven by the importance of African American Baptists in the civil rights movement, however, misses the important ecclesiastical concerns within the NBC as it sought to define its polity throughout the first half of the twentieth century. Contradictory ideas of ministerial leadership, the presidential role, and the understanding of congregational autonomy figured prominently in the denominational debate, even as NBC ministers sought to define the role of their president. The aura of office versus democratic fears of autocracy competed alongside with the need for unity, which resulted in long terms for NBC presidents, versus the ambitions of talented ministers. These issues combined to produce important and on-going ecclesiastical tensions within the convention. Because the schism occurred during the civil rights movement of the mid-twentieth century, historians have often overlooked the long origins of the schism and have privileged secular political concerns over issues of denominational politics and policy. Both William D. Booth and Prof. Sandy Dwayne Martin remind scholars that faction relations and ministerial ambitions provide ample illustrations of the internal origins of the denominational schism.[5] A trek through the presidential and political history of the NBC demonstrates the soundness of their conclusions, but it also highlights how personality, politics, generational and regional declensions—and, of course, the power figure of Joseph H. Jackson—gave shape to defining the issue in this significant ecclesiastical schism.

Clayton Powell, Jr. (New York City: Pilgrim Press, 1978); and Charles V. Hamilton, *The Black Preacher in America* (New York City: William Morrow, 1972).

[5]Booth, *Call to Greatness*, 26; Sandy Dwayne Martin, "The Formation of the Progressive National Baptist Convention: Gardner Calvin Taylor and the PNBC in Historical Context," *Baptist History and Heritage* 46 (Spring 2011) 23 ff. Martin notes that tenure and "the scope of civil rights activism" caused the schism in 1961 between the NBC and PNBC. As I hope to show in this chapter, ministers had been debating the tenure issue and had nearly ruptured the convention long before the question of non-violent direct action was under consideration. However, there is no doubt that many young ministers were acculturated to the political frustration already extant when the question of a more assertive posture toward civil rights with Baptist support compelled a powerful minority to exit the NBC. Here, I absolutely agree with Martin: "The formation of the ... PNBC cannot be understood apart from the larger historical currents. More than one hundred years of Baptist divisions and racial struggles played a critical role in shaping the divergent philosophies and commitments" (26).

A glance as the roster of NBC presidents from 1895 to Jackson's elevation to the august office in 1953 contains only three names: Elias Camp Morris, who served from 1895 to his death in 1922, Lacy Kirk Williams, who held the office from 1922 until his death in 1940, and David V. Jemison, an eloquent speaker who succeeded Morris in 1940 and served with distinction before failing eyesight led him to withdraw from the NBC presidential election in 1953. An average presidential tenure of eighteen-plus years is sure testimony to both a conjoined saga of the power of incumbency and a pronounced desire for unity within the denomination. However, the neat and unbroken chronology of long presidential terms masks the larger story of contingency. Periodically, other ministers and their supporters mounted powerful challenges to the incumbency, and they frequently bolstered their campaign by referencing the tenure issue. These challengers often pledged to serve but four years, when they would agree to relinquish office for at least one year. The consistency in the platform of these challengers suggests the creation and continuation of a consistent minority interest, one which threatened the fabric of the convention, but was obscured by the triumph of incumbency and the need for a united front in a Jim Crow world. Secular African American leadership recognized the power of the NBC to project both African American dignity and unity. As the specter of division appeared in 1931, Prof. Carter G. Woodson, the "father of black history," appealed to the NBC to avoid schism: "I object to the further division of the Negro Church because it is the only institution the Negroes control. Everything else in America and Europe is controlled by traducers of the Negro race."[6]

The evolving political culture of the NBC found ways to contain the tension of presidential politics, often an expression of regional pride as well as the personal ambition of preachers, during those rare times of a vacant presidency. Following the death of President Morris, the editor of the *National Baptist Voice* lamented the loss of "one of the best beloved men that ever lived and died in this country," but confidently asserted that "there is another, under the providence of heaven, … to fill his place, and this servant will be selected and chosen by an honest ballot vote of the Convention," which was to gather in St. Louis on December 6. E. C. Morris's death

---

[6] *National Baptist Voice*, 5 September 1931, 1. The *Voice* was the official organ of the NBC, hereinafter cited as *NBV*.

produced both lamentation for the loss of a leader and, according to James A. Mitchell, NBC missions superintendent in Tennessee, the potential for "mean competition and green-eyed jealous rivalry." Some ministers supported a "cleaning of the slate" proposal, presumably calling for the removal of incumbent vice-presidents in addition to selecting a new leader. In this contested election, interim President Wesley G. Parks, at the time a pastor in Philadelphia, seemed to be the frontrunner, and his handlers arrived in St. Louis with his nomination and a proposal to conduct the election by secret ballot. In addition, they called for an amendment to the NBC constitution that would limit the presidential term. To serve more than four consecutive one-year terms, the incumbent would require a unanimous vote by the convention. Perhaps a harbinger that their faction had not effectively counted votes, the move to prescribe new electoral procedures and introduce "tenure" into the NBC constitution failed. And, in what the *Voice* would subsequently style, "the fairest election ever held by any convention or other organization at any time or anywhere," Lacy Kirk Williams of Chicago prevailed 800 to 764, whereupon someone moved from the floor and adopted to make the election unanimous. Soothing the feeling of the Parks faction, Williams sought to "put the Convention on higher ground" and "pledged a fair and square deal to all alike." In a prescient prediction of the procedural outcome, the *Voice* presaged that for the NBC constitution and the political culture it reflected consistently mediated tensions between partisan ambition and the need for denominational unity:

> The method of election is fixed by the Constitution of the Convention, and is about as fair a methods as could be adopted by any religious assembly.... However fierce the contest may be each candidate knows that only one man can reach the goal. When this has been done, a generous concession is made on the part of the defeated candidate which is evidenced by the making of a motion that 'the election will be made unanimous.'.... Each candidate and his friends will do all he can to be elected; in the case of failure he will bow, as is customary, to the will of the majority, and take his place, agreeably and harmoniously in the ranks of the followers.[7]

---

[7] *NBV*, 25 November 1922, 16; *NBV*, 2 December 1922, 2; *NBV*, 16 December 1922, 3; *Minutes of the National Baptist Convention, Incorporated, 1922*, 79, 88. Microfilm copy Southern Baptist Historical Society and Archives, Nashville, TN. Over time, the technical title and publisher changes. Hereinafter cited as *Minutes*.

The *Voice* was more hopeful than accurate in predicting the responses of the political partisans, who in the wake of Parks' defeat suggested that the electoral scales were tipped in favor of their opponents. In its election post mortem, the *Voice* expressed amazement: "How any preacher or other delegates ... could go forth and say it was unfair almost baffles belief. There is something fundamentally wrong with such a person."[8]

The death of Lacy Kirk Williams in 1940 triggered another election with no incumbent. David V. Jemison, a longtime supporter of Williams and currently the vice president-at-large in the convention, delivered an address that afforded his supporters the opportunity to give "a 'Jemison' yell." However, J. C. Austin's supporters nominated their candidate, endorsed by "a fiery address." The election was not a close one: Jemison, 1019; Austin, 193.[9]

In these rare elections with no incumbent, one would expect some partisan rancor, and the historical record reveals this sentiment in abundance, but the larger point remains that the convention appears to have contained the heated politics and rallied behind newly elected leaders, who were then carried for long presidential terms. However, even during these long incumbencies, there were regular, but unsuccessful, challenges to continuing the annual terms of the sitting president for several reasons. The first one is easily overlooked. Long-serving presidents sometimes wanted to pass the torch because of the demands of the job. President Morris, for example, in his presidential address in 1911 intoned: "This is the seventeenth time I have had the distinguished honor of delivering an annual address as the president of your great Convention. If my own feelings are to be consulted and you are to be governed by them, I am now making my final report as president of this great body." His wishes were not heeded. As was

---

[8] *NBV*, 23 December 1922, 8.

[9] *Minutes, 1941*, 45–46. Williams died in a plane crash en route to a fete for Republican Candidate Wendell Willkie. A fire erupted at Williams's funeral causing some NBC members to see his death as "divine retribution" because of an episode involving the NBC books in 1930. Edward D. Pierson, the NBC auditor, had been mysteriously murdered and elements in the NBC continued to believe that somehow Williams might have been complicit in the homicide. The point is that NBC presidents had supporters and detractors, and detractors often perceived the presidents to be morally challenged leaders. Nevertheless, the forces of unity tended to predominate in the convention. Best, "Right Achieved," 199.

the ritual at most NBC conventions, a member from the floor, Dr. E. J. Fisher, a Chicagoan, first acknowledged his approbation of Morris's address, "moved that the rules [governing elections] be suspended[,] and Dr. Morris be elected President by acclamation." This time, convention members debated the motion, perhaps because there was a candidate who some in the convention preferred to the continued the incumbency of Morris, and a regular vote occurred. Its result showed that "Dr. Morris was overwhelmingly elected in spite of his expressed inclination to retire from an office which he had filled so acceptably for seventeen years." Just seven years later Morris again indicated his desire to step down. Again, his wishes were not heeded, perhaps because many preferred his leadership and some feared an election might divide the convention. He was re-elected anyway in 1918, 1919, 1920, and 1921, three times by acclamation, before he died on 5 September 1922.[10]

A second reason came from the regional divisions within the convention, which operated alongside the divisive ambitions of rivals. J. Pius Barbour, longtime editor of the *Voice*, provided an astute analysis of presidential politics during the 1920s, '30s, and '40s. Holding forth on why David Jemison continued in office for so many years despite the desires of able challengers and the limitations imposed by Jemison's failing eyesight, Barbour schooled his readers in the realities of NBC politics with the following:

> When I first came into the National Convention, I was in a group that wanted to get Dr. E. C. Morris out. Then when Dr. Williams became president, I was a ring leader in the group that wanted to get him out, until my brother got an office and then I became a Williamsite with a vengeance. I am a member of the Jemison administration and, of course, what I say is in his favor. But underneath all this wiggling and turning of mine was an unconscious urge. I WANTED TO GET IN MYSELF. The difference between my revolutionary actions and some of my friends was: I knew why I was trying to stir up something and they tried to cover up theirs by talking about "The Good of the Work" and "the promotion of the Lord's Work." Some of these men hold office now and I have not heard a peep out of them since....

---

[10] *Minutes, 1911,* 28, 44; *Minutes 1918,* 31, 33, 39; *Minutes 1920,* 54; Minutes, *1921,* 46; *Minutes, 1922,* 27.

Are the present Bolsheviks made of more noble stuff than those off my younger days? Not one bit. The same thing that stirred us in those days stirs them: AMBITION FOR LEADERSHIP. And this is why Dr. Jemison is still President![11]

To Barbour, Jemison was more than a convenient figurehead; he was a man of exemplary moral leadership. However, even worthy rivals were not able to mount a challenge to Jemison's presidency because these rivals cancelled out one another. While each rival had a strong base of potential voters, none had a majority in the convention, and because Jemison hailed from Alabama, attacking him earned any rival the ire of Alabama Baptists. Jemison noted that in former times, the convention was almost "monarchal [*sic*]," but under Jemison, the operation had become more democratic. However, it was lower member satisfaction and more transparency in NBC operations that resulted in long presidential terms. Mostly, the executive secretaries of convention boards, the likely challengers to a sitting president, tended to run little fiefdoms. However, because not one of them was able to mount a successful challenge and become president—because the other convention officials would not unite behind a single challenger—these officials quickly became advocates of the presidential *status quo*. "Now put all these things together," concluded Barbour, "and you see the reason why the Chief is re-elected almost before he can get off the train."[12]

A third reason involved the experience with serious challenges to incumbency. These challenges did portend of the real potential for schism in the convention. As one might expect, the *Voice* worked to dissuade potential aspirants to the presidential office from seeking elevation to it, reinforcing the notion that presidential stability was a major desideratum because the ongoing fiscal and management concerns made "the swapping of horses in the middle of the stream" quite unwise. Such sentiments appear to have been designed to dissuade both potential presidential aspirants and the denominational rank and file from dissension, which was made to seem worldly and unchristian.[13]

This dominant political culture, however, proved barely adequate to preserve stability in a denomination that mixed human ambition and the

---

[11] *NBV*, 1 October 1948, 4.

[12] Ibid.

[13] *NBV*, 4 September 1926, 8.

Baptist ideas of congregational autonomy and democracy. In 1926, early in the long presidency of Lacy Williams, rumblings of discontent against Williams's serving longer than four years surfaced in the months leading up to the annual convention meeting in Fort Worth, Texas. A movement surfaced to amend the constitution preventing succession for longer than four years without at least a year out of office. Others, including Williams's active supporters and many other National Baptists, held to the ideas that change for the sake of change was an unwise policy and that constitutional reform actually threatened a Baptist right to choose one's own leaders. A majority at the Fort Worth Convention stood with Williams and the current constitution, choosing to not limit presidential terms.[14]

In 1931, again during the presidency of Lacy Williams, rivals mounted a serious challenge to unseat him. The division on the eve of the national convention appeared so deep that observers queried: "Is the National Baptist Convention to live?"[15] This drama provided a lesson in the understanding of the politics of the convention, evidence of growing frustration with long presidential terms and constitutional provisions that permitted it, among some members of the NBC, but especially a demonstration of the omnipresent frustration and ambition that might potentially break apart the NBC. A massive debt accrued by the Sunday School Publishing Board of the NBC pitted against convention impecuniousness animated by the Great Depression, as well as the ethnic frustration coming from the fact that Williams's financial manager was "a Chicago Jew," created a complex collage of issues making the meeting of the NBC in Atlanta particularly stormy. Two interrelated topics provided the proxies for this critical debated in NBC life. Voters could endorse Williams or Rev. J. C. Jackson, who pledged himself to "a four year term of office." And voters could continue the current convention constitution, last altered in 1925, or ratify a major constitutional revision, which included limiting the presidential term to four years and adjusting the power of the executive committee, seen by the revisers as an extension of Williams' presidential prerogatives and a violation of Baptist prerogatives to govern themselves through direct democracy. Under the

---

[14] J. H. Jackson, *A Story of Christian Activism: The History of the National Baptist Convention, U. S. A., Inc.* (Nashville: Townshend Press, 1980) 151–53.

[15] *NBV*, 8 August 1931, 12.

proposed new constitution, the board of directors would need to ratify executive board action.[16]

Partisanship abounded. J. D. Burdett called for continuity, blaming the bad economy, not the president, for convention woes. Continue Williams as president, he urged, for Williams is "the tallest tree in the forest." E. L. Harrison, whose nomination in 1922 began Williams's long service in the presidential chair, had decided to abandon his former chief, concluding "HE IS FAILING." After six years of effective leadership, Williams allegedly overly centralized the operation of the convention, and this lack of transparency led to both the financial woes and the resurrection of the issue of Williams's presidential legitimacy in the convention. Concluding that Williams should step down, Harrison thundered, neither "his pride nor the urge of enthusiastic parasites should be allowed to persuade him to cling to the presidency."[17]

In some ways, the politics of the national level convention trickled down to the state conventions, and commentary by the *Voice* on the conduct of state conventions provides insight into the workings of NBC politics, especially human feelings and Baptist polity. In July 1931, African American Baptists in Mississippi endured quite a row between the longtime state moderator and his challengers. The moderator's actions had, according to his opponents, "produced an anti-administration force that keenly feels your partial ruling," despite other achievements by the moderator and his administration. The editor of the *Voice* noted that state conventions were operating just like the NBC. Indeed, the Mississippi moderator, who was removed by his opponents, said, "I got my methods from the National Baptist Convention."[18]

Such a highly charged political atmosphere produced quite a donnybrook at the national convention. As the meeting approached, an observer noted that full trainloads of delegates were heading for Atlanta, with all the

---

[16] "There was considerable secrecy about how the Hebrew Manager would raise the prospective … million dollars [to pay off the publishing debt]. President Williams and the inner circle of his administration gave the impression that this Jew would sell the bonds to some wealthy white concerns; but when the board members insisted on knowing how he would raise the money the Jew positively refused" (*NBV*, 15 August 1913, 1).

[17] *NBV*, 14 August 1931, 11, 14; 5 September 1931, 1–2.

[18] *NBV*, 8 April 1931, 8.

zeal of a secular partisan nominating convention. The meeting was certainly spirited. Following a speech by United States Representative Oscar De Priest of Chicago, the time came for Williams's presidential address. While most convention addresses were political events cloaked in partisan enthusiasm, and so often led to a re-election of the speaker by acclamation, this event had no precedent in the convention annals. Before Williams could begin, his supporters paraded in the convention hall, carrying their state banners, "shouting 'Williams,' while the mammoth audience, equally thrilled with enthusiasm mingled their voices and joined in the great ovation accorded" the convention president. At the conclusion of his address, Williams's supporters presented him with flowers and made financial offerings to the NBC in Williams's honor. In the wake of these demonstrations, Rev. J. C. Jackson's supporters offered his name in opposition to the Williams presidency and uttered "fiery and eloquent" speeches urging his election. Williams's supporters followed suit. Williams prevailed in the election, 564 to 145. After a stormy session, noted the *Voice*, perhaps with some journalistic interpretation, "No sign of bitterness followed. The people had rendered their verdict and it was accepted as final."[19]

Williams's seemingly easy re-election blunts the significance of the 1931 convention. The non-schismatic event was nearly a schismatic event. In soothing language, the *Voice* asserted that "it is no crime for a Baptist pastor to aspire on the highest office within our gift. Our denomination needs these leaders and their good influences." At the same time, National Baptists who were frustrated with the operation of the convention could rally around constitutional reform, specifically limits on the number of terms that a president could serve successively, as an acceptable manner to express their dissent, a tactic that substituted politics of process for the politics of the presidency. A minority of NBC members who became stymied by convention and presidential-level policies could express their ire by advocating for a revision of the constitution. However, as events were to eventually

---

[19] *Minutes, 1931*, 40–41; *NBV*, 7 November 1931, 3. De Priest, the first African American elected to Congress in the twentieth century, and the first ever elected from outside the Deep South, sat in the House of Representatives from 1929 through 1935. See Kristie Millier, "Oscard de Priest," in Henry Louis Gates, Jr., and Evelyn Brooks Higginbotham, eds., *Harlem Renaissance Lives: From the African American National Biography* (New York City: Oxford University Press, 2009) 148–49.

show, relocating dissent away from the annual election and toward a constitutional model to limit presidential tenure simply rearranged frustrations, especially for long-standing, self-conscious minorities in the convention. Inability to amend the constitution underscored the lack of power a minority had in the convention. And the politics of the presidency simply transmogrified the politics of the constitution.[20]

Because the NBC fundamentally consisted of congregations united in support of missions, due to the exigencies of the Great Depression and World War II, and perhaps animated by the danger of presidential and constitutional politics affecting denominational unity, a number of years passed before the issue of tenure rose from dormancy again after the knock-out blow of the 1931 convention. Indeed, rumors that Rev. J. C. Jackson would again challenge Williams for the presidency, a report of which appeared in an African American newspaper on 7 September 1935, so moved members of the convention that a committee was appointed to investigate and, when it found no substance to the rumor, formally acted:

> In-so-far as no act or known inclination of Dr. Jackson substantiates this newspaper statement, but to the contrary, his every act with regard to the National Baptist Convention has been in full and unquestioned loyalty to the President of the Convention, be it.
>
> Resolved, that this Convention in session, go down on record as condemning the newspaper article referred to, and commend Dr. Jackson as one of her most loyal members and one of President Williams' ardent and staunch supporters.[21]

Given the mission of the convention, much of its activity involved foreign missions, an arena in which a young minister born in Rudyard, Mississippi, was fast acquiring a name for himself as a tireless advocate and eloquent champion. In 1934, Joseph H. Jackson had become the Executive Secretary for the Foreign Mission Board. His formal address to the

---

[20] *NBV*, 7 November 1931, 1. Jackson, *Story of Christian Activism* mentions challenges to long-serving presidents, including the 1931 challenge, and in other portions of his massive history, he provides great detail about convention meetings, but he does not treat the 1931 convention, even though he addressed the convention for the first time that year. See Jackson, *Story of Christian Activism*, 217; and *Minutes, 1931*, 39, which style his inaugural speech, titled *The Holy Ghost in Regeneration*, as "one of the most brilliant and inspiring of the session."

[21] *Minutes*, 1935, 54.

convention in 1935 "stirred the Convention with practical thoughts from his earnest, fiery soul, as he, in a masterly manner, gave convincing proof of the onward march of the church, defying the gates of hell." Simultaneously, the convention continued its advocacy work for the earthly condition of its members by endorsing the National Association for the Advancement of Colored People (NAACP), its executive leader, Walter White, and the Legal Defense Fund of Charles Houston and his able assistant Thurgood Marshall. In urging its members to support this work, the Convention called the NAACP "the fighting arm of the church."[22]

The NBC missionary and domestic advocacy continued in the years after World War II. For the generation of NBC leaders who were born at the turn of the century, these were challenging times. Vigorous demands for change abroad melded into the reality of the Cold War and the domestic Red Scare at home. African Americans had flirted with Communism during the 1920s and 1930s, but Stalin's alliance with Hitler in August 1939 exposed the hypocrisy of Soviet advocacy of oppressed people, as Jim Crow continued to make a mockery of the US Bill of Rights. NBC leadership tended to focus on obtaining the fulfillment of US rights within the existing constitutional system rather than advocating radical structural change at the governmental level. However, even gradualism, cloaked in pastoral language, invited scrutiny from conservative elements who considered advocacy for improvement at home to provide support for what was believed to be international communism. In testifying before the House Committee on Un-American Activities in 1948, Rev. Sandy F. Ray, a classmate of Martin Luther King, Sr., (Morehouse, 1930) and pastor of the Cornerstone Baptist Church in Brooklyn, challenged the conservative fear and captured the consensus of the NBC's idea about church and state in a Jim Crow America in an era of Cold War:

> We believe that it is the business of a prophetic religion to speak boldly in defense of justice and freedom. We believe we have a clear mandate, as successor to the prophets, to resist all forms of oppression, and to preach universal good will, and global brotherhood. We cannot escape the passion for social justice. We believe that our material, political, and military powers have too greatly out-distanced our moral and spiritual strength. As religious leaders, we have no thought of overthrowing this government by violence. We do, however, seek to overthrow and intangible empire which exists in our

---

[22] *Minutes*, 1935, 40; *Minutes*, 1934, 105.

government and many of our institutions throughout the land. It is that empire which shelters injustice, oppression, exploitation, segregation, discrimination, ill will, and all of the inconsistencies which makes for separation, tension and strife.

Genuine democracy realized in the United States and support for democratic governments abroad, concluded Ray, offered the surest bulwark against global communism and anti-Americanism.[23]

The African American struggle for secular democracy, and those who were allowed to define it, paralleled ongoing constitutional struggles within the NBC. Ongoing electioneering within the convention resulted in a vocal display of displeasure at the teller's report of the election for vice president-at-large in 1947. Despite the dispute, and consistent with past practices of placing unity before partisanship, candidate Joseph H. Jackson urged his supporters to accept his rival, E. W. Perry, as vice president-at-large, while withdrawing his own candidacy, making the election unanimous. The growing tension between the power of the board of directors in the convention and the rank-and-file delegates proved more difficult to resolve. Constitutional revisions had made the board responsible "to complete the unfinished business of the [annual] Convention, and to adjust such matters as may be referred to it by the Convention, and to fill any vacancies which may occur in the roster of the Convention." According to George Crawley of Baltimore, the board had accomplished important things, but it was increasingly viewed as both anti-democratic and weak in its efforts to promote "practical vocational Christianity." Its allegedly tepid support of social Christianity meant that African Americans were turning to other

---

[23] *NBV*, 15 June 1949. 1, 14; A longtime friend of the King family, Rev. Ray allowed his home to serve as a place of convalescence following the stabbing of Martin Luther King, Jr., in 1950. For more on Ray, see Martin Luther King Papers Project, http://mlk-kpp01.stanford.edu/index.php/encyclopedia/documentsentry/doc_400118_000/ (accessed 14 April 2013). The scholarship on the tortured relationship between the Cold War and African American civil rights is excellent and ubiquitous. See Mary L. Dudziak, *Cold War Civil Rights: Race and the Image of American Democracy*, reprint ed. (Princeton: Princeton University Press, 2011) 18–46.

supports than the NBC and its churches to deal with the vicissitudes of life.[24]

The political tensions within the convention, perhaps animated by the emergence of new leadership and the maelstrom of racial change during the years of the Eisenhower Presidency exploded in the 1950s. Debates over constitutional change, the elevation of Joseph H. Jackson to the NBC presidency, and the frustration with his alleged manipulation of executive power and the constitution melded to create denominational schism. When the convention met in Chicago in September 1952, it heard a report reflecting the aspirations of "a coalition of primarily younger ministers," to amend its constitution to prohibit a president who had "served four consecutive years" from serving again "until at least one year has elapsed" since his last term. Some suggested that the report be tabled until 1953, but President Jemison instructed the convention to take up the matter on Friday, 12 September 1952, the third day of the convention. At 10:30 a.m., with Joseph H. Jackson presiding in his capacity as vice president, the convention heard extended debate on the proposal, and then, the convention voted to affirm the revision. Thus, the NBC had placed term limits into its constitution, on the surface at least, bringing to an end the long presidencies that had characterized its denominational history.[25]

In January 1953, ailing President Jemison announced his resignation, which took effect in September of that year, permitting his presidency to continue until the NBC convened to elect a new chief. This logical plan worked to mask the deeper turmoil underneath the surface of the convention, in which six candidates were nominated to replace Jemison in a

---

[24] *Minutes, 1947*, 56–57; *Minutes, 1948*, 4; *NBV*, 15 August 1948, 1. Jackson's own version of his quest for the vice-presidency-at-large is found in Jackson, *Story of Christian Activism*, 208–9.

[25] *Minutes, 1952*, 4, 62–63; Jackson, *Story of Christian Activism*, 209–13. Historian Nick Salvatore's view links youth, a burgeoning civil rights movement, and Jackson's autocracy as causes of the schism. His *Singing in a Strange Land: C. L. Franklin, the Black Church, and the Transformation of America* (New York City: Little, Brown and Co., 2005) 193–96, is a splendid analysis, as the whole study is simply magisterial on the African American migration and Christian-informed social change in twentieth-century America. Salvatore lists five candidates for the 1953 election, because there were five tellers named to conduct the presidential election, but on the floor, six ministers were actually nominated for NBC president in 1953.

hyper-partisan atmosphere. Jemison, for his part, believed it necessary to declare before the assembled delegates that "he had never accepted a bribe with respect to his retirement from the presidency." Four of the six candidates, Marshall Shepard, J. R. Henderson, H. B. Hawkins and Sandy Ray, withdrew from contention, with Henderson and Hawkins urging their supporters to back E. W. Perry, longtime NBC vice president and pastor of Tabernacle Baptist Church of Oklahoma City. Facing Perry was Jackson, pastor of Olivet Baptist Church, a post he had held since resigning as Foreign Mission Board Executive Secretary in 1941, a pulpit once occupied by Lacy Kirk Williams. In 1947, Jackson had stepped aside for Perry in a contested election for vice president-at-large. This time, Jackson boasted electoral strength and prevailed in the balloting 2,035 to 1,555. Jackson would remain NBC president for the next twenty-nine years. Already well-traveled, having visited Africa, and Europe, the Mississippi-born Jackson represented the great migration, having moved out of the South in 1927, strident in his anti-communist sentiments, and a powerful interracial and international advocate of ecumenism, mostly under the aegis of the World Council of Churches. A mixture of deep Baptist convictions and powerful personal ambition, Jackson earned respect from his friends, ire from his foes, and serves as an example of go-slow accommodation and conservatism when compared to both the civil rights activists within the Southern Christian Leadership Conference and the black theology movements. As Wallace Best has shown, Jackson's beliefs and actions "defied easy generalization." Although Jackson's advocacy of social change lacked the militant stridency of Malcolm X or Martin Luther King, Jr., his brand of conservative and constitutional social change included a large role for governmental action, according to Sandy Dwayne Martin, which places Jackson at odds with the conservatism of the late 1990s and early 2000s. At the time of his elevation to the presidency, he seemed not at all controversial, having the support of Martin Luther King, Sr., and his soon-to-become-famous son, and he was viewed by his supporters as an example of "more intelligent leadership" within the NBC. Additionally, given the rancor that would soon erupt over his presidency, Jackson was unanimously re-elected by the NBC in 1954.[26]

---

[26] *Minutes, 1953*, 59–61; *Minutes, 1954*, 70; M. J. Proffitt to J. H. Jackson, 4 September 1953, in Rev. Joseph H. Jackson Papers, Box. 11, Chicago History Museum Research Center [hereafter Jackson Papers]. Best, "Right Achieved," 198;

Perhaps the changing expectations of successive generations serve to explain the contradiction between the eventual negative characterizations of Jackson as an accommodationist and denominational dictator by his detractors and the continuing adulation by his supporters who found him to be a symbol of optimism and racial progress in the 1950s. Having earned graduate degrees from Colgate-Rochester Seminary, Creighton University, and the University of Pennsylvania, and having passed his qualifying exams from the University of Chicago (although he never completed his dissertation), Jackson typified the idea of uplift that had traditionally characterized the African American tradition of self-help, progress, and the attainment of greater legal and social rights. Residing in Chicago's south side, Jackson was a member of the African American establishment, was politically well-connected with both the political scenes in Chicago and in the Democratic Party (although Jackson later became a Republican). For a generation who had escaped poverty and racial violence in the rural South and who represented economic and social progress in the promised land of Chicago, Jackson provided evidence that one could move toward the American dream even as a black man. At the same time, the long line of Cadillacs that conveyed Jackson and his entourage from the Dearborn Street Station in Chicago to Olivet Baptist Church following his return from Miami and election as NBC president became easy evidence that Jackson enjoyed the

---

Sandy Dwayne Martin, "Uncle Tom, Pragmatist, or Visionary? An Assessment of the Reverend Dr. Joseph Harrison Jackson and Civil Rights," in Peter Eisenstadt, ed., *Black Conservatism: Essays on Intellectual and Political History* (New York City: Garland, 1999) 170; Sherman Roosevelt Tribble, Jackson's biographer, calls Jackson a "progressive accommodationist," and Jackson's writings and advocacy sustain an accommodationist label only when comparing him to more radical spokespersons for social change in the 1960s; his writings read not so differently from the ideas of Roy Wilkins or Walter White. See his *Images of a Preacher: A Study of the Reverend Joseph Harrison Jackson* (Nashville: Townsend Press, 1990). In recent years, a robust scholarship on African American responses to Jim Crow posits alternatives to an activist versus accommodationist alternative and notes that the apparent accommodationism of African American conservatives did in fact place significant demands on the white power structure. See Eisenstadt, ed., *Black Conservatism*, xi–xii.

trappings of prestige and office, even as other African Americans endured systematic poverty and were repeated targets of racial violence.[27]

In defending British soldiers accused of murder at what was subsequently dubbed the Boston Massacre, John Adams held that "facts are stubborn things and whatever may be our wishes, our inclinations, or the dictums of our passions, they cannot alter the state of facts and evidence." The schism in the NBC arose out of perceptions of very clear facts about the presidency and the legality of the 1952 revisions that term-limited the president and the frustrations of the political factions who supported Jackson and his policies and those who wanted change in leadership. In his massive, *Story of Christian Activism*, written twenty-eight years after the controversial constitutional change, Jackson mused that the convention at the time should have been aware of a technicality that the tenure amendment passed on the third day of the 1952 convention—in that the convention could not consider constitutional amendments after the second day of the convention in which the amendment was introduced—and it should have taken immediate action to correct the constitutional misstep. His retrospective sentiment was both understandable and self-serving, especially given the inconvenient fact that Jackson was presiding over the actual mechanics of amending the constitution, and by 1955, Jackson was calling for a process "to re-vamp, reshape, amend or to re-affirm" the term limit provisions now in the NBC constitution. He initiated a process in 1955 so that, prior to the next NBC Convention meeting in 1956, the board would consider recommendations from a special committee charged with reporting on both the constitutionality and

---

[27] W. L. Dawson to J. H. Jackson, 18 October 1952; "New Church Head Greeted by Flock," *Chicago Daily News*, 16 September 1953, in Jackson Papers, Box 11. *Uplift* is an idea that is prevalent in the African American community that an emerging African American middle class had a duty to help their less fortunate brethren by providing a moral and educational example for racial improvement while, at the same time, serving as a cultural bridge between African Americans and majority culture. See Kevin K. Gaines, *Uplifting the Race: Black Leadership, Politics, and Culture in the Twentieth Century* (Chapel Hill: University of North Carolina Press, 1996). The generational theme is ironic: Young progressives were critical of Jackson and others; later a younger generation of African Americans would deride King as "de lawd" and reject his strategies for racial advancement. See Harvard Sitkoff, *King: Pilgrimage to the Mountaintop* (New York City: Hill and Wang, 2008) 188–92.

efficacy of term limits in each of its three regular meetings, mid-winter, June, and September. At this point, the recommendation from Jackson did not seem especially controversial, and the process Jackson called for received unanimous endorsement, moved by Gardner C. Taylor, who would later become Jackson's rival for the presidency and eventually part of the Progressive secession movement in the early 1960s.[28]

The apparent calm in the wake of the committee process inaugurated in 1955 yielded to tempest at the June 1956 board of directors meeting in Chicago. When that body began its discussion of the tenure issue, Dr. L. K. Jackson, a prominent pastor from Gary, Indiana, took the floor and denounced the "present administration" of the NBC as "immoral for seeking a change in the Constitution." Despite a motion made by Martin Luther King, Sr., that he apologize, L. K. Jackson did not.[29]

In early September, the 1956 NBC convened in Denver. The revision committee was evenly divided between those favoring term limits and those wishing to revert to the long-standing practice of long presidential terms. The committee recommendations also linked presidential tenure with a welter of convention offices. While many NBC members did want to end what J. H. Jackson's critics called "one man rule," other convention officials and their supporters realized that the committee was now recommending that rotation-in-office provisions apply to NBC board members, including the salaried executive secretary, and vice-presidents. Jackson himself had strong floor support and, in fact, was unanimously elected for a fourth term. In the maelstrom that followed, the NBC took up the committee report, with the convention at a deadlock. Jackson recalled that he simply retired from the convention meeting place, while Charles King recalled that Jackson said to his detractors "they can have the convention," and stormed out.[30] While the convention attempted to continue its business, NBC attorney A.

---

[28] *Minutes, 1955*, 65; Jackson, *Story of Christian Activism*, 332–36. Adams quoted in David McCullough, *John Adams* (New York City: Simon & Schuster, 2001) 68.

[29] *Minutes, 1956*, 47; Lewis V. Baldwin, *There is a Balm in Gilead: The Cultural Roots of Martin Luther King, Jr.* (Minneapolis: Augsburg Fortress, 1991) 215–16; Charles H. King, Jr., *Fire in My Bones* (Grand Rapids: Eerdmans, 1983) 82.

[30] *Minutes, 1956*, 59, 62, 65; King, *Fire in My Bones*, 83; Jackson, *Story of Christian Activism*, 332–40.

T. Walden sought an *ad hoc* committee of ministers to find Jackson and get him to return to the convention.

A fair inference for a reader of Jackson's *Story of Christian Activism* suggests that efforts by such a committee constituted a fool's errand. Jackson was not especially happy with Walden and was unlikely to accede to the request to return initiated by the barrister. He asserts that Walden had advised him in writing that the 1952 amendments were improperly adopted and, therefore, of no effect, but Walden had become reticent to repeat that advice from the convention rostra to those NBC members who favored the tenure provisions in the constitution. The convention minutes are silent about the on-going tenure debate during what remained of the convention. However, for the first time, Martin Luther King, Jr., addressed the convention, thanking Jackson for his rhetorical and monetary contributions in support of the recently concluded Montgomery Bus Boycott, before delivering what the minutes style as a "fresh and dynamic" address entitled *Paul's Letter to American Christians,* a version of which he later delivered at Dexter Avenue Baptist Church. Because anti-Jackson forces began to tout King as a possible successor to Jackson in the wake of the successful reception that King's address garnered from NBC members, and given Jackson's later antipathy toward King, some have viewed the convention address and the potential for King to rival Jackson's control over the NBC as the starting point of the fracture between these two African American Baptist leaders. However, scholars directed by Clayborne Carson at the King Papers Project have conclusively demonstrated that the break between these two men stems from a later date. And, it was the use that anti-Jackson men wanted to make of King, not necessarily how King and Jackson regarded one another in September 1956, that would initiate their eventual feud.[31]

---

[31] Clayborne Carson, et al., *The Papers of Martin Luther King, Jr., Volume III: Birth of a New Age, December 1955–December 1956* (Berkeley: University of California Press, 1997) 27. Charles King cites the best evidence for Jackson's being jealous of the reception that MLK received at the Denver convention in 1956 as the root of the personal schism between the two men (85–86). At the same time, he notes that MLK sat down rather than continue his address, as prodded by the anti-Jackson faction in the NBC at the conclusion of his address. A stronger case can be made for Jackson's sensing MLK as a possible rival when he was unanimously chosen as vice president of the Sunday School and Baptist Training Union Congress following the Denver meeting. Nonetheless, MLK asked Jackson to serve on the

However, the divisions within the convention were deepened, and its ability to place unity over platform was threatened by conflicting devotion to partisanship and principle. With Jackson's presidency formally terminated by the current tenure amendments, with his supporters clamoring for repeal, and given his presidential role of chairing the convention until his successor was declared, the 1957 Convention in Louisville promised drama. And it delivered. Politically astute and supported by a powerful base, Jackson was determined to remain president and relied on his own political skill and the zeal of his supporters. Pastor Herbert Brewster of East Trigg Avenue Baptist Church in Memphis was one such Jackson supporter. He arranged for a special Jackson cheering squad to attend the convention in support of a continued Jackson presidency and had even song written extolling Jackson as the proper Baptist leader in difficult times. Brewster's Jackson voters were to "wear a [pro-Jackson] badge and vote" for him in Louisville. Other Jackson supporters sought a logical and evidentiary base to justify continuing Jackson's presidency. Rev. Steve H. Banks of Amos Chapel and Union Missionary Baptist Church in Pine Bluff produced a pro-Jackson pamphlet evoking the sentiment of Isaiah 1:18: "Come Let Us Reason Together." He offered six reasons for opposing term limits: there was no record of it in the early church, it found no support in the texts of the Old or New Testaments, it deprived people of the opportunity to continue under the leadership of someone acceptable to them, it prompted office seeking by materially motivated candidates, it was foisted on the NBC by an unconstitutional amendment process, and it was unnecessary because Jackson was such a good president. Banks concluded: "WE DO NOT NEED tenure. To-DAY WE NEED Dr. J. H. Jackson for President."[32]

The board of directors met just prior the full NBC meeting in 1957. The question of tenure dominated their discussion, and neither attorney A. T. Walden's conflicted legal advice nor an ambiguous stance on the issue by the board lent clarity to the opening session of the Convention when the

---

National Advisory Committee of the Southern Christian Leadership Conference's *Crusade for Citizenship*, MLK to J H. Jackson, 17 December 1957, Box 11, Jackson Papers. Sherman Tribble, *Images of a Preacher*, locates the breach in the tempestuous 1960 convention (88). However, for a recent and different characterization of these same events, see Hitchmough, "Missions of Patriotism," 3–4.

[32] Herbert Brewster to J. H. Jackson, 1 August 1957; Stephen Banks, "Facts about Tenure," Box 22, Jackson Papers.

initial gaveling called it to order on Wednesday, September 4. Amazingly, the complex procedural issue was now reduced to which way the convention's presiding officer, Jackson, would rule on the constitutionality of the 1952 amendment process. He did not disappoint his supporters or detractors. Dr. Charles H. Williams rose to a point of order and averred that the 1952 constitution, having been wrongly adopted, was "null and void." At this procedural signal, as presiding officer, Jackson had to rule.

What follows is a brilliantly deliberate process of legal and constitutional proceedings that ensured the rejection of the previously ratified constitution limiting the term limits of the convention president. He summoned his convention secretary to read the mechanics for amending the constitution, the constitution of 1951, in effect when the tenure amendment passed in 1952. The secretary's reading of the convention minutes for 1952 clearly showed that the tenure amendment received ratification on day three, in clear violation of the constitution.[33] In a carefully worded apology, Jackson said he did not know until July 1956 that the amendment had been improperly, as opposed to unwisely, adopted. He then read a letter from NBC attorney Walden into the record, which opined that the 1952 tenure amendment had been inappropriately adopted. He then read a concurring letter from attorney W. S. Bodman, affirming the dubious constitutionality of the offending amendment. At this point, Jackson turned to the cultural and procedural authority of Henry Martyn Robert, whose *Rules of Order* have been used properly and improperly since its first edition appeared in the centennial year of the United States: "Any measure adopted contrary to the constitution of the body are null and void."[34]

The NBC *Minutes*, which reflect the voice of those in power, recorded that "the huge delegation was delirious with joy that they were now free to select the man of their choice." And in a refrain dating to the earliest days of the convention, "Dr. T. S. Harten moved that the rules be suspended and Dr. Jackson be re-elected president. The motion was seconded ... by many more. The president was elected by acclamation." The old constitution was thus restored and the current president was thus retained. At the same time,

---

[33] *Minutes, 1957*, 54–55; Jackson, *Story of Christian Activism*, 340–48.
[34] Ibid.

the minutes note that the vote was not unanimous, a harbinger of continued fracturing in the convention.[35]

Charles King's memoir adds some clarity and color, while agreeing on essential points with both Jackson's *Story of Christian Activism* and the *Minutes*: "While conceding the fact that it was voted on in violation of the constitution, the progressive forces contended that the 'spirit of the constitution was as the majority directed.' ... It was not the legal issue they argued, it was a matter of ethics." When Jackson ruled, "All hell broke loose," as Jackson's organization flooded the hall with demonstrators and banners, which had been housed outside the convention hall in trucks. "There was a struggle for the microphone, and Jackson's forces commandeered it," calling for the suspension of the rules, and an election, "*a full day before it was programmed*, ... an old convention trick," according to King.[36]

Jackson's memoir-history seeks to assign responsibility for the confusion on the attorneys, especially Walden, who in separate written communiques from July 1956, had held that mechanics of the tenure amendments was unconstitutional, a legal opinion supported subsequently by Attorney W. S. Bodman. In addition, he suggests that he really was not aware of the problematic nature of the tenure amendments until 1955, when he sponsored the committee to solve the problem. And he assigns the date of July 1956 when he learned that the amendments were not adopted properly. He implies that Walden had given inconsistent counsel to board members, including J. Pius Barbour, who then asked him why the attorney had not made the editor of the *Voice* aware of his opinion that the tenure amendments were improperly adopted.[37]

Jackson asserted that Walden never answered Barbour's query and that Jackson considered Walden's inconsistent tactics a "double cross."[38] Charles H. King, however, asserts that Jackson's supporters sold him to the convention as the proper candidate precisely because his platform both endorsed term limits and indicated that he would abide by it. Jackson's personal papers shed no light on the possibilities. Jackson may have supported tenure to get elected and then employed his power to nullify it. He may not have

---

[35] *Ibid.* For the restored constitution, see *Minutes*, 1958, 6.

[36] King, *Fire in My Bones*, 83–84.

[37] Jackson, *Story of Christian Activism*, 347-8; King, *Fire in My Bones*, 82.

[38] Ibid. A reader scouring Jackson's Papers will not find evidence of Jackson's relation to the tenure issue, especially whether or not it was a tool to get him elected.

understood the significance of what he was doing in presiding over the 1952 amendments, as he sometimes claimed. He may have initially supported term limits and then changed his mind. His subsequent actions do indicate that he thought he acted in a principled manner.

Regardless, the thin record on Jackson's motivations for his subsequent actions does not support a definitive judgment, but it is clear that NBC members could and did form clear opinions about the propriety of Jackson's actions. Many thought his ruling to be high-handed; he should not have acted legalistically, because the convention had overwhelmingly supported tenure in 1952. Jackson, himself, suggested that he sought to resign in 1956 but was dissuaded in doing so because he was, as one unanimously elected, the people's choice. Those throngs who broke with Jackson had failed to garner majorities to unseat him in subsequent annual elections and, for a variety of reasons, most NBC members followed Jackson's opponents into the PNBC. That is, depending on how one frames the question, majoritarian principles either affirm or condemn Jackson, his supporters, and his detractors.[39]

The NBC returned to Chicago for its 1958 convention. Jackson bestrode the convention world as Colossus, a dominant figure in Chicago, the dominant figure in the NBC, an important figure in the world of secular politics and, from his perspective, a significant figure in the efforts to end racial discrimination. Both Chicago mayor Richard J. Daley and Illinois governor William J. Stratton addressed the NBC. Greetings came from Baptists in India and Russia, lands Jackson had previously visited. The Reverend Vernon Johns thundered that social justice on earth was required before the kingdom of God would be realized. Southern Baptist Convention president Brooks Hayes then addressed the convention calling for interracial unity in the great task of promoting human brotherhood, calling for "human institutions [to] … be brought into conformity to the laws of God, for the establishment of justice is an act of God." At this point, Jackson informed the convention that the United States Supreme Court demanded

---

[39] Wallace Best assigns the responsibility for the 1952 constitutional revisions to Jemison, and he notes that some of Jackson's supporters hoped he would resist tampering with tenure, once elected. At best, circumstantial evidence would show that "Jackson worked slowly toward the effort of revising the tenure amendment." Best, "Right Achieved," 202.

the immediate integration of Central High School in Little Rock, Arkansas. As the conventioneers sang, "Hold to God's Unchanging Hand" and "Rock of Ages, Cleft for Me," Jackson could easily believe that the NBC and African Americans stood on the threshold of racial and religious betterment. The $3,000 gift from the NBC board of directors and a new 1958 Chrysler presented by Olivet Baptist Church seemed like upward mobility and the providence of God to Jackson's supporters, but Jackson's detractors formed a different view.[40]

Jackson and his NBC supporters moved through the 1950s, aware of denominational growth and discord. They reveled in the promise of social change, demonstrated by the decision of the Supreme Court in *Brown v. Board of Education*, handed down on 17 May 1954, a day that Jackson worked for two decades to have designated a national holiday. At the same time, the murder of Emmitt Till and the lynching of Mack C. Parker, both victims of the intractable racism in Jackson's home state of Mississippi, provoked responses from Jackson and the NBC. The NBC leadership continued to press for social change in its traditional ways. At its 1959 convention, the NBC adopted Jackson's statements on the progress of school integration and a statement affirming faith in the fundamental goodness and fairness of the United States. At Jackson's behest, the executive board sent a resolution to Mississippi governor James C. Coleman, calling for the governor's support to end the violence that compelled Rev. Harrison DuPree to flee the Magnolia State.[41]

While Jackson had supported the activities of the Montgomery Improvement Association to achieve "first come, first serve" seating on city buses, Jackson believed strongly in social change through law and order. He thought that racial equality and social justice would ensue if people obeyed the laws and extended their full protection to everyone the law was to cover. Beginning 1 February 1960, a wave of sit-ins by college students in Greensboro, North Carolina, quickly spread to twenty states and one hundred cities

---

[40] *Minutes, 1958,* 54, 56; Jackson, *Story of Christian Activism,* 351, 353.

[41] *Minutes, 1959,* 50–51, 55, 58; Jackson, *Story of Christian Activism,* 360–67. In many ways, Jackson typified the consensus outlook of the post-World War II era in the United States. See Best, "Right Achieved," 208–13. Sam Hitchmough notes that "Jackson planted his patriotism firmly within a more consensual civil framework that revolved heavily around concepts of individualism, meritocracy and materialism, more the 'official' narrative of patriotism," Hitchmough, "Missions of Patriotism," 2.

by September, when the NBC gathered again for its convention in Philadelphia. Jackson found himself the target of tactics he already loathed philosophically and his practical experiences with them as a challenge to his continued presidency, confirmed his pre-existing philosophical stance. Having supported John F. Kennedy for president in the Democratic primary and then for president in 1960, a move that posed some risk to his standing among the culturally and religiously conservative Protestantism in Olivet Baptist Church, Jackson could understandably consider himself a champion of religious inclusion. Similarly, his advocacy of the 1960 Civil Rights Act put him on the side of vigorous pursuit of racial justice. However, frustration with the slow pace of social change outside of the NBC coincided with internal weariness of Jackson's seemingly pontifical presidency.[42]

As the board of directors conducted its pre-convention meeting, Jackson supporters sought to challenge the convention agenda, especially the time set for electing a president. Jackson's opponents had settled behind the candidacy of Gardner Calvin Taylor, a native of Louisiana but now pastor of Concord Baptists Church of Christ in Brooklyn, New York. Nearly twenty years younger than Jackson, Taylor was a dynamic preacher and the individual behind whom younger Baptists, who wanted a more democratic presidency in the NBC, would rally. Taylor supporters literally "sat in" and, according to Jackson, substantially disrupted the convention. The real threat to Jackson's incumbency, however, was political. Leading the so-called Taylor faction was Rev. Marshall Shepard, whom Jackson had fired as head of the Foreign Mission Board. Its goal was to have a vote on the floor, where Taylorites believed they had the numbers to defeat Jackson. A railroad strike also made travel more difficult to Philadelphia for Jackson's supporters who hailed form the South and Midwest, strengthening the hands of Jackson's opponents. However, the convention machinery rested in the hands of many Jackson supporters. Despite a gentleman's agreement that the nominating committee would place two names before the convention and then allow for voting by states, only Jackson's name went to the floor. The committee then

---

[42] *Minutes*, 1960, 52–55; Jackson, *Story of Christian Activism*, 406–30; King, *Fire in My Bones*, 91–94. J. H. Jackson, *Unholy Shadows and Freedom's Holy Light* (Nashville: Townshend Press) 121.

moved that its report—nominating only Jackson—be accepted, tantamount to electing Jackson.[43]

Bedlam rose in defiance of order. No one truly knows what happened next. Jackson attempted to ask the choir to sing; someone cut his microphone cord. Jacksonites and Taylorites attempted to determine what had happened. Taylor's supporters brought in a loud bass drum and released balloons into the air, urging the voice of the people to select their new champion as president. Amid the turmoil, someone moved that the report of the nominating committee be accepted by the NBC. The *Minutes* and Jackson's *Story of Christian Activism* assert that the motion seconded and, with the key word, "approximately," 3,500 in favor of the report and Jackson and 500 against. All reports agree that bedlam, not order, continued to hold the floor so that Jackson was not able to give the full presidential address. In the wake, many Taylorites, including Martin Luther King, Sr., were stripped of convention offices. But Taylor's forces did not yield. They held their own election in which Jackson received but 536 votes to Taylor's 1,864. The police commissioner, in an attempt to calm the waters, called for a meeting among Taylor, King, Jr., Shepard, and Jackson. He was told that such a meeting, at the behest of the police commissioner, violated the constitution of the NBC. Jackson believed King was behind the movement to unseat him as president and that King wished to transform the NBC into a civil rights organization. Jackson's view was that the church was an instrument of the gospel, a social gospel to be sure, but its fundamental purpose was souls, not the state. Jackson's determined dismissal of sit-ins, repeated most famously in *Unholy Shadows and Freedom's Holy Light*, clearly was shaped and assumed crystalline form during this 1960 convention in the City of Brotherly Love.[44]

Taylor and his supporters, including Martin Luther King, Jr., left Philadelphia claiming to be the legitimate leadership of the NBC, and they filed a lawsuit to gain control of NBC assets. Jackson countered by employing A. Leon Higginbotham to represent his faction. The attorney argued successfully that courts in Pennsylvania had no jurisdiction over the NBC,

---

[43] Ibid.

[44] Jackson, *Unholy Shadows*, 120–25; Jackson, *Story of Christian Activism*, 426–30, especially 430, for discussion of "one clergyman." Jackson's *Unholy Shadows* reads clearly as a screed attacking Dr. King. A wise, sympathetic, yet critical analysis of Jackson's ideas of civil liberty and self-help, styled by Jackson himself as "from protest to production," is found in Martin, "Uncle Tom," 177–95.

which was chartered in Washington, DC. However, the federated nature of the convention complicated efforts further than legal jurisdiction by the anti-Jackson forces in their attempt to take over the NBC. Boards and auxiliaries, long staffed with Jackson loyalists and supporters or, conversely, operating in practical independence of national leadership, eluded the grasp of the anti-Jacksonites. However, the anti-Jacksonites considered Taylor to have been legitimately elected, and they believed Jackson's supporters' ratification of the nominating committee report to be Nazi-like in its dismissal of Baptist and democratic principles. Taylor likened the escapade to "the worst days of Hitler... If Negroes stand for this they will let the world know they are not prepared for leadership."[45]

Both factions worked to ensure that the next convention, held in 1961, would clearly determine who controlled the convention presidency. Jackson's regulars held eight board meetings, each ostensibly to deal with the education, missionary, and charitable ministries of the church, but largely re-affirming the current governmental and board structure under President Jackson. *Voice* editor Caesar Clark extolled Jackson's virtues while labeling his opposition as ill-informed. The so-termed Taylorite faction registered delegates, rented hotel space, and prepared for what was later termed a "march-in," to complete the ouster of Jackson and the take-over of the NBC. What followed, according to Nick Salvatore, was "the closest approximation to open warfare in the convention's long history." While only one delegate, the elderly Arthur Garfield Wright, died during the actual march-in on 6 September 1961, it ultimately required legal adjudication to move forward with the business of the convention. Jackson claimed he wrote the rules to which both sides agreed that permitted the annual election of an NBC president. Given the advantages the rules gave to Jackson in these terms, this assertion may well be legally defensible. The Taylor faction had to dissolve itself as an organization (it nominally claimed to be the real NBC), and in order to receive recognition, its delegates had to receive new credentials from Jackson's faction. Election rules required voting by states. Jackson received 2,732 votes to Taylors 1,519. After such a melee, the election ended in apparent harmony. Taylor "congratulated" Jackson "and said that the 'Supreme Court' of the Convention (the people) had spoken and he was now satisfied. He called for a closing of the ranks by the brethren

---

[45] King, *Fire in My Bones*, 94-5; Best, "Right Achieved," 204.

and said the he was falling in and would follow the leadership of Dr. Jackson." It appeared that the crisis had passed.[46]

It had not. While Gardner Taylor remained in the NBC for a year, many younger ministers bolted the convention beginning in the fall of 1961. A faction of NBC pastors had been working in concert since 1959, and L. Venchael Booth and Cornell Talley—along with at least 230 other ministers—clearly identified themselves with the vision of Martin Luther King, Jr., and the Southern Christian Leadership Conference and were determined to seek new leadership in the NBC. They had persuaded Taylor to run against Jackson in 1960 and 1961, and Martin Luther King, Jr., was clearly a supporter and mobilizer of this movement to "move Dr. Jackson" out of the NBC presidency, urging "an organized effort … [in] Philadelphia" to elect Taylor, stating, "We can no longer passively accept the moral degeneracy which has infiltrated the top echelon of our convention."[47] When Jackson prevailed in both the 1960 and 1961 presidential elections, a rump of this larger anti-Jackson group consisting of thirty-three delegates from fourteen states, led by Booth, gathered in Cincinnati from 14–15 November 1961 to found a new progressive convention. Although each of these ministers had powerful connections to the larger African American crusade for equality and justice, what bound them together was their opposition to Joseph H. Jackson and "tenure." Booth and his supporters set out their version of denominational schism:

> The record should be set straight about who is splitting the Convention. We who separate at this time are not. We are simply trying to make the most of a tragic condition. The leader who creates disunity, expels members, throws out officers and banishes opponents is the real convention splitter. We who separate are simply trying to salvage the dignity of a life-time of struggle, preserve the contributions of our Fathers and bequeath to our children the best of our heritage. Our separation is for the purpose of restoring men to a sense of responsibility, spirituality, and service. Ours is a high call to greatness.[48]

In its statement of principles, the Progressive National Convention asserted that "long forbearance and democratic effort seeking reformation

---

[46] *Minutes*, 1961, 23; *NBV*, June 1961, 1, 16; July 1961, 4; August 1961, 4; Jackson, *Unholy Shadows*, 128; Salvatore, *Singing in a Strange Land*, 228.

[47] Booth, *Call to Greatness*, 5, 60.

[48] Ibid., 75.

within the framework of our Communion have brought no hope for redress … [so] therefore now nothing [is] left for the aggrieved to do" but to begin a new African American Baptist Convention. Consistent with its concern with term limits, the new convention limited all officers to two one-year terms, after which they were to remain out of that office for two consecutive years before being eligible for re-election.[49]

In an era characterized by its quest for social justice, African Americans were a people divided along the lines of means and ends. Older accommodationists found themselves assailed by younger, frustrated people demanding direct action. Mainstream organizations such as the NAACP faced rivals from the Congress of Racial Equality, the Student Non-Violent Coordinating Committee, and countless local groups organizing to achieve social betterment in the inner-cities and small hamlets across the United States. Gendered liberation among African Americans competed against the desire for masculine empowerment. Existing organizations groaned under strains of unmet and competing expectations. And irony abounded. The PNBC never enjoyed the support of a majority of African American Baptists, despite its own important record in mobilizing efforts for civil rights and religious conversions. As Albert Avant noted, "[T]he PNBC has stressed racial advancement and deplored racial injustice, … [while assisting] America's constitutional democracy … to … live up to its ideals."[50] The

---

[49] *Minutes of the Progressive National Baptist Convention, 1962.* 5–6, 13. Microfilm copy, Southern Baptist Historical Library and Archives, Nashville, TN. King to Thomas Kilgore, 6 October 1959, in Clayborne Carson, et al., *The Papers of Martin Luther King, Jr., Volume V: Threshold of a New Decade, January 1959–December 1960* (Berkeley: University of California Press, 2005) 305. About half a million NBC members went with the progressives. Best, "Right Achieved," 215. While a student at the University of Chicago, Booth was a member of Olivet Baptist Church. For an insightful interpretation of Booth's life and work, especially as "founder" of the PNBC, see Clarence G. Newsome, "L. V. Booth as the Founder of the Progressive National Baptist Convention, Inc.: A Religious Perspective," *Baptist History and Heritage* 46 (Spring 2011): 28–48. Bill J. Leonard, "'In the Name of Our God and Our Baptist Heritage': Reflections on History and the Progressive National Convention," *Baptist History and Heritage* 46 (Spring 2011): 11–12, offers a succinct summary of the road from Jackson's overturning tenure to the founding of the PNBC.

[50] Albert A. Avant, *The Social Teachings of the Progressive National Baptist Convention, Inc., Since 1961: A Critical Analysis of the Least, the Lost, and the Left-Out*

schism within the NBC did not end challenges to Joseph H. Jackson, even though the NBC continued to exert its own powerful call for social justice. Jackson himself was ousted as NBC president in 1982. Admirers erected a massive statue in his honor outside of Olivet Baptist Church. However, considering it idolatrous, a later pastor had the statue removed.[51]

Jackson is remembered for changing the main entrance of Olivet Baptist Church and for changing its official mailing address, after Chicago officials renamed South Parkway, the street address for Olivet, as Martin Luther King, Jr., Boulevard. He continued his enmity for King and for Jesse Louis Jackson, one of King's important Chicago mentees. Ironically, J. H. Jackson's most famous denunciations of King came when King travelled to Chicago to lead a civil rights campaign in the Windy City. By this time, King was already buffeted by dissent from younger activists who sometimes derided him as an "Uncle Tom," out of touch with the lives of many African Americans. Both men, Jackson and King, came of age in the National Baptist Convention, shaped by its politics and electoral culture, and the NBC offered a vehicle for moral and professional advancement and showed resilience through eras of growth and change. However, the NBC could not withstand the thunder of egos, perceptions, and competing needs of its leaders and parishioners. The presidency became both a real office and a symbol for the democratic and Baptist legitimacy of the convention. The political skill and grass-roots support of Joseph Jackson, manifested in his long, albeit contested, tenure as NBC president, proved to be the rock upon which denominational unity broke apart. Hence, William D. Booth is correct when he writes, "Tenure was the bedrock issue spawning the new convention and that is the unimpeachable verdict of history."[52]

(New York City: Routledge, 2004) 146; and Steve Lawson and Charles Payne, *Debating the Civil Rights Movement, 1945–1968*, 2nd ed. (Lanham, MD: Rowan & Littlefield, 2006) provide an excellent introduction to the top-down, bottom-up approaches, respectively, to the African American civil rights movement.

[51] Best, "Right Achieved," 195; "Church Casts Aside Famed Pastor's Statue," *Chicago Tribune*, 4 April 2001, http://articles.chicagotribune.com/2001-04-04/news/0104040264_1_monument-noble-father (accessed 20 April 2013).

[52] Best, "Right Achieved," 195; Booth, *Call to Greatness*, 26; Memphis *Commercial Appeal*, 22 June 1983, B 1; J. H. Jackson's Thought of Rev. Jessie L. Jackson's Candidacy for the Office of President of the U. S. A., Jackson Papers, Box 77.

9

Hilarity and Hope:
The Homegoing of Fred Shuttlesworth

Andrew M. Manis

My phone rang one warm fall day in 2011, and the grapevine revealed that Fred Shuttlesworth's condition was declining rapidly. By that time, the health of Birmingham's principal civil rights leader had nowhere to go but down, and did not have very far to go at that. For five years after the publication of my biography of him, *A Fire You Can't Put Out*, he always showed up as the picture of health in periodic joint appearances with me at special lectures (his, mine, and/or ours) and other book events.[1]

But in August 2005 he suffered a seizure caused by a brain tumor. Surgery revealed it to be benign, but not before health concerns forced his retirement from the active ministry. After thirty-nine years, his tenure as pastor of Cincinnati's Greater New Light Baptist Church came to an end. On the brighter side, he recovered from his brain tumor and surgery enough to enter into marriage with Sephira Ann Bailey, a member of his church who had shared caretaking responsibilities with his grown children during his convalescence. Ten months later, the new Mrs. Shuttlesworth was again acting as a nurse for her husband. In mid-August 2007, doctors were forced to insert a pacemaker in his heart, and three weeks later, he suffered a stroke from which he never fully recovered.

Now, it was time to lay aside my calculated objectivity. Knowing my portrayal of his life was generally affirmative, I had often found myself keeping emotional distance from him and his family, with whom I had spent upwards of seventy hours of taped interview time, not counting informal and telephone conversations. But I did not want my fellow historians to accuse me of moving past sympathetic biography to hagiography, so I resisted the impulse to become an honorary Shuttlesworth.

---

[1] See Andrew M. Manis, *A Fire You Can't Put Out: The Civil Rights Life of Birmingham's Reverend Fred Shuttlesworth* (Tuscaloosa: University of Alabama Press, 1999).

I expressed my concerns and good wishes to Sephira, who in turn encouraged me to speak to her husband. Thirty-three years and fifty-eight percent of my life had passed since we first met in my uncle's living room in Cincinnati. This time, however, the eighty-nine-year-old body that had literally, deliberately, and repeatedly been put in harm's way was now curled into the fetal position, bed-ridden, and the voice that had demanded racial justice in Birmingham, Cincinnati, and all of America was now silent. A Fred Shuttlesworth who was unable to speak seemed, to me, the ultimate oxymoron. Ever since the mid-1950s, he had been speaking in God's name, speaking truth to the powerful and to the powerless alike. Now here we were, summoned to one last exchange on the telephone, both unable to speak, waiting for a one-way conversation to begin.

"Here," she said, "Say a few words to him now. He'll hear you." Only very rarely ever letting myself call him by his first name, I realized these last words to him had to dispense with the formality of titles. "Fred, this is Andrew Manis," I began. "I wanted you to know I'm praying that you will feel God's presence in these days as you always have. I want to tell you how much it has meant to me to have told your story over these last years and how honored I am that you trusted me with it. Thank you for using your life to help liberate America—whites as well as blacks—from the evils of racism and Jim Crow. Thank you for leaving America better than you found it. Goodbye, Fred." Thus ended a thirty-three-year conversation between two Baptist preachers from Birmingham.

Knowing that Mrs. Shuttlesworth and I would speak again soon, I assured her of my continuing prayers and good wishes and hung up the phone. Fighting back tears, I instantly remembered a poignant moment in our conversations when he detected that his narration was plucking some emotional strings in his interviewer. Almost as a taunt, he said to me, "About to cry, aren't you? ... I didn't have time for no tears in Birmingham. When the child is sick, somebody's got to be strong enough to give the medicine."

As funerals go, there were relatively few tears at the service for Fred Shuttlesworth. Such would typically be the case with one so near the end of nine decades, and even more so with a life as consequential as that of Fred Shuttlesworth. Friends and family also expected an imminent death and felt the pain of seeing relegated to a wheelchair a loved one who had, for so long, been so strong, so active, and seemingly so indestructible. Such sentiments gave them a sense of peace more prone to sending the prophet back to the One who sent him than to weep over his departure.

On 5 October 2011, a few days after our last "conversation," he finally succumbed. Within minutes, the first of many reporters from around the country called to ask for a quote from his biographer. Mostly, they asked about his legacy. Most often I told them, "If Fred Shuttlesworth was not martyred for the cause of civil rights in America, it was not for lack of trying."[2] Immediately I phoned Mrs. Shuttlesworth to express my condolences. She asked if I would be coming to Birmingham for the memorial services. When I assured her I would be there, she indicated she wanted me to say a few words.

Of course, I accepted. I wondered, however, whether or not to take the invitation seriously. Initial newspaper accounts indicated that Shuttlesworth's children were at odds with the new wife. Older than Sephira, who was thirty-five years their father's junior, the children of his first marriage, as is common in such domestic situations, had strong reservations regarding their father's decision to remarry, as well as the particular woman he chose.

When Shuttlesworth's health began to decline, Sephira helped convinced her new husband to leave Cincinnati, where the Shuttlesworths had lived since 1961, to return to Birmingham permanently. She believed both that Birmingham's medical resources exceeded those in Cincinnati and that the black community in Birmingham was more indebted to Shuttlesworth than the citizens of Cincinnati. She reasoned that in gratitude for his role in the civil rights movement, African Americans in Birmingham would be more likely to contribute to the new Fred Shuttlesworth Foundation created by Mrs. Shuttlesworth in August 2011.

At the end of September, in response to the new foundation, all four of the Shuttlesworth children issued a joint statement to the press that "their father's Birmingham legacy" was secure and that he himself was not destitute nor in need of charity."[3] These disputes loomed like the proverbial "elephant

---

[2] Among the many reporters and commentators used the quotation, see Marian Wright Edelman, "Remembering Fred Shuttlesworth: The Most Courageous Man in America," 30 December 2011, http://www.childrensdefense.org/newsroom/child-watch-columns/child-watch-documents/remembering-fred-shuttlesworth.html.

[3] Joseph D. Bryant, "Civil Rights Icon Rev. Fred Shuttlesworth's Children Resist Foundation," *Birmingham News*, 30 September 2011, http://blog.al.com/spotnews/2011/09/shuttlesworths_children_resist.html.

in the room" five days later when their father died. As a result, the first announcements of funeral arrangements signaled the possibility of dueling services, one presumably in Cincinnati and the other in Birmingham. Fortunately, the tensions were smoothed over, and the younger Shuttlesworths deferred to the spouse. In any case, the multiple events memorializing the leader were postponed for two and a half weeks, until October 23–24, to allow the African American and civil rights communities to attend the dedication of the new Martin Luther King, Jr., memorial in Washington, DC.

So on Sunday, October 23, I wished my daughter a happy twenty-eighth birthday, apologized for not being able to celebrate her day with her, and headed west toward Birmingham. Flying east to meet me there was a young screenwriter from Los Angeles named Denise (Dax) Snaer. She had just committed to writing a screenplay for a feature film version of *A Fire You Can't Put Out*, and we both believed that attending Shuttlesworth's funeral would give her a clearer sense of not only the physical lay of the land, but of this particular civil rights leader and his following around Birmingham.

Our first stop was the Birmingham Civil Rights Institute. Filling the courtyard in front of the museum, several hundred visitors prepared to begin the institute's formal tour before attending two Shuttlesworth events scheduled for three and six p.m. The bridge between the tour and a historic speech by the attorney-general of the United States, Eric Holder, was the opportunity to pay our respects to Shuttlesworth himself, whose body lay in state at the institute's rotunda. As hundreds of persons filed past his casket, I immediately thought of the public mourning connected with the death of President John F. Kennedy. Few leaders could have had more contrasting lives or deaths. Shuttlesworth had neither Kennedy's wealth, education, nor family heritage. Instead of confronting Jim Crow "on all fronts," as had Shuttlesworth, Kennedy was slow on coming to attack it all. Most tellingly of all, Kennedy became a martyr despite doing remarkably little to advance civil rights during his administration. By contrast, Shuttlesworth remains relatively unknown despite plunging headlong into the fight throughout a life almost nine decades long. Dax, however, despite her rookie status as a Shuttlesworth observer, noticed perhaps the most powerful irony of the entire cluster of memorial events: that members of the Birmingham police and fire departments, which had so frequently impeded the minister's civil rights activities and threatened his life, now served as his official pallbearers.

Having sped through her copy of *A Fire You Can't Put Out*, Dax had fallen in love with Fred Shuttlesworth, or at least had been captured by his charisma. A native Jamaican of African descent with an eclectic spirituality, Dax sought a spot as near the departed as possible, in hopes of feeling his spirit in preparation for writing about his life and life force. As we arrived at the casket, we were greeted by Sephira, who assertively protected the distance between her husband's remains and his admirers. In that moment, as I peeled off to take refuge in my own emotions, Dax lingered in her meditations before the deceased, finally parting after promising him not to rest until she had written his story and helped bring it to the silver screen.

Next, we hurried over to Steiner Auditorium, part of the Birmingham Museum of Arts. Some days before, between my classes at Middle Georgia State College, I answered my cellphone and was surprised to find a Pulitzer Prize-winner on the other end. Diane McWhorter, author of *Carry Me Home: Birmingham, Alabama: The Climactic Battle of the Civil Rights Revolution*, and I had never met, despite our both having chased Shuttlesworth around for twelve years or so. She and Robert G. Corley, two of several civil rights historians who hail from Birmingham, organized and moderated a three-hour panel discussion titled, "Historians and History Makers Pay Tribute to the Reverend Fred Shuttlesworth."[4] Two categories of speakers offered their thoughts on Shuttlesworth's importance as a civil rights leader: (1) Historians and/or journalists who made historical comparisons of Shuttlesworth to King and other prominent civil rights leaders; and (2) Shuttlesworth's contemporaries in Birmingham and members of Shuttlesworth's Bethel Baptist Church or his civil rights organization, the Alabama Christian Movement for Human Rights (ACMHR).

Once the welcomes and introductions were out of the way, the first speaker made it clear that even the three hours allotted for the event would

---

[4] See S. Jonathan Bass, *Blessed Are the Peacemakers: Martin Luther King, Jr., Eight White Religious Leaders, and the "Letter from Birmingham Jail"* (Baton Rouge: Louisiana State University Press, 2001); Robert G. Corley, "The Quest for Racial Harmony: Race Relations in Birmingham, Alabama, 1947-1963," (PhD diss., University of Virginia, 1979); Glenn T. Eskew, *But for Birmingham: The Local and National Movements in the Civil Rights Struggle* (Chapel Hill: University of North Carolina Press, 1997); Manis, *A Fire You Can't Put Out*; Diane McWhorter, *Carry Me Home: Birmingham, Alabama: The Climactic Battle of the Civil Rights Revolution* (New York City: Simon & Schuster, 2000).

never suffice for this particular "cloud of witnesses." In a fifteen-minute sermon, Woods harked back to "movement days" to sing praises to Shuttlesworth and the ACMHR. While Woods had played a role in the Birmingham struggle, having been arrested for preaching a boycott of segregated facilities in the city, he led the reflections more for the longevity of his association with Shuttlesworth than for the centrality of his specific contributions to the success of the movement. Despite being the pastor of the Shiloh Baptist Church in Birmingham, his use of the title of "bishop" in a theological tradition that rejected hierarchy suggests either an oversized ministerial ego or a black Baptists' inattention to the subtleties of Baptist polity. His oratory, however, elevated the spirit of the audience while intimidating the speakers who followed him.

Burdened by the task of immediately following Woods to the dais was Shuttlesworth's biographer, who by training is both historian and preacher. In reality, as has been suggested before, the two roles are indeed similar: they both read old writings from which they seek to draw insights for contemporary life.[5] Probably a bit carried away by the tone that had been set, the speaker exceeded his narrow time limit, proving, no doubt, his ministerial credentials. He told of one of Shuttlesworth's early experiences that had crucial, long-terms implications. In 1948, Shuttlesworth was a recently ordained a Baptist minister and was called by First (African) Baptist Church in Selma, Alabama, a year later. Seven months later, he was named the regular pastor of the congregation. Class tensions quickly surfaced, however, between the middle-class professional deacons and their unpolished, working-class pastor. After months of tension, Shuttlesworth found himself "grievously vexed" and on a train to Oklahoma City for a meeting of the National Baptist Convention. Out between railroad cars for some fresh air at two a.m., the young minister prayed, "Lord, I'm not asking you to relieve the suffering but I am asking you to fix me so I don't worry so much."[6] Could a situation be any more Baptist than this? Perhaps never has a prayer been more definitively answered in the affirmative. After this spiritual experience, the word "fear" seemed to drop out of his vocabulary altogether, and by his own testimony rendered him "ready" for Birmingham and Bull Connor.

---

[5] See Andrew Manis, *Macon Black and White: An Unutterable Separation in the American Century* (Macon, GA: Mercer University Press, 2004) Epilogue.

[6] Manis, *A Fire You Can't Put Out*, 63–4.

Subsequent speakers struggled to stay within their time limits and did so with even more limited success. The big story of the event, however, began innocently enough about two-thirds of the way through the proceedings. Sephira Shuttlesworth and Ricky Shuttlesworth Bester dropped by to offer thanks from the family to the conveners for organizing the event and to the audience for attending. As Ricky finished her brief remarks, Sephira made her way to the podium but tripped and fell headlong off the stage. Surviving the fall without severe injuries, she was hospitalized overnight for back strain. As the audience dispersed and headed a few ~~city~~ blocks over to the Sixteenth Street Baptist Church for a meeting of black church (predominantly, but not exclusively Baptist) leaders, most who attended the event wondered whether Mrs. Shuttlesworth would overcome her injuries enough to be present at her husband's funeral.[7]

Spirits were flying even higher, the African American version of the Social Gospel was being proclaimed more eloquently, black evangelical religion and liberal politics were tied together more tightly, and the liberal

---

[7] Laura Newland, "Historians and History Makers Pay Tribute to the Rev. Fred Shuttlesworth: The Birmingham Museum of Art hosts a panel discussion on the legacy of the Rev. Shuttlesworth, Sunday, Oct. 23–3:00 p.m.," http://www.linkedin.com/groups/Historians-History-Makers-Pay-Tribute-4139336.S.76687132. Confirmed panelists included Howell Raines, former editor of *The New York Times* and author/editor of *My Soul is Rested: Movement Days in the Deep South Remembered* (New York City: Penguin Books, 1983); Marjorie White, director of the Birmingham Historical Society and co-editor with Andrew M. Manis, *Birmingham Revolutionaries: Fred Shuttlesworth and the Alabama Christian Movement for Human Rights* (Macon, GA: Mercer University Press, 2000); retired US District Court Judge U. W. Clemon; Andrew Manis, award-winning author of the Shuttlesworth biography *A Fire You Can't Put Out*; Mark Kelly, publisher of *Weld*; Jim Baggett, Director of the Department of Archivist, Birmingham Public Library, and author of what will be definitive biography of Eugene T. "Bull" Connor; Odessa Woolfolk, educator, activist and Birmingham Civil Rights Institute founder; Bishop Calvin Woods, president of the Birmingham Chapter of the Southern Christian Leadership Conference; longtime Shuttlesworth associate Colonel Stone Johnson; activist Eileen Kelley Walberg; Freedom Rider Catherine Burks-Brooks; lifelong Sixteen Street Baptist Church member and activist Carolyn McKinstry; former detective Dan Jordan; and Judy Hand-Truitt, who worked with Shuttlesworth in the post-Civil Rights era.

version of American civil religion was being expressed more loyally at the Sixteenth Street Baptist Church. There, a cadre of activist ministers who had sometimes reluctantly, but most times enthusiastically, followed Shuttlesworth's leadership (if not his example) paid a series of silver-tongued ministerial tributes to the departed leader. Had it not been for the decision to turn the pulpit over to two lawyers, the entire congregation might have been launched into ecstatic orbit. Hearing from a white lawyer in a context like this, one might have expected the fervor-meter to come down a notch or two.

On the contrary, however, the lawyer in question was a "saint" returning to a sacred place. Attorney G. Douglas Jones had served as the US attorney who led a team of prosecutors and investigators in re-opening the case of the Sixteenth Street Baptist Church bombing. He also became a hero to the sort of Birminghamians most likely to attend Fred Shuttlesworth's memorial service, having prosecuted two former Ku Klux Klansmen for the murder of the four young girls killed in the bombing. Jones's job was, ostensibly, only to introduce the main speaker for the evening. On this night, however, Jones rose to the occasion, inspired by both the context and the company, put his oratorical motor into overdrive, and brought his audience to their feet. The ensuing cheers were clearly more the audience's response to Jones's introductory remarks than a welcome for Attorney-General Eric Holder, who himself mockingly complained, "Now I'm supposed to follow *him*?"

On their own, Holder's remarks would have been fairly boilerplate and quite anti-climactic compared to those of the ministers who held forth in the best of the black homiletical tradition. The prestige of his position as the highest-ranking public official at the Shuttlesworth memorial events and his role as a stand-in for the President of the United States—the first African American president—added great import and great celebration to the occasion. By his presence, he indicated that he was joining with the crowd in appreciating Shuttlesworth's legacy and reminded the congregation of "our collective responsibility to carry on his critical work and to live up to the example of service that he left to each and every one of us." Shuttlesworth was, he noted, "a trailblazer who "never sought the spotlight and never stopped reaching back to help those who struggled to follow in his steps." Thinking of his own position as America's first African American attorney general, Holder made the personal connection explicit:

Let me be very clear: Without him there would be no me....He became, as President Obama recently noted, "nothing less than a testament to the strength of the human spirit....He showed us what it means to be dedicated to a cause that is greater than yourself. And along with Dr. King, Reverend Abernathy, Reverend Lowery, and other distinguished Alabama preachers... AlaBAMA preachers...he demonstrated the quiet power of selflessness, kindness, and obviously self- sacrifice. Reverend Shuttlesworth helped lead the movement that remade this nation and renewed its promise that all its citizens would be created and treated as equals.[8]

As the curtain fell on the attorney-general's performance, it became clear that when the clerical trumpets lifted the next day in praise of Fred Shuttlesworth, the notes they would hit would be those of celebration instead of sorrow. They would also be notes with roots sunk deep in the traditions of ancient Christianity. Since at least the second-century Christian congregations have honored the memory of their martyrs and looked past the sorrow of their deaths by renaming the anniversaries of their honor roll of martyrs' deaths as their "natalitia" or their "births into eternal life." Still other traditions emphasize life on earth as a Christian "sojourn" of "aliens" whose "kingdom was not of this world." More recently, at least one hit song in the genre of country music celebrated one's "temporary home."[9]

This interpretation is traceable to the American revivalistic tradition, including the thought and practice of both white and black Baptist churches in the American South. As white Baptists have prospered economically and ascended the socio-economic ladder, such anti-worldly themes have become muted as they have become a characteristic of an earlier era of white Baptist

---

[8] See video of Holder's speech at http://www.youtube.com/watch?v=vYm-KOL2NJmw.html.

[9] See F. L. Cross and E. A. Livingstone, eds., *Oxford Dictionary of the Christian Church*, 2nd ed. (New York City: Oxford University Press, 1974) 954–55; W. H. C. Frend, *Martyrdom and Persecution in the Early Church: A Study of a Conflict from the Maccabees to Donatus* (London: Basil Blackwell, 1965; Baker Book House, 1981) 257, 380, 383. See also the 2009 country hit "Temporary Home," written by Luke Robert Laird, Zachary Maloy, and Carrie Underwood, Universal Music Publishing Group, Sony/ATV Music Publishing. Earlier expression of similar sentiments are widespread in the genre of gospel music, both southern (white) and black. Clear examples are to be found in the songs of Albert E. Brumley (1905–77). Among them were *I'll Fly Away* (1929) and *This World Is Not My Home* (1952), http://www.brumleymusic.com/Bio_-_Albert.html.

history.[10] As such religions prosper, a proportion of their members grow increasingly comfortable with life in this world and conversely uncomfortable with the language of "homegoing."

Among American slaves and their descendants, however, this theology has remained a living legacy of African American theological and funerary traditions. For slaves, especially those who had spent long lives in bondage, death was often greeted as a release of the soul from physical bondage, wherein one's soul was emancipated for a "homegoing" or a return home to ancestral Africa. From this specific setting in the African American slave experience, the funeral services of slaves celebrated both the life and the homegoing of the departed. They also "served to honor the body of someone who had not been honored in life," providing a gathering of the living where the deceased's life and "path to freedom" could be celebrated.[11]

One would be extremely hard pressed to find a person more perfectly suited to be eulogized in this "homegoing" tradition than Fred Shuttlesworth. A nonviolent gladiator who challenged segregation's champion, Eugene Theophilus "Bull" Connor, Shuttlesworth lived up to the admiration of those who knew him best, but without the national acclaim that has greeted other figures of the civil rights movement. But this day—which began early and ended late—would bring him in death the historical significance that had eluded him in life.

Expecting larger crowds than could be accommodated even by the largest African American congregations, arrangements were made to hold the service at one of Birmingham's newest mega-churches, Faith Chapel Christian Center. Heralded as the world's largest monolithic dome, the church's physical facility occupies 137 acres of land, and its main sanctuary

---

[10] Baptist connections to this mentality can be seen in the influence of Pastor Rick Warren's book, *The Purpose-Driven Life,* where the author uses the same phrase to describe life on earth.

[11] On the "homegoing" theme of African American funerary customs, see Elaine Nichols, ed., *The Last Miles of the Way: African American Homegoing Traditions, 1890–Present* (Columbia: Commissioners of the South Carolina State Museums, 1989); Suzanne E. Smith, *To Serve the Living: Funeral Directors and the African American Way of Death* (Cambridge: Harvard University Press, 2010). See also the documentary film based on these works, "Homegoings," http://www.pbs.org/pov/homegoings/African american-funeral-director.php#.UpNlKLEo7MM.

seats three thousand.[12] Having arrived at a holding area at 8:30 a.m., persons scheduled to speak began filing into the sanctuary half-filled with an audience that was probably 90 percent African American, and prepared at 10:30 a.m. to hear a parade of prayers, hymns, scripture readings, choir and solo selections, thirty-six tributes, and an official eulogy.

At least one mystery hung over those in attendance, namely whether President Barack Obama, whose name was listed in the program, would, in fact, appear to pay tribute to the fallen civil rights leader. The mystery was solved fairly quickly upon entering the building given the dearth of Secret Service security measures in place. After a short speech by the local US attorney, Alabama governor Robert Bentley was introduced. As a white, middle-aged Republican governor who was clearly unaccustomed to speaking before a black church audience, the governor nevertheless felt at home addressing a Christian congregation. He also knew that testimonies of conversion were always welcomed in such company. Leaders of the civil rights movement such as Fred Shuttlesworth had been instrumental in helping convert a younger Robert Bentley from the "gospel" of Jim Crow. Neither growing up white in Shelby County, Alabama, nor attending the University of Alabama had given the young Bentley over to the "culture of discrimination" that had hung over Alabama and the South. Shuttlesworth and other leaders of the movement, he confessed, had helped him see the truth. After noting how different both he and his home state were from the days of his youth, he concluded by thanking Shuttlesworth for undoing "the teachings of a misdirected society."[13]

The conclusion of the governor's remarks, however, did not bring an end to references to them by the Reverend Joseph Lowery, one of Martin Luther King's successors as president of the Southern Christian Leadership Conference, who poked fun at Bentley's efforts by feigning ignorance and asking, "I thought the governor was a Republican." He began these mock inquiries from his seat in the audience even while the governor was finishing his speech, and went back to this rhetorical device a bit later when his own

---

[12] See the church's website, www.faithchapel.net/index.cfm//pageid/2472/index.

[13] "Funeral services held in Birmingham for Civil Rights leader Rev. Fred Shuttlesworth." *Birmingham News*, 24 October 011. Accessed at http://www.masslive.com/news/index.ssf/2011/10/funeral services held in birmi.html.

turn at the podium came. Each speaker had been instructed to hold his or her remarks to a three-minute limit. Although almost every speaker violated that guideline, Lowery's violation was the most egregious. His initial remarks wondered why Republican governor Bentley did not use his newly discovered anti-racial sentiments to veto his state's recent anti-immigration law. Once he moved into his prepared material, he reiterated sentiments he had once told me in an interview: that God had perfectly placed Fred Shuttlesworth in the strategic position of being the nemesis of Birmingham's arch-segregationist political leader, Bull Connor. Connor's commitment to maintaining Jim Crow was an exact match to Shuttlesworth's radical commitment to its destruction. "Fred and Bull were simply made for each other." Most impressive, however, was the jocular attitude with which Lowery praised Shuttlesworth's ability to mock the forces so dead set against him. In the process, Lowery added, Fred left a powerful legacy: "Fred's real reward was that little black children can find the history of a black man who didn't scratch where he didn't itch, didn't grin when he wasn't tickled, didn't bow down, and didn't sell out..."[14]

Following Lowery was Andrew Young's impressive tribute. Striking the homegoing theme, he also made a powerful argument regarding Shuttlesworth's historical legacy. "It was on his legacy in Birmingham," he explained, "that we were able to get the 1964 Civil Rights bill and the March on Washington." After the six years between the Montgomery Bus Boycott and the campaign in Albany, Georgia," King's movement had seen no significant victories that it could authentically claim as its own. With his repeated insistence that King bring SCLC forces to join with his ACMHR in Birmingham, Young claimed "Fred probably saved the civil rights movement.... we had been bogged down in Albany, Georgia, and people were saying nonviolence wouldn't work. But Fred said, "Look, the only thing we can do is nonviolence. You have to come to Birmingham." And then there was his unmatched courage, which Young tied closely to Fred's homegoing:

> ...that courage, that determination was sort of contagious when you were around Fred. Because Fred didn't have sense enough to be afraid. Fred thought he was going to die at twenty-nine. He never thought he'd live to

---

[14] See video of Shuttlesworth funeral, http://www.youtube.com/watch?v=b ECqoCTT-8SY.

eighty-nine. So don't anybody get sad about his going home to glory now, he's lonnnnnng overdue![15]

After two sets of leaders from the civil rights movement had given their tributes, punctuated by musical interludes led by the combined mass choirs of Faith Chapel Christian Center and the Bethel Baptist Church, a set of historians took their turns at "eulogizing" Shuttlesworth. My own turn came sandwiched between Pulitzer Prize winners Taylor Branch and Diane McWhorter. Weighing on me more heavily than comparisons with my historical colleagues was how my remarks—as far as I could tell the only ones on the program from a white minister—would measure up to the homiletic masterpieces that came before and after me. Mentally, I tossed away the academic historians' hat in favor of the preacher hat, determined to prove that a white preacher could hold his own in that context. I strode to the pulpit intent on "bringin' it," as one of my students watching online later commented, and began:

Fred Shuttlesworth and I grew up a few miles from each other. Ironically, he lived in "Bombingham," while I lived in the "city of churches." Eventually, Shuttlesworth became a Baptist minister on the north side of Birmingham, while I studied for the Baptist ministry on the Southside. My education turned me into a historian and, by and by, the biographer of Fred Shuttlesworth. While I was working on that book, he once told me this story:

Nineteen fifty-nine was a year of battling Bull Connor. Bull thrust with the fire department, while Fred parried with his lightning quick mind. They said churches were fire hazards and mass meetings needed to be shut down. So one night Fred looked the fire chief in the eye and said: "Chief, you know there ain't no fire in here. The kind of fire we have in here you can't put out with hoses and axes."

In a flash, he had given me the metaphor for his life. Because if anybody embodied the movement's fire to be free, … if anybody personified what Cornel West called the "combative spirituality" of the Black Church, … if anybody could be both "fiery mad" at the realities of race in America, but "fiery glad" in the confidence that God would make "a way out of no way," it was Fred Shuttlesworth.

If he never died in the fires of martyrdom, it was not for lack of trying. No one in this historic movement put himself in a position to lose his life

---

more often than did Fred Shuttlesworth. In so doing he helped liberate his people from the evils of racism. But he also helped liberate us white people from our ancient arrogance that white skin made us superior.

For eighty-nine years he carried out the promise uttered by every child in every Sunday school in America: "This little light of mine, I'm gonna let it shine!" With that light he ignited "a fire you can't put out," a fire that burned away some of our impurities and left Birmingham much brighter and America much better than he found them. "Red and yellow, black and white," we should be grateful for his light, now burning eternally in "another country."

And now as he joins that "great cloud of witnesses" and cheers us on to "keep the movement moving," our response is simple. We look up and say, "Thank you, Honored Brother, for lighting your light and helping us inch closer to finding that city 'not made with hands, whose builder and maker is God.'" Rest in peace, Brother Fred, rest in peace.[16]

Before the congregation had heard all the tributes to Fred Shuttlesworth and exited Faith Chapel and headed for Oak Hill Cemetery for the graveside service, six and a half hours had passed. Invariably, most people, black as well as white, roll their eyes at this extreme length. But how many of the rest of us would like to think that at the end of our lives a thousand or so would come and pay their respects by hearing thirty or so of our closest colleagues stand up and praise us and thank God that we had come and gone and left the world better than we found it?

But the pinnacle of these preachers' offerings came as it should have, in the official eulogy by Shuttlesworth's closest friend, the Reverend Dr. Otis Moss, Jr., emeritus pastor of the Olivet Institutional Baptist Church in Cleveland, Ohio. Moss and Shuttlesworth had shared a friendship of more than fifty years, and Moss had presided ministerially at Fred's installation as pastor of the Greater New Light Baptist Church, at the funeral of his first wife, Ruby Keeler Shuttlesworth, at the marriage of daughter Ruby Fredricka Shuttlesworth to Harold Bester, and at the wedding of Fred and Sephira Shuttlesworth. Giving one last gift to his friend, Moss spoke on "the Eternal Worth of Fred Shuttlesworth." The sermon was a work of art, a

---

[16] The author is, of course, unsure that these remarks made up for the absence of the white clergy from the occasion. As biographer, however, he would say that the reality at his death certainly matched the reality of his life. The speech did elicit this later Facebook response from daughter Ruby Fredricka Shuttlesworth Bester: "Thank you for the words you spoke at the funeral. Daddy loved you. Blessings, Ricky."

masterpiece that not only involved the homegoing theme, but perfectly depicted the importance of the life he was called to praise.[17]

He began by combining an Old Testament text with one from the new. Genesis 49:22 compared Shuttlesworth's life to that of the patriarch Joseph: "Joseph is a fruitful bough, a fruitful bough by a spring; his branches run all over the wall." Next came 2 Corinthians 4:16–18:

> We do not lose heart. Even though our outer nature is wasting away, our inner nature is being renewed day by day. For this slight momentary affliction is preparing us for an eternal weight of glory beyond all reason, because we look not at what can be seen; for what can be seen is temporary, but what cannot be seen is eternal. (2 Corinthians 4:16-18, NRSV)

Like Joseph, said Moss, Fred Shuttlesworth was "a fruitful tree by a spring of living water whose branches stretch far beyond his time, place and space ... an abiding tree by a spring of living water whose prophetic and redemptive leadership will be a blessing to generations not yet born."

He continued:

> When we think of his life, we think of courage. When we think of his life, we think of nonviolent direct action. When we think of his life, we think peaceful revolutionary. Think of a freedom fighter with mountain moving faith. Think of a servant leader with mountain climbing faith.... That is the eternal worth of Fred L. Shuttlesworth. His value, contributions, victories, scars and stars are much larger than Birmingham, Alabama, and stretch beyond the borders of his beloved nation, Shuttlesworth has a global address, an ecumenical witness, and an interfaith embrace. This is the eternal worth of Shuttlesworth.

The sermon then moved to rehearsing a series of the signature milestones in his eventful life. He told of his earliest work in Birmingham and his role in the founding of SCLC. He told of their being arrested together in Cincinnati for protesting discriminatory policies of the Drake County Hospital. In quick thrusts, he recounted Shuttlesworth's promise of desegregated bus riding on the day after Christmas. Someone asked, "When do we march?" Fred said, "Tomorrow morning," as he brushed himself from the debris and dust of sixteen sticks of dynamite that turned his house into

---

[17] All quotations from the eulogy come from a typescript copy of the eulogy graciously provided the author by the Rev. Dr. Otis Moss, Jr.

rubble. "Shuttlesworth, you are a fruitful tree by a well of water whose branches hang over the wall." Moss continued:

> When parents Fred and Ruby decided to enroll three of their children in Phillips High School, they sought to "educate the education system of the State of Alabama. They were seeking to democratize and civilize the entire State. At Philips High, they met a mob armed with chains, bats, and pikes; they were attacked by a mob unloving, unrighteous, uneducated, ungodly, unethical and uncivilized."

But then, a surprise stop in Moss's tour. Instead of Freedom Rides and Project C and a March on Washington, instead of wrestling with the Klan in Tallahassee or in Selma, instead of praise from the Kennedy brothers or the Nobel Prize committee, this preacher detoured into a Birmingham courtroom. The event where the eulogist lingered was comparatively little-known, yet perfectly conceived as the central, signature episode that embodies the very meaning of Fred Shuttlesworth's fight with segregation.

After several years of effort by Connor to intimidate Shuttlesworth and his followers into submission, Shuttlesworth and Rev. Charles Billups decided to sue the city of Birmingham, hopefully enjoining Connor's police and fire departments from attending, interrupting, surveilling, or otherwise intimidating citizens from participating in the weekly mass meetings.

With no illusion of winning such a case in the courtroom of another committed segregationist, Judge Seybourne Lynn, and against the advice of his lawyers, Shuttlesworth undertook this role as what Moss insightfully called "an act of prophetic drama." In that setting he could, as Shuttlesworth himself phrased it, "harass the harassers." In the process, Moss explained, he could encourage his followers by cross-examining "the great 'Bully'–Bull Connor himself." Moss added:

> Bull Connor took the witness stand, shackled by the weight of decades of hate … Thirty plus years before he met the Bull Connor, Shuttlesworth had already encountered scores of Bull Connors, little size, medium size, and extra-large Goliaths, He discovered that all the Goliaths and all the Bull Connors of the world are bloated bullies filled with countless insecurities, surrounded by mobs devoid of spiritual content.... The bullies of history seek to conquer through ridicule, terror, fear, smear, threats of death, and death itself.... Shuttlesworth's life was planted in this Alabama soil, but the branches of the Shuttlesworth tree had a national outreach and the fruits from the branches were global fruits. A tree planted in Alabama by a well of living water whose roots were local, whose branches were national, whose fruits are global.... God sent a prophet of love to a city ruled by hate and

fear. Fred had no tanks but truth, No rifles but righteousness. No guns but the goodness of the Lord. With this faith he proceeded to remove the shackles of despair and fear from the psyche of the African American community.... "His legacy is courage, his lesson is truth, his weapon is love. His life is his monument. He now belongs to humankind." I say that because he always belonged to God.

Why linger on this relatively obscure episode in a sermon whose purpose is to epitomize the entire life of the deceased? Because in the one image—of Bull and Fred face-to-face, of segregation versus integration, of hate versus love, of the symbol of violence and repression being mocked and cross-examined by the symbol of peace and liberation—we see in their clearest forms the hilarity and the hope of the black freedom struggle. In it, we see the essence of Fred L. Shuttlesworth. So reasoned and so preached the friend and confidant who knew him best.[18]

And then the eulogist brought Fred home:

In Fred's final years, his physical frame stood up against the challenge of a brain tumor and, subsequently, a stroke. Yet, he carried the sacred mission in a wheelchair. There is a famous and historic photo.... President Barack Obama pushing Rev. Fred Shuttlesworth in a wheelchair, reliving the 1965 Selma March across the Edmund Pettus Bridge. President Obama was pushing the wheelchair and the prophet was still leading, saying "We are on our way!" Fred would not allow his spirit to be broken. His body was challenged, but his soul was fired up on the way to the ballot box and to the White House....

A few days ago Fred moved from wheelchair to chariot.... Mr. Courageous, our activist plenipotentiary from the rugged school of anointed prophets. Mr. Human Rights personified. A seven star general in the nonviolent army of love and justice. Jailed between 35 and 40 times, more individual federal cases for civil rights than any single human being....

The other day when Fred transitioned from wheelchair to chariot, I believe a vast host gathered on the balcony of eternity to welcome him home:

Rosa Parks, Fannie Lou Hamer. Ed Gardner. James Phifer, Charles Billups, and N.H. Smith.

Ralph Abernathy. Ruby Doris Smith....

Albert Luthuli and Steve Biko ... Gandhi and Anne Frank ... JFK, RFK and LBJ ... Hubert Humphrey and Medgar Evers.

---

[18] The phrase "hilarity and hope" come from Rev. Dr. Otis Moss, Jr., telephone interview by Andrew Manis, 15 August 2013.

On the front lines of the Welcome Committee I see the four little girls from the Sixteenth Street Baptist Church. At the front and center of the line, I see Dr. King and Mrs. Coretta King flanked by Dorothy Height, Jimmie Lee Jackson, and Viola Gregg Liuzzo.

I hear them saying, with smiles and outstretched arms: "Welcome home, Fred. You have a crown of victory. It was wrapped up in your cross. You have stars that were consecrated and concealed behind collective scars. Welcome, May the next generation be worthy of your eternal worth. Thanks be to God! Amen."

Dear God, we thank and praise your name for the fruitful life and eternal worth of your servant, our brother, prophet of non-violence, proclaimer of truth, apostle of freedom and justice, ambassador of Jesus Christ and disciple of love, Fred Shuttlesworth. Amen.

Afterword

Wayne Flynt

When I first began to take photographs, I adjusted the lens of my camera to obtain the largest, widest frame possible. The result was predictable. Lots of vague, big stuff; some useful general impressions, but no detail. Though I could identify the scene, that is about all I could do. No complex smaller, intriguing elements to confuse me about what I was seeing. No confusing individual details that made me wonder exactly what this scene meant.

My son, a *real* photographer who has won jury shows for his images, taught me another way of understanding what I saw in the lens. Focus on details, constituent parts, stark contrasts. Understand the whole by seeing the intersection of the elements. Even if the larger image no longer makes the same kind of sense, the mind can reconstruct the large picture by paying attention to the detailed building blocks of reality.

In some ways, historians are like that. Most begin by trying to describe too much, to derive too general a meaning from insufficient information. Being the first to observe, having never read much about it, they jump to the first obvious conclusion about what they see. Sometimes they get it right. Most times they get it partly right. Many times they completely miss the point. By adding layers of detail, historical reality almost always becomes more complicated, nuanced, even confusing.

America's "Black Church" provides a perfect case study. For decades, white historians ignored the subject (and mostly American religion in general). When they discovered it, their lens of discovery was usually wide and wrong, arbitrary and artificial in assigning meaning to what they saw. Too often they concluded that black Christians thought alike. Baptists and Methodists leapt out of the landscape. Black Catholics, Jews, Presbyterians, Pentecostals, Holiness people, faded into a vague and nearly indiscernible background. Even being a Methodist or Presbyterian triggered Baptist jokes about that resulting from some white folks messing with the mind of an otherwise pious black Baptist.

A later historical generation tuned to activism saw in black Baptists the spearhead of the civil rights movement. Diversity there was, of course: Afrocentric revolutionaries sought to channelize democracy and the black church in one direction; "Uncle Toms", religious accommodationists, denominational bureaucrats beholden to white donors, became the lap dogs of the white religious community or self-serving narcissists who profited personally from their control of black institutions that flourished as a result of apartheid, not in spite of it.

In this refreshing lens adjustment of a book, a diverse group of scholars focusing on lots of different details manage to change our vision of an entire denominational landscape. The result is a much more complex, complicated narrative about the big stuff. In 1821, black Baptists utilized a "theology of Ethiopianism" to win the support of white co-religionists in Virginia, creating the Richmond African Baptist Missionary Society and dispatching Lott Cary and Collin Teague, both former slaves, to Africa because it was better for African Americans to carry the gospel to those far shores than whites who might not fare so well. Following the Civil War, not all freedmen rushed to leave their white-controlled churches for churches of their own. Confident black Baptist women subverted, challenged, or ignored black male autocrats. They also spun webs of friendship with white Woman Missionary Union leaders despite their differing racial agendas. Older, conservative black Baptist pastors differed strategically with more confrontational younger ones. National Baptist conventions erupted into chaos, requiring litigation to resolve control. Black folk culture slipped the boundaries of elite black religious institutions that sought to intellectualize evangelicalism. Black Baptists such as Mahalia Jackson and Aretha Franklin, who came from Baptist preacher families newly relocated in the North from the South, created a new genre of American music by grafting blues elements onto traditional hymns, plantation, and gospel songs.

Nor do the revelations stop at the cusp of the civil rights revolution. Fred Shuttlesworth and Martin Luther King, Jr., both derived their outrage about American society from a Biblical standard of justice outrageously transgressed by apartheid. Both claimed the proud heritage of black Baptists. But there the similarities ended. Shuttlesworth was a theological fundamentalist with limited education. King was a cerebral product of neo-orthodoxy at Boston University Divinity School, even if he did learn to preach in the old-time way. Whereas King pondered, feared, often even seemed suspended in the awful complexities of options and strategies available in Christian Realism, Shuttlesworth blasted straight ahead as a Biblicist who saw only one meaning and one destiny in history. He believed God had hand delivered to him a detailed description of how the freedom journey would end. To Shuttlesworth, heaven and hell were as palpable as if they had been alternative black and white churches in Birmingham, Alabama, in 1963. Get ready for jubilee or get ready for judgment.

No one who reads these stories will ever think of America's black Baptists in the same way again.

Index

Index

Smith, N. H. 253
Smitle, Esther O. 147
Snaer, Denise (Dax) 239
Sobel, Mechal 1, 48(n)
Social Gospel 7, 117, 165, 230, 243
Southern Baptist Convention (SBC)3,
  6, 8, 81, 83(n), 88-89, 91-95, 100,
  102-104, 108-109, 122, 127, 137,
  139, 156, 204, 227
Southern Christian Leadership
  Conference (SCLC) 7, 117, 167-
  168, 205(n), 219, 224(n), 232, 247,
  251
Stowell, Daniel 31(n), 32, 33(n),
  118(n)
Stratton, William J. 227
Straughton, William 65
Student Nonviolent Coordinating
  Committee (SNCC) 7, 117, 165,
  166(n), 167-172, 175, 176-199,
  233
Talley, Cornell 232
Taney, Roger 16
Taylor, Gardner C. 206(n), 222, 229,
  232
Teague, Collin 58, 65, 68, 70-71, 158,
  255
Tenure 204-208, 215, 221-227, 232,
  233(n), 234-35
Theodicy 9, 17, 20, 148(n), 151(n),
  154(n)
Thomas, E. L. 77, 83
Thurman, Howard 3
Tichenor, I. T. 93, 102-103
Till, Emmitt 228
Tokenism 123
Triennial Convention 66, 68-71, 73-74
Tupper, Henry Martin 39, 40
Turner, Henry McNeal 33, 59
Turner, Nat 47(n), 49
Tyler-McGraw, Marie 63
Union Church of Africans 13
Union League 115
Unionists 10
University of Pennsylvania 32(n), 220

Uplift 3-4, 6, 24, 59, 60(n), 62, 78, 84,
  89, 118, 123, 135, 164, 204, 220,
  221(n)
Virginia Baptist State Convention
  (VBSC) 20, 77-78, 84, 117(n),
  119(n)
Virginia Theological Seminary and
  College 136, 138-140, 145, 149,
  162
Virginia Union University 138
Walden, A. T. 223-227
Walker, David 11-12
Walker, Wyatt Tee 173
Ward, Elizabeth 157
Washington, Booker T. 128(n), 204
Washington, George 151-153
Washington, James Melvin 73, 113,
  121(n)
Welch, M. M. 105
Wells, Samuel 192, 196
Wheatley, Pillis 60
White, Walter 216, 220(n)
Whitted, J. A. 29, 34(n), 35(n), 38(n),
  40(n)
Williams, Charles H. 225
Williams, Lacy Kirk 207-219
Williams, Roger 146
Willingham, R. J. 100, 103(n), 104(n)
Wilson, Charles Reagan 12(n), 13
Woman's Baptist Home Mission
  Society of Maryland (WBHMS)
Woman's Congress 98
Woman's Convention (WC) 88,
  106(n), 107(n), 108(n), 109
Woman's Home Mission Society 98
Woman's Missionary Union (WMU)
  87-89, 90-98, 100-111, 156
Wood, Minerva 28, 30, 33, 46-47
Woodson, Carter G. 2(n), 16(n), 207
Wright, Abraham Garfield 231
Wright, Arthur Garfield 205
Yores, Aura 190-191
Young, Andrew 247-248
Zellner, Bob 171(n), 172-173
Zion Colored Baptist Association 35